The Protection of Intellectual Property Rights in Outer Space Activities

The Protection of Intellectual Property Rights in Outer Space Activities

Tosaporn Leepuengtham

Research Judge, Intellectual Property and International Trade Division, Supreme Court of Thailand

 Edward Elgar
PUBLISHING

Cheltenham, UK • Northampton, MA, USA

Published by
Edward Elgar Publishing Limited
The Lypiatts
15 Lansdown Road
Cheltenham
Glos GL50 2JA
UK

Edward Elgar Publishing, Inc.
William Pratt House
9 Dewey Court
Northampton
Massachusetts 01060
USA

A catalogue record for this book
is available from the British Library

Library of Congress Control Number: 2016949978

This book is available electronically in the **Elgar**online
Law subject collection
DOI 10.4337/9781785369629

MIX
Paper from
responsible sources
FSC
www.fsc.org   FSC® C013604

ISBN 978 1 78536 961 2 (cased)
ISBN 978 1 78536 962 9 (eBook)

Typeset by Columns Design XML Ltd, Reading
Printed and bound by CPI Group (UK) Ltd, Croydon, CR0 4YY

Contents

Introduction

The space era commenced with the successful launch of Sputnik I by the Soviet Union into outer space on 4 October 1957, followed by the first US satellite, Explorer I, a few months later.[1] Since then, states have been interested in exploring and exploiting this spatial area. Joining the United States and Russia as another space-faring nation, China has increased its technological capability and plans to send its first international space station into outer space in 2020.[2] Space technology has been developed aggressively and space applications have proved very beneficial for mankind. Outer space has been explored not only for scientific purposes but also for commercial uses. Private enterprises have gradually expanded their involvements in space venture during the last decades.[3] Commercial revenue and government budgets for the global space industry jumped to US$304.31 billion in 2012, representing growth of 6.7 per cent from the total of US$285.33 billion in 2011 and in 2013, the space economy grew by 4 per cent, reaching a new record of US$314.17 billion and continued to grow to the total of US$330 billion in 2014.[4] The global space

---

[1]   Christopher M. Hearsey, 'A Review of Challenge to Corporate Expansion into Outer Space' (AIAA Space 2008 Conference & Exposition, San Diego, September 2008) 2. <http://www.astrosociology.org/Library/PDF/Hearsey_CorporateExpansion.pdf> (accessed 5 July 2015).

[2]   'Chinese Space Station to Benefit World', Xinhua News Agency (16 June 2012) <http://news.xinhuanet.com/english/china/2012-06/16/c_123293484.htm> (accessed 12 March 2016).

[3]   David J. Salt, 'Space Operations for a New Space Era' in Craig A. Cruzen, et al. (eds), *Progress in Astronautics and Aeronautics*, vol. 236: Exploration, Scientific Utilization, and Technology Development (American Institute of Aeronautics and Astronautics, Inc. 2011) 4.

[4]   'Space Foundation's 2013 Report Reveals 6.7 Percent Growth in the Global Space Economy in 2012', Space Foundation Press Release (2 April 2013) <http://www.spacefoundation.org/media/press-releases/space-foundations-2013-report-reveals-67-percent-growth-global-space-economy> (accessed 16 June 2013); Space Foundation, *The Space Report, 2014* <http://www.spacefoundation.org/sites/default/files/downloads/The_Space_Report_2014_Overview_TOC_Exhibits.pdf> (accessed 5 July 2015); Space Foundation, *The Space*

industry experienced a significant growth of 37 per cent between 2007 and 2012.[5]

Space tourism transitioned from science fiction to reality when the first space tourist travelled on a Russian spaceship to the International Space Station in April 2001.[6] Shortly after that, the world's second space tourist travelled to the International Space Station and spent eight days there conducting scientific experiments including those relating to the HIV virus.[7] These two space tourists paid up to US\$20 million for their space journey.[8] The Virgin Galactic company plans to send tourists into outer space in the near future and more than 500 people have already booked its first space trip.[9] Once vehicles are available for paying space tourists, the space tourism industry will probably be the most profitable industry for suborbital flights.[10] In addition to these existing space industries, new space projects are being developed. These new projects include space hotels, orbital laboratories (providing zero-gravity biotech manufacturing), solar satellites (with the potential to convert solar radiation into usable electricity), space elevators (less costly than conventional rocket launches and premised upon raising an elevator car along a cable extending 62,000 miles above earth) and solar sails (collecting and utilizing solar radiation instead of conventional rocket fuel to propel spaceships and weather satellites).[11]

In addition, the special 'weightless' characteristic of the environment in outer space has proven to be enormously advantageous in the

---

Report, 2015 https://www.spacefoundation.org/sites/default/files/downloads/The_Space_Report_2015_Overview_TOC_Exhibits.pdf (accessed 29 December 2015).

    5   'Space Foundation's 2013 Report' (n 4).
    6   Nikhil D. Cooper, 'Circumventing Non-Appropriation: Law and Development of United States Space Commerce' (2009) 36 *Hastings Constitutional Law Quarterly* 457, 457; 'First Space Tourist Sets Sights on a Mars Mission', National Public Radio (27 February 2013) <http://www.npr.org/2013/02/27/173056144/first-space-tourist-sets-sights-on-a-mars-mission> (accessed 5 July 2015).
    7   Steven S. Freeland, 'Up, Up … Back: The Emergence of Space Tourism and Its Impact on the International Law of Outer Space' (2005–2006) 6 *Chicago Journal of International Law* 1, 3.
    8   Ibid.
    9   Elizabeth Howell, 'Virgin Galactic: Richard Branson's Space Tourism Company', Space.com (17 February 2016) <http://www.space.com/18993-virgin-galactic.html> (accessed 31 January 2016).
    10   Salt (n 3) 13.
    11   Cooper (n 6) 477.

manufacture of commercially valuable products in various fields, particularly in the pharmaceutical and electronics industries. The study of biochemical protein structure is enhanced and cheaper medicine can be produced effectively under zero gravity.[12] The purified atmosphere in space also enhances the production of silicon or gallium arsenide crystals for semiconductor manufacture.[13] These valuable industrial processes are definitely of great importance and arguably need intellectual property protection to encourage the necessary investment.

Space activities require sophisticated technology, which results in high operating costs and significant ongoing investment. Therefore, at the start of the space age, space activities were the exclusive reserve of governmental agencies. At that time, space activities were mainly for exploration and experiment, including military operations. However, with advances in technology, space activities have become more commercialized and privatized. The United States, for example, began to privatize its space industry some decades ago by implementing statutory and regulatory changes to encourage private entrepreneurs.[14] Thus, the trend in many areas of space activities is a marked shift towards more participation by private entities. Some people may not realize how these outer space activities, including remote sensing data from space, satellite broadcasting and telecommunication services, have become part of our daily lives. Since the development of space activities needs huge investment, states now encourage private entrepreneurs to participate in space activities. Such private entity participation depends upon their ability to generate a return on their investment.

The protection of the intellectual property rights in outer space activities is one potential way to serve and guarantee the interests of private enterprise in return for their investment.[15] However, the scope and application of principles of 'freedom of exploration', 'use' and 'non-appropriation' of outer space provided for in the 1967 Outer Space Treaty raise concerns for any space investor. These principles imply that benefits and information derived from outer space activities will be shared; but those who own space technologies are likely to be reluctant and unwilling to share such technology without first obtaining a reasonable return. In addition, the underlining principles in outer space and intellectual property laws are different. The main principles of outer space law

---

[12] Dan L. Burk, 'Protection of Trade Secrets In Outer Space Activity: A Study in Federal Preemption' (1992–1993) 23 *Seton Hall Law Review* 560, 565.

[13] Ibid 567.

[14] Ibid 563–564.

[15] Ibid 577.

aim to secure benefits for all mankind whereas the tenet of intellectual property law is the protection of private property. Due to the commercialization and privatization of space activities, the underlining principles in the existing space treaties are considered to be a key hindrance to space development. It is arguably unfair for the party who has invested his effort and resources to exploit space activities to be unprotected and lose his control of the benefit of his output. Therefore, a protection regime is necessary to guarantee an investment in outer space. But what is the best way to balance the public benefits of space activities with the interests of private entities regarding intellectual property protection in outer space activities?

RESEARCH QUESTIONS

Despite the different approaches between space law and intellectual property law, current state practice shows that intellectual creation resulting from space activities is being protected.[16] Questions arise whether this application of intellectual property law to outer space activities is a breach of the state's obligation under the existing space treaties. Should right holders be made to relinquish intellectual property protection in works or inventions created or made in outer space as a result of the 'non-appropriation' and the 'common heritage of mankind' principles in outer space treaties? What exactly do these space law 'benefit' principles mean and to what extent do they apply to the intellectual property protection in space activities?[17] These questions will be analyzed in more detail in this book.

With regard to intellectual property protection, there are various forms of intellectual property rights which can be applied to space activities. Nevertheless, at present, only patents and copyright play a potential role in space industry.[18] However, both types of intellectual property protection pose questions and problems as to their applications to outer space activities in terms of subsistence and enforcement. Thus, it is necessary

---

[16]   See Chapter 3, p. 56.

[17]   For instance, in the case of geostationary satellite orbit where the allocation of this limited orbit is based on the first-come-first-serve basis, it is questionable that the utilization of such orbit is contrary to the non-appropriation principle in the 1967 Outer Space Treaty. Or whether medicine produced in a zero gravity environment meets the requirement of patentability. See Section 5 in Chapter 1 and Section 1.2.1 in Chapter 3, respectively.

[18]   WIPO Doc (n 118).

to examine whether space activities are well-protected under present patent and copyright regimes.

Moreover, intellectual property law is based upon territoriality, whereas outer space falls outside the scope of any sovereignty. Currently there is no global or international form of intellectual property (IP) protection which enables a right holder to gain protection without any territorial limitation; rather, it is necessary to seek protection in any individual protecting country. Thus, questions arise when applying national IP law in outer space where there is no law available. Moreover, the question of jurisdiction in outer space is also legally challenging. Can a state extend its jurisdiction for any act which occurred in outer space? What are the legal grounds for asserting jurisdiction? Should territoriality or nationality or any other principles be adopted in determining jurisdiction over outer space activity? In addition, can the state of registration assert its jurisdiction on the principle of quasi-territorial jurisdiction if an incident occurs in the International Space Station (ISS)? These questions lead to issues of appropriate jurisdiction and applicable law, as well as recognition and enforcement of foreign judgments, which all need deeper investigation.

METHODOLOGY

Since this legal research relates to intellectual property law and space law, the main objective is to determine how these two legal regimes, with their distinct characteristics, may be best integrated for the optimum benefit of both rights holders and the public. Thus, the doctrinal approach, which examines the principles enshrined in the relevant laws through both statutes and cases, plays a dominant role in most parts of this research. However, due to general limitations of the doctrinal approach (in terms of investigating possible 'real world' answers), and more specifically since in this subject area there is limited statutory and case law for investigation, it is important to draw upon other approaches. Therefore, this work is based on a comparative study of law.

The study of comparative law begins by setting a question or a hypothesis.[19] The next step is to investigate other legal systems to find out how these deal with the same problem.[20] Given the lack of available case law relating to intellectual property rights in outer space activities,

---

[19]   Konrad Zweigert and Hein Kotz, *An Introduction to Comparative Law* (Oxford: Clarendon Press 1998) 34.
[20]   Ibid.

hypothetical cases will be examined and discussed in order to propose appropriate solutions. This comparative legal study of intellectual property law and space law draws from the United States and the United Kingdom, cases chosen for several reasons. Firstly, both of them are space-faring nations. Although the United Kingdom may not be directly comparable to the United States in term of space technology, the United Kingdom is one of the founding members of the European Space Agency (ESA), an intergovernmental organization and a major leader in the space industry today. Also, both the United States and United Kingdom (by ESA) are participants in the International Space Station (ISS) project. Secondly, the intellectual property laws of the United States and United Kingdom have been developed consistently to keep pace with new technologies. In addition, as a result of EU harmonization of law in this field, intellectual property law in the United Kingdom is generally similar to – or the same as – equivalent laws of other European Union countries.

OUTLINE OF THE BOOK

This book consists of seven parts. After the introduction, Chapter 1 will deal with the international space law treaties. The main principles, namely the province of all mankind, the common heritage of mankind and the non-appropriation principles, will be examined to find out how these principles are applied to space activities and to assess whether these principles might prevent an assertion of intellectual property protection in space activities.

Chapter 2 will deal with the international conventions relating to intellectual property rights. Attention will be paid only to the major and relevant conventions. In this chapter, the principles embedded in these IP conventions (national treatment, the territoriality of IP rights and the most-favored nation provisions, as well as the priority rights of the Paris Convention) will be researched to investigate whether there is any obstacle when applying these conventions to outer space activities, e.g., how and to what extent do these main principles apply to the outer space activities in issue?

Chapter 3 focuses on patents in outer space, including patentability issues such as patentable subject matter. The chapter will seek to answer a number of specific questions. Do the characteristics of space activities hinder the results from being patented? How should the patentability requirements of novelty, non-obviousness and industrial application be assessed in relation to space activities? Do they need to have different assessment standards compared to earth-based inventions? In addition, the so-called temporary presence exception will be examined to determine whether this rule would apply to space vehicles or not. Attention will also be paid to the International Space Station (ISS), its legal structure and any implications which might result in respect of IP rights, especially patents, in outer space activities which take place on board.

Chapter 4 will investigate the application of copyright law to outer space activities. The discussion will focus on space telecommunication and satellite remote sensing to determine to what extent these activities are copyrightable. In the case of remote sensing data, the analysis will cover an understanding of whether the difference in character between 'unenhanced' and 'enhanced' data will require different levels of protection.

Chapter 5 will be devoted to the private international law matter which will come to fill the gap of the non-availability of specific remedies for intellectual protection of outer space activities. This chapter begins with a discussion on the competency of courts, followed by analysis of the applicable law. The recognition and enforcement of foreign judgments will be discussed in the last part of this chapter. Hypothetical cases will be introduced and used as parts of the discussion in this chapter.

Based upon the findings in previous chapters, the solutions or alternatives which would better suit for the protection of intellectual property rights in outer space activities will be proposed in the conclusion as the last part of this research.

LIMITATIONS

The study of this research is limited to the application of two forms of IP rights to outer space activities – patents and copyrights. This is because at present only patents and copyrights play a significant role to the protection of IP rights in outer space activities. While this book focuses on US and UK law, EU law will be addressed when necessary and relevant as a result of the UK's membership of the European Union. Case laws primarily cover the two jurisdictions, whereas case law from other jurisdictions will be examined when they are relevant to the research topic (e.g., Chapter 4). The main literature is from the US, UK and Europe, although other resources will be taken into account if necessary. The court cases used in this book are from several databases[21] as updated until 31 May 2014.

---

[21] Westlaw, LexisNexis and the Thai Supreme Court database.

1. International space law and its implications for outer space activities

The importance and potential of space activities have drawn the attention of the world community to intellectual property law's protection of such activities. To appreciate how and to what extent space activities should be protected, it is first necessary to analyze the principles set forth in space law instruments and find out how these legal rules are applied to space activities. This chapter begins with a categorization of space activities. The next part is devoted to defining and delimiting 'outer space' to provide a better understanding of the boundary to which this legal regime properly applies. Then, space law treaties will be briefly examined. The fundamental principles of space law (freedom of use and access, non-appropriation, the 'Province of all Mankind' and the 'Common Heritage of Mankind') will be shown to be based upon common, or shared, 'ownership' among states. These space law principles and basic principles of private intellectual property rights – which exclude others from exploiting the protected work without the right holder's consent – would appear to conflict, such that it would seem problematic to apply both legal regimes to intellectual works created in outer space. This problem will be discussed in more detail, together with an analysis of its implications to space activities, in the last part of this chapter.

1.   SPACE ACTIVITIES

There are a number of activities that take place in outer space. Satellites are presently the dominant commercial activity in the spatial area. These satellites operate in various fields, such as telecommunication, navigation, remote sensing of the earth's resources and meteorology.[22] Satellites are employed in either earth-oriented activities or space-related activities;

---

[22]   James J. Trimble, 'International Law of Outer Space and Its Effect on Commercial Space Activity' (1984) 113 *Pepperdine Law Review* 521, 523.

i.e., activities which are carried out in outer space but which directly affect the earth by capturing images of the earth or transmitting signals to the earth. Finally, space-created activities exploit space resources, for example, using Helium-3 available on the Moon as a component of nuclear power or producing cost-effective pharmaceuticals and electronics under zero gravity.[23]

2. THE DEFINITION AND DELIMITATION OF OUTER SPACE

At present, there is no precise definition of either 'outer space' or 'delimitation of outer space', and these two terms are used interchangeably. This book will use 'delimitation of outer space'. Although the delimitation question has long been discussed under the auspices of the Legal Sub-Committee of the Committee on the Peaceful Uses of Outer Space, a body of the United Nations since 1966,[24] no agreement has yet been reached. While there is no delimitation of outer space under any international regime, some states include definitions in their national legislation. For example, Australia amended its Space Activities Act of 1988 in 2002 to define 'outer space' as an area beyond the distance of 100 km above mean sea level.[25]

One important factor preventing agreement on the definition and delimitation of outer space is the lack of consensus on the criteria for setting such delimitation. Two main approaches, the 'spatial' approach and the 'functional' approach, have been put forward for consideration.

2.1 The Spatial Approach

Under the spatial approach, the boundary of outer space is based upon scientific and technical criteria. These, in turn, split into several theories,[26] namely:

---

[23] David Lamb, *The Search for Extraterritorial Intelligence: A Philosophical Inquiry* (Routledge 2001) 124.

[24] UN DOC. A/AC.105/769 (18 January 2002) para 3.

[25] UN DOC. A/AC.105/865/Add 11 (21 February 2012) p. 2.

[26] UN. Doc. A/AC.105/C.2/7 (7 May 1970) and UN Doc A/AC/C.2/7/Add. 1 (21 January 1977). See more in I.H.Ph. Diederiks-Verschoor and V. Kopal, *An Introduction to Space Law* (3rd ed., Wolters Kluwer 2008) 17–20; Marietta Benkö et al, *Space Law in the United Nations* (Martinus Nijhoff Publishers 1985) 127–130; Bin Cheng, *Studies in International Space Law* (Clarendon Press Oxford 1997) 444–451; and Rhys Monahan, 'The Sky's the Limit? Establishing

A.   Demarcation based upon an equation of the upper limit of national sovereignty with the concept of 'atmosphere';

B.   Demarcation based upon the division of atmosphere into layers;

C.   Demarcation based upon the maximum altitude of aircraft flight (theory of navigable air space);

D.   Demarcation based upon aerodynamic characteristics of flight instrumentalities (von Karman line);

E.   Demarcation according to the lowest perigee of an orbiting satellite;[27]

F.   Demarcation based upon the earth's gravitational effects;

G.   Demarcation based upon effective control; and

H.   Demarcation based upon the division of space into zones.

Of these, E – the lowest perigee of an orbiting satellite – has gained most attention from those states which favor a spatial delimitation.[28] This theory suggests that a boundary be set at an altitude of approximately 100–110 km above sea level.[29] This altitude is close to one that the USSR submitted in a working paper to the United Nations Committee on the Peaceful Uses of Outer Space (UNCOPUOS) Legal Sub-Committee for consideration during its 22nd session in 1983,[30] which proposed the boundary between air space and outer space at an altitude not exceeding 110 km above sea level.

2.2   The Functional Approach

Contrary to the spatial approach, the boundary adopted under the functional approach is based upon the nature, type and circumstances of various space activities.[31] States favoring this approach suggest that a distinction be made between aeronautical and astronautical activities. Thus, activities are regulated in accordance with the particular mission

---

a Legal Delimitation of Airspace and Outer Space' (D.Phil thesis, Durham University 2008) 23–25 and 37–52.

[27]   The perigee is the point where the orbit is nearest to the earth while the apogee is farthest away from the earth. See Benkö (n 26) 124.

[28]   Ibid 127.

[29]   Ibid 128.

[30]   UN Doc. A/AC.105/C.2/L.139 (4 April 1983).

[31]   Benkö (n 26) 129; Diederiks-Verschoor and Kopal (n 26) 18.

and objectives under a single legal regime of either air law or space law.[32] Implicitly, there is no need to establish a delimitation of outer space.[33]

Those states which favor the precise demarcation of outer space support the spatial approach, whereas those who oppose to such demarcation prefer the functional approach, as the latter allows more flexibility in terms of the development of space technology.[34]

This lack of a definition and delimitation of outer space is problematic, since certain particular areas are neither explicitly defined as 'air space' or 'outer space'. For example, it is vague whether an area located between 80 km and 120 km above sea level would be classified as either air space or outer space in the absence of demarcation, since 80 km is the maximum attitude for convention aircraft, and 120 km is the lowest attitude in which space activities could be carried out.[35] Satellites which are stationed in a geostationary orbit are a good example of this ambiguity. Owing to this lack of any internationally recognized delimitation, equatorial states claim sovereignty over that part of the geostationary orbit which is located over their respective territories;[36] whereas technologically developed countries believe that the geostationary orbit is an integral part of outer space.[37] This uncertain status of areas leads to legal jurisdictional problems.

According to international law, a state has sovereignty over the airspace above its territory.[38] However, national sovereignty does not extend into outer space.[39] Thus, it is necessary to determine where a state's airspace ends to ensure that the appropriate legal regime is applied. One possible scenario which might occur and which is relevant to the subject of this book is the creation or infringement of an intellectual work is in just such an ambiguous location. This would cast doubt on the 'legal' location of creation or infringement, and the question of which applicable legal regime arises. Should we apply the law of the

---

[32] Ibid.
[33] Ibid.
[34] Trimble (n 22) 556–557.
[35] Diederiks-Verschoor and Kopal (n 26) 17.
[36] The Bogota Declaration was issued on 3 December 1976 by the equatorial states, claiming their sovereignty over the geostationary orbit. The text of the Bogota declaration is available at <http://www.spacelaw.olemiss.edu/library/space/International_Agreements/declarations/1976_bogota_declaration.pdf> (accessed 31 January 2016).
[37] Diederiks-Verschoor and Kopal (n 26) 21 and Benkö (n 26) 138.
[38] Article 1 of the 1944 Chicago Convention.
[39] Article II of the Outer Space Treaty.

underlying state or is there no law to apply? For example, would satellite signals transmitted from a satellite stationed in a geostationary orbit located over equatorial countries be considered as works created or, if intercepted, be infringed, in outer space or in the sovereign air space of those respective countries? These hypothetical examples highlight why a boundary is necessary if unpredictability arising from different legal application is to be avoided. While it might be argued that this issue is being overemphasized at this stage, given increasing use of space technology, this problem is worth considering now rather than later.

3. AN OVERVIEW OF INTERNATIONAL SPACE LAW

In the realm of international space law, there are now five treaties under the auspices of the United Nations. These are: the 1967 Treaty on Principles Governing the Activities of States in the Exploration and Use of Outer Space, including the Moon and Other Celestial Bodies (hereinafter referred to as 'the Outer Space Treaty'), the 1968 Agreement on the Rescue of Astronauts, the Return of Astronauts and the Return of Objects Launched into Outer Space ('the Rescue Agreement'), the 1972 Convention on International Liability for Damage Caused by Space Objects ('the Liability Convention'), the 1976 Convention on Registration of Objects Launched in Outer Space ('the Registration Convention') and the 1979 Agreement Governing the Activities of States on the Moon and Other Celestial Bodies ('the Moon Agreement'). Only the Outer Space Treaty and the Moon Agreement are relevant to this book, and so the main focus will be on these treaties. However, this chapter will touch upon the other three instruments briefly.

3.1   The Outer Space Treaty of 1967

The Outer Space Treaty is the first international instrument on space law. It established regulations for activities carried out in outer space and on celestial bodies. Other subsequent international agreements on outer space have been enacted mainly to amplify and explicate the rules embodied in the Outer Space Treaty.[40] While there is no explicit provision on intellectual property rights in outer space in this treaty, this

---

[40]   Trimble (n 22) 528.

does not render it irrelevant to this research, because it includes provisions which are relevant when considering the exploitation of intellectual property rights in this extraterritorial area. Only these relevant provisions will be discussed in this chapter.

Article I(1) of the Outer Space Treaty states that any exploitation and use of outer space must be carried out 'for the benefit and in the interest of all states irrespective of their economic and social capabilities and shall be the province of all mankind'.[41] However, the treaty itself lacks either an explicit definition of the term 'province of all mankind' or any further explanation.[42] The United States has interpreted this term as being equivalent to 'benefit of all mankind', which has led to a divergence of interpretations.[43] We shall return to this later in the chapter.[44]

Article I(2) sets out a principle of freedom of exploration and use of outer space on the basis of equality and in accordance with international law.[45] Article III of the treaty further provides that the space activities are carried out in accordance with the international law including the Charter of the United Nations.[46]

Article II establishes the 'non-appropriation principle' by stating that outer space is not subject to 'national appropriation ... by any means'.[47] It is arguable whether private appropriation is allowed under this article, since the provision refers to *national* appropriation and does not explicitly mention private appropriation. However, most scholars are of the

---

[41] Article I(1) of the Outer Space Treaty states, 'The exploration and use of outer space, including the Moon and other celestial bodies, shall be carried out for the benefit and in the interests of all countries, irrespective of their degree of economic or scientific development, and shall be the province of all mankind.'

[42] Diederiks-Verschoor and Kopal (n 26) 25.

[43] *Treaty on Outer Space*, Hearing before the Commission on Foreign Relations Senate Executive D. 90th Cong, 1st Session 56, 1967, 69–70.

[44] See Section 5 of this chapter.

[45] Article I(2) of the Outer Space Treaty states, 'Outer space, including the Moon and other celestial bodies, shall be free for exploration and use by all States without discrimination of any kind, on a basis of equality and in accordance with international law, and there shall be free access to all areas of celestial bodies'.

[46] Article III of the Outer Space Treaty states, 'States Parties to the Treaty shall carry on activities in the exploration and use of outer space, including the Moon and other celestial bodies, in accordance with international law, including the Charter of the United Nations, in the interest of maintaining international peace and security and promoting international co-operation and understanding.'

[47] Article II of the Outer Space Treaty states, 'Outer Space, including the Moon and other celestial bodies, is not subject to national appropriation by claim of sovereignty, by means of use or occupation, or by any other means'.

view that the purpose of Article II's non-appropriation rule is to prevent any appropriation of outer space, irrespective of who is making the claim.[48] In other words, this provision identifies the legal nature of outer space as *res communis*, in which all states are equally free to access, use or exploit, but all are prohibited from any kind of appropriation.

Article VIII of the treaty establishes jurisdiction for a state of registry 'to retain jurisdiction and control over such object, and over any personnel thereof, while in outer space or on a celestial body'. Such jurisdiction and control applies to personnel only and does not extend to any third party.

When the Outer Space Treaty was concluded, its drafters probably would not have considered the issue of intellectual property rights in outer space, perhaps because it seemed premature to discuss the issue at that time. However, it is questionable how the two fundamental principles of space law, i.e., the province of all mankind and non-appropriation principles, are to be accommodated when applied to intellectual property creations in space activities. Thus, it is worth examining whether these two principles would recognize the intellectual property rights in outer space. Accordingly, this issue will be discussed in detail later in this chapter,[49] together with a related 'common heritage of mankind' principle, which was established in the Moon Agreement.[50]

3.2   The Rescue Agreement of 1968

The Rescue Agreement sets forth the obligations for States Parties on assistance to astronauts in case of an accident, distress or emergency, including those practical measures for rescuing and assisting the crew.[51] In addition, States Parties are bound to notify the launching authority and the Secretary-General of the United Nations immediately about any such relevant situation.[52] This Agreement is not pertinent to the subject of this book.

---

[48]   Fabio Tronchetti, *The Exploitation of Natural Resources of the Moon and Other Celestial Bodies* (Martinus Nijhoff 2009) 29–33.
[49]   See Sections 4.2, 4.3 and 5.0 of this chapter.
[50]   Article 11 paragraph 1 of the Moon Agreement.
[51]   See more in Diederiks-Verschoor and Kopal (n 26) 31–34 and Bin Cheng (n 26) 263–285
[52]   Article 1 of the Agreement.

3.3 The Liability Convention of 1972

The Liability Convention establishes liability principles for any damage caused by space objects and measures of compensation for victims of such damage. Pursuant to Article I of this Convention, four States potentially qualify as the 'launching State', which is defined as: (1) the state which launches; (2) the state which procures the launching; (3) the state whose territory is used for launching; and (4) the state whose facilities are used for launching.[53] Victims have flexibility to obtain compensation from one of these four launching states for damage caused by a space object.[54] Reference to the concept of 'launching state' will be discussed, where relevant, in following chapters.[55]

3.4 The Registration Convention of 1976

The purpose of the Registration Convention is to establish an identification system for objects launched into outer space. Specified information must be furnished to be recorded on a UN register in each case.[56] Unlike registration of an aircraft or ship, registration of a space object does not automatically confer the nationality of the registering state on that object.[57] This Convention is therefore only relevant to this book insofar as it is necessary to identify the state of registry when dealing with jurisdiction and choice-of-law matters, as discussed in Chapter 5.[58] The Convention is silent on the issue of jurisdiction and control over unregistered space objects.[59]

3.5 The Moon Agreement of 1979

The Moon Agreement includes provisions which are pertinent for our study. In compliance with the Outer Space Treaty, Article 4 of the Moon

---

[53]   The 'launching authority' has been addressed in Article 6 of the Astronaut Agreement as the State responsible for the launching. The meaning of such authority has been made clearer by giving definition of 'launching State' in Article I (c) of this Convention.

[54]   Article II of the Convention, see more explanation about this Convention in Diederiks-Verschoor and Kopal (n 26) 35–44 and Cheng (n 26) 286–356.

[55]   See Chapter 3, Section 4 on infringement.

[56]   Article IV of the Convention.

[57]   This issue will be examined again in section 1.2.4 in Chapter 5.

[58]   See Chapter 5, the hypothetical cases number 1 and 3 under the choice of law section.

[59]   Diederiks-Verschoor and Kopal (n 26) 46.

Agreement requires that 'the exploration and use of the Moon shall be the province of all mankind and shall be carried out for the benefit and in the interest of all countries, irrespective of their degree of economic or scientific development'.[60] This provision restates the province of all mankind principle, as contained in the Outer Space Treaty. Thus, the exploitation and the use of outer space, including the Moon and other celestial bodies, must be carried out for the benefit of all countries.

The Moon Agreement reaffirms the non-appropriation principle, as stated in the Outer Space Treaty. This is established in Article 11(2) of the Moon Agreement and further elaborated in Article 11(3) of this Agreement. In addition, Article 11(4) confirms the right to exploit and use the Moon on the basis of equality without any kind of discrimination. The discussion of these provisions will be examined later in this chapter, in Section 4.3.[61]

4. FUNDAMENTAL PRINCIPLES OF INTERNATIONAL SPACE LAW

4.1 Freedom of Exploration and Use of Outer Space

The doctrine of freedom of exploration and use of outer space, set out in the Outer Space Treaty, establishes the legal status of outer space as *res communis*: an area which is not subject to any claim by any state; a characteristic which outer space shares with the high sea.[62] Article I(2) of the Outer Space Treaty embodies three basic rights: the right of free access, the right of free exploration and the right of free use.[63] Thus, every state has an equal right to explore, use and access outer space and its resources, provided that such exploration and use are carried out for the benefit and in the interest of all countries, as required by Article I(1). However, the Treaty itself contains no further explanation of the meaning of these rights or the proviso. The provision of Article I(1) could be interpreted to mean that all countries not only have the right to take part in these activities, but also to enjoy a right of access to those technologies involved. Some scholars view the obligation (that all exploration and

---

60   Article I of Outer Space Treaty.
61   See below, Section 4.3.
62   Article 2 of the Geneva Convention on the High Seas and Article 89 of the 1982 Convention on the Law of the Sea and outer space (see UN General Assembly Resolutions 1962 (XVII), 1721 (XVI), and 1884 (XVIII).
63   Article I(2) of the Outer Space Treaty (n 45).

use be carried out for the benefit and in the interest of all countries) as a general provision which sets a guideline for any space-faring nation in conducting their activities in outer space.[64] Such an interpretation of this provision would enable a state or private entity to enjoy the fruit arising from its activities in outer space, including any intellectual property rights. In my opinion, it would be an overly broad interpretation of Article I of the Outer Space Treaty to require all benefits, including intellectual property rights, arising from any space venture to be relinquished.

Rather, this Article merely affirms the freedom of access and use of outer space, as long as such activities do not hamper or prevent others from likewise freely accessing and exploiting outer space. Applying this interpretation, any party *is* entitled to reap any benefit from any value-added intellectual work created in outer space. Hence, enjoyment of a proprietary interest in technology of space activities is not in conflict with the principles enunciated in Article I of the Outer Space Treaty.

4.2 Non-appropriation of Outer Space

The non-appropriation principle was originally included in UN General Assembly Resolutions 1721 and its declaration of 1962, before later becoming legally binding by its incorporation as Article II of the Outer Space Treaty.[65] The principle of non-appropriation in Article II of this Treaty confirms outer space as a *res communis*.[66] It has been agreed that the aim of this Article is to ban any claim of national sovereignty or exclusive property rights in outer space and its celestial bodies.[67] Articles 11(2) and 11(3) of the Moon Agreement reaffirm the non-appropriation

---

[64] Trimble (n 22) 530 and Roger K. Hoover, 'Law and Security in Outer Space from the Viewpoint of Private Industry' (1983) 11 *Journal of Space Law* 115, 122.

[65] The UN General Resolution 1721 (XVI) (20 December 1961) namely 'International Cooperation in the Peaceful Uses of Outer Space' and UN Declaration 1962 (XIII) (13 December 1963) namely 'Declaration Of Legal Principles Governing the Activities of States in the Exploration and Use of Outer Space.' The text of these two documents are available online at <http://www.oosa.unvienna.org/oosa/SpaceLaw/gares/html/gares_16_1721.html> and <http://www.unoosa.org/oosa/SpaceLaw/lpos.html>, respectively (accessed 31 January 2016).

[66] Glen Reynolds and Robert Merges, *Outer Space Problems of Law and Policy* (2nd ed., Westview Press 1997) 78.

[67] Ibid.

of the Moon and the prohibition of the property rights in the Moon, respectively.[68]

Questions arise as to the exact meaning of this non-appropriation principle and whether it is possible for states to exploit and explore outer space without violating it. Does the non-appropriation principle mean that states and private entities are prevented from reaping the fruit resulting from their effort and investment in outer space? Since the drafters of the Outer Space Treaty chose to declare outer space *res communis*,[69] rather than a *res nullius*,[70] the non-appropriation principle has to be read and interpreted in conjunction with the freedom of the exploration and exploitation principle set out in Article I of the treaty.[71] Thus, one possible conclusion is that states and natural or legal persons are entitled to free and equal access to the environment of space which is in the interest of all countries, but in doing so, no assertion on any claim of ownership over these extraterritorial areas is permitted.[72] However, some scholars view the term "national appropriation" in Article II as referring only to states, such that private appropriation is not forbidden.[73]

It would seem overly broad to interpret Article II as an absolute bar to property rights in natural resources in outer space. Taking into consideration the language of Article 6(2) of the Moon Agreement, which allows states to collect and remove samples of Moon minerals and substances, it appears that property rights over natural resources on the Moon is permissible, even only for a scientific purpose as stated in this provision.[74] In addition, Article 11(3) of the Moon Agreement states that

---

[68]   Article 11(2) and Article 11(3) of the Moon Agreement.

[69]   A territory that is not subject to national appropriation in Bin Cheng (n 26) 80.

[70]   A territory that is not subject to the territorial jurisdiction of any recognized subject of international law but susceptible of national appropriation, ibid 80.

[71]   Glen Reynolds and Robert Merges (n 66) 80.

[72]   Leslie Tennen, 'Towards a New Regime for Exploration of Outer Space Mineral Resources' (2010) 88 *Nebraska Law Review* 794, 807; Fabio Tronchetti, 'The Non-Appropriation Principles as a Structural Norm of International Law: A New Way of Interpreting Article II of the Outer Space Treaty' (2008) 33 *Air and Space Law* 277, 280.

[73]   Tronchetti (n 72) 280–281 and Daniel A. Porras, 'Comment: The "Common Heritage" of Outer Space: Equal Benefits for Most of Mankind' (2006) 37 *California Western International Law Journal* 143, 154.

[74]   Article 6(2) of the Moon Agreement provides: 'In carrying out scientific investigations and in furtherance of the provisions of this Agreement, the States Parties shall have the right to collect and remove from the Moon samples of its

'Neither surface nor the substance of the Moon, nor any part thereof or natural resources in place, shall become property of any state'. This text leads some scholars to interpret that provision as allowing some acquisition of property from the Moon, since the Article only prohibits the acquisition of that which is 'in place'. This might permit appropriation of that which has already been removed from its place.[75] But, one might also argue that since most space-faring nations have yet to ratify the Moon Agreement, its provisions cannot stand as a legal norm for the world community.[76] Therefore, the non-appropriative nature of outer space which prohibits the acquisition of outer space from both public and private entities is still well-founded as a legal norm.

Some experts have suggested that the non-appropriation principle should be abrogated because it is considered an obstruction to the commercialization of outer space.[77] However, the majority of states believe otherwise.

As the non-appropriation principle aims to prevent the acquisition of any part of outer space or its resources, it may be concluded that this rule is only designed to govern tangible property, not intangible property. This view has gained support from some scholars.[78] This is because recognizing intellectual property rights in outer space or in works created in outer space would not result in physical appropriation either of parts of outer space or its resources. In addition, the past practice of some states to recognize intellectual property rights in works created in outer space supports the view that intellectual property rights in such works is possible and is justified.[79]

---

mineral and other substances. Such samples shall remain at the disposal of those States Parties which caused them to be collected and may be used by them for scientific purposes'.

[75] Kemal Baslar, *The Concept of the Common Heritage of Mankind in International Law* (Martinus Nijhoff 1998) 167–169.

[76] The United States, the USSR, and China are not parties to the Moon Agreement. For the status of the international agreements relating to outer space activities as of 8 April 2015 see UN doc A/AC.105/C.2/2015/CRP.8 available online at <http://www.unoosa.org/pdf/limited/c2/AC105_C2_2015_CRP08E.pdf> (accessed 29 December 2015).

[77] Tennen (n 72) 807–809.

[78] Christopher Miles, 'Assessing the Need for an International Patent Regime for Inventions in Outer Space' (2008) 11 *Tulane Journal of Technology and Intellectual Property* 59, 64.

[79] For example, the US Patent in Space Act.

However, the situation might be more complex if an intellectual property work created involved using outer space resources as a component of its output. Take, as a hypothetical example: Scientist A, a national of the United States, discovers a process to produce nuclear power using Helium-3 as its major constituent. Helium-3 is known to be a valuable resource for generating nuclear power which is rare on earth, but abundant on the Moon.[80] The production of nuclear power using this process would be cost-effective if produced in outer space. But would the process of producing this nuclear power violate the non-appropriation principle if the Moon's natural resources are taken as part of this process? A strict interpretation would see use of Helium-3 as a type of appropriation of the Moon's resources, and so a breach of the non-appropriation obligation. But, if neither the production of such nuclear power nor intellectual property rights protecting the process are allowed, the world community would lose the benefit of this additional source of power. However, a compromise could be put forward which would allow exploitation of this intellectual property work based upon licensing. Any such licensing scheme would need to ensure third parties fair and equitable access to this process in order to uphold the principle of freedom of exploration and use, but with appropriate safeguards in place, exploitation via licensing would guarantee Scientist A an opportunity to enjoy some benefit from his effort and investment.

The situation is essentially the same when considering application of the non-appropriation principle to remote sensing and satellite telecommunication. This is because situating a satellite in orbit within a specific spatial area could be considered as an appropriation of outer space, particularly when taking into account the fact that geostationary orbits are considered a 'limited natural resource', and access to such resources must comply with the International Telecommunication Union (ITU) Constitution.[81]

---

[80]   Shameem Kazmi, 'Moon Mining: Myth or Reality?' Earth Times (27 September 2012) <http://www.earthtimes.org/energy/moon-mining-myh-reality/2201/> (accessed 31 January 2016).

[81]   Article 44(2) of the ITU Constitution which stipulates that '*In using frequency bands for radio services, Members shall bear in mind that radio frequencies and the geostationary-satellite orbit are limited natural resources and that they must be used rationally, efficiently and economically, in conformity with the provisions of the Radio Regulations, so that countries or groups of countries may have equitable access to both, taking into account the special needs of the developing countries and the geographical situation of particular countries*' (emphasis added). The full text of the ITU Constitution is available

However, pharmaceuticals and electronics produced under zero gravity should not be considered as a violation of the non-appropriation principle because those works are only *created* in outer space, without physically taking any space resources.

4.3   The Province of All Mankind and Common Heritage of Mankind

The 'province of all mankind' principle in the Outer Space Treaty (hereafter 'the Province principle') and the 'common heritage of mankind' principle in the Moon Agreement (hereafter 'the Common Heritage principle') both guarantee that outer space and its resources are a common heritage. However, they differ since the Province principle grants all states freedom of access to natural resources in outer space and its celestial bodies on an equal basis, whereas the Common Heritage principle, while providing for equal freedom of access, also requires the exploiter to share any benefit with all states.[82] These two principles are the most controversial principles in space law, and no agreement has been reached as to their precise definition.

What is the implication of these two principles for intellectual property rights? Firstly, it is significant that the Outer Space Treaty, which establishes the Province principle, has been ratified by 102 states, whereas the Moon Agreement, which establishes the Common Heritage principle, has only 15 states parties, and these do not include the main space power countries: the United States, Russian Federation and China.[83] Thus, the Province principle is more widely accepted than the Common Heritage principle. However, this does not mean that the Common Heritage principle gains less attention within the space law world community. A significant quantity of legal scholarship is devoted to the dominant role which the Common Heritage principle plays in space activities.[84] Thus, it is appropriate to take account of the Common

online at <http://www.itu.int/dms_pub/itu-s/oth/02/09/s02090000115201pdfe.pdf> (accessed 31 January 2016).

[82]   David Tan, 'Towards a New Regime for the Protection of Outer Space as the "province of all mankind"' (2000) 25 *Yale Journal of International Law* 145, 161.

[83]   The current status of the treaties as of 29 December 2015 is available online at <http://www.unoosa.org/pdf/limited/c2/AC105_C2_2015_CRP08E.pdf> (accessed 29 December 2015).

[84]   Tan (n 82) 161; Tronchetti (n 48); Baslar (n 75); Carl Q. Christol, 'The Common Heritage of Mankind Provision in the 1979 Agreement Governing the Activities of States on the Moon and Other Celestial Bodies' (1980) 14 *International Lawyer* 429; Rudiger Wolfrum, 'The Principle of the Common

Heritage principle when considering the international law implications of any utilization of outer space and space resources, including the Moon.

Since neither the Outer Space Treaty nor the Moon Agreement include precise definitions of these principles, it is necessary to look at the texts of these treaties to obtain guidance for the proper interpretation of these principles.

Article I(I) of the Outer Space Treaty provides that 'the exploration and use of outer space ... shall be carried out for the benefit and in the interest of all countries, irrespective of their degree of economic or scientific development, and shall be the province of all mankind', and Article I(II) states that 'Outer Space, including the Moon and other celestial bodies, shall be free for exploration and use by all states ... and shall be free access to all areas of celestial bodies'.

Taking the requirements of Article I(I) and I(II) together, the Province principle as established in Article I(I) proclaims outer space as *res communis*, where all States can freely and equally access its resources regardless of their technological capability and contribution to the exploitation.[85] The use of outer space resources is allowed as long as it does not interfere with others' uses.[86] In addition, the *res communis* doctrine forbids states from claiming sovereignty and property rights over this common area and its parts, a doctrine which is also embodied as the non-appropriation principle in Article II of the treaty.[87]

Nevertheless, some scholars believe that the Province principle in Article I(I) of the Outer Space Treaty is not intended to be *legally* binding, but rather imposes only a *moral* obligation upon states.[88] The

---

Heritage of Mankind' (1983) *Max-Planck-Institut für ausländisches öffentliches Recht und Völkerrecht* 312 available online at <http://www.zaoerv.de/43_1983/43_1983_2_a_312_337.pdf> (accessed 31 January 2016). Also, Scott Ervin, 'Law in a Vacuum: The Common Heritage Doctrine in Outer Space Law' (1984) 7 *Boston College International and Comparative Law Review* 403; Edward Guntrip, 'The Common Heritage of Mankind: An Adequate Regime for Managing the Deep Seabed?' (2003) 4 *Melbourne Journal of International Law*, 376; John Adolph, 'The Recent Boom in Private Space Development and the Necessity of an International Framework Embracing Private Property Rights to Encourage Investment' (2006) 40 *International Lawyer* 961.

[85]   Tronchetti (n 48) 23, see also Scott J. Shackelford, 'The Tragedy of the Common Heritage of Mankind' (2008) 27 *Stanford Environmental Law Journal* 101, 110.

[86]   Shackelford (n 85) 107.

[87]   Tronchetti (n 48) 87.

[88]   Opinions cited in Tronchetti (n 48) 24.

basis of this position is explained on the grounds that Article I(I) neither elaborates how the exploration of outer space for the benefit of all States is to take place, nor how the benefits arising from space activities are to be shared.[89] On the other hand, other scholars regard the Province principle of Article I(I) of the Outer Space Treaty as customary law binding all States.[90] This school refers to legal documents which preceded the treaty, namely the UN General Assembly Resolution 1721 and 1962 Declaration, to support their conclusion.[91] These documents, which were finally translated into Article I(I) of the Outer Space Treaty, recognize the common interest of all mankind and express a desire that states should have legal binding principles governing space activities.[92]

Reference to a 'common heritage of mankind' principle, such as that in the Moon Agreement, has been employed elsewhere in international law in relation to the high seas and Antarctica. Like outer space, these areas are beyond national jurisdiction, and they are also enriched with valuable resources which are held non-appropriable by states.[93] A 'common heritage of mankind' principle was first put forward in 1910 when it was suggested that Antarctica should be an area commonly owned by all nations.[94] It was later formally introduced to the world community in 1967, when United Nations Ambassador Arvid Pardo suggested that the seabed and oceans, being areas beyond any national jurisdiction, should be considered as a common heritage of mankind to be administered by an international authority for the benefit of all people.[95] This principle was later embodied in Articles 11(1) of the Moon Agreement and in the Law of the Sea Convention of 1982.[96]

As mentioned above, the Common Heritage principle of the Moon Agreement shares some common characteristic with the Province principle in term of free access on an equal basis, but differs from the latter in some aspects.[97] The Common Heritage principle has been interpreted

---

[89]   Ibid.

[90]   Ibid.

[91]   See UN documents cited above (n 65).

[92]   Tronchetti (n 48) 24.

[93]   Tronchetti (n 48) 86; Carl Q. Christol, *The Modern International Law of Outer Space* (2nd ed., Pergamon Press 1984) 286; Wolfrum (n 84) 313.

[94]   Tronchetti (n 48) 91.

[95]   Ibid 92–93.

[96]   Article 11.1 of the Moon Agreement states, 'The Moon and its natural resources are the common heritage of mankind, which finds its expression in the provisions of this Agreement, in particular in paragraph 5 of this Article.'

[97]   Tan (n 82) 161. For more details on this issue, see, Tronchetti (n 48); Baslar (n 75); Christol, et al. (n 84).

to mean that the protected areas and their natural resources form a human heritage, such that the interest of future generation must be taken into account when these common areas are being exploited.[98] It prohibits any one state or person from exclusively using these areas or their resources. Thus a sharing of benefit arises from exploitative activities in these protected areas, in accordance with principles and rules established by an international regime.[99]

The concept of equitable sharing of benefits through an international regime has been addressed in Articles 11(5) and 11(7) (d) of the Moon Agreement.[100] The concept of benefit sharing comes from the belief that natural resources should be held in trust by all mankind.[101]

The Common Heritage principle has been interpreted differently among states. Developing states tend to hold that since common areas belong to 'all nations', any benefit derived from exploitation of such common resource should be shared equally among states, regardless of their respective contribution to the particular exploitation.[102] Under this interpretation, nations would derive benefit from exploitative activities without making either a financial or intellectual investment. On the other hand, developed countries consider reference to equitable sharing extends only to mean that every state has an equal right to exploit natural

---

[98]   Tronchetti (n 48) 88.

[99]   Ibid.

[100]   Article 11(5) states that 'States Parties to this Agreement hereby under-take to establish an international regime, including appropriate procedures, to govern the exploitation of the natural resources of the Moon as such exploitation is about to become feasible. This provision shall be implemented in accordance with article 18 of this Agreement.'

Article 11(7) states:

The main purposes of the international regime to be established shall include:

(d) an equitable sharing by all States Parties in the benefits derived from those resources, whereby the interests and needs of the developing countries as well as the efforts of those countries which have contributed either directly or indirectly to the exploration of the Moon, shall be given special consideration.

[101]   Baslar (n 75) 172. It should be noted that this concept of benefit sharing is comparable to the access and benefit sharing (ABS) regime in the Convention on Biological Diversity (CBD). Article 8(j) of the Convention establishes ABS regime requiring that the use of genetic resources be treated on a fair and equitable basis.

[102]   Ibid 165.

resources freely, such that states have no legitimate claim to the technology or investment in other's exploitation.[103]

It is noted that a provision in the Moon Agreement which establishes an international 'policing' regime is ambiguous in terms of its implementation. While the Convention on the Law of the Sea ('UNCLOS') of 1982 includes the same provision,[104] pursuant to part XI of the UNCLOS, an International Seabed Authority has been set up with its clear authorization for the management of the exploration and exploitation of the deep seabed.[105] In contrast, while Article 11(5) of the Moon Agreement requires States Parties to set up an international regime to oversee utilization of the Moon, the treaty does not directly establish such entity itself. In addition, this provision does not seem to be compulsory as it relies upon the good faith of States Parties to establish such an entity. Moreover, the Moon Agreement does not provide any direction for how to equitably share the benefits and what exactly such 'benefits' mean.[106] Taking into account the lack of clear guidance in the Moon Agreement itself, and the divergent interpretation of equitable sharing concept among states, it is questionable how the Common Heritage principle set out in the Moon Agreement should be implemented. However, it is likely that the interpretation of the non-space power nations might prevail based on the fact the space power countries are all reluctant to ratify the Moon Agreement.

Additionally, the Common Heritage principle is limited to the Moon, its resources and other celestial bodies within the solar system; it does not govern outer space more generally.[107] In other words, except for the Moon (its resources and other celestial bodies), outer space (and its resources) is subject only to the Province principle which does not oblige states to share the benefit through the international authority, as specified in the Common Heritage principle.

Another pertinent point is Article 4 of the Moon Agreement, which states that: 'The exploration and use of the Moon shall be the *province of all mankind* and shall be carried out for the benefit and in the interests of all countries, irrespective of their degree of economic or scientific

---

[103] Carol R. Buxton, 'Property in Outer Space: The Common Heritage of Mankind Principles vs. The "first in time, first in right, rule of property law"' (2004) 69 *Journal of Air Law and Commerce* 689, 692–693.

[104] Tronchetti (n 48) 54.

[105] Part XI Section 4 of the UNCLOS.

[106] Tronchetti (n 48) 55 and Shackelford (n 85) 137.

[107] Articles 1.1 and 11.1 of the Moon Agreement.

development'. So, whereas Article 11(1) of the Moon Agreement identifies the Moon and its natural resources as the 'common heritage of mankind', Article 4 of the *same* treaty refers to the 'province of all mankind'.

While some scholars therefore view 'province of all mankind' and 'common heritage of mankind' as equivalent and interchangeable terms,[108] I conclude otherwise. If the two terms were equivalent, why would a single instrument, the Moon Agreement, feature two different terms in the different provisions, rather than consistently adopting a single term? My view is supported by the fact that the two terms are not contradictory and can be interpreted in a consistent way: the Moon Agreement recognizes the legal status of the Moon and its resources as a common heritage of mankind (Article 11(1)) and provides that the method of management for the exploration and use of the Moon must be in line with the province of all mankind principle (Article 4). In other words, the 'common heritage of mankind' principle is an extension of the 'province of all mankind' principle, which further requires an equitable sharing benefit and establishment of a legal regime to regulate exploitation of the Moon.

Thus, it is reasonable to conclude that an intellectual output resulting from outer space activities may be protected, and that only the contributing states can reap the fruit of their investment. In addition, application of the Province and Common Heritage principles are consistent with the exclusive private rights arising from intellectual property protection regimes.[109]

Since the Province and Common Heritage principles share common characteristics (the latter requiring an additional equitable sharing of benefit), analysis of their implications to space activities in term of intellectual property rights will be addressed concurrently.

---

[108] Bess C.M. Reijnen, *The United Nations Space Treaties Analysed* (Editions Frontieres 1992) 96; Yun Zhao, *Space Commercialization and the Development of Space Law from a Chinese Legal Perspective* (Nova Science 2009) 6.

[109] See conclusion chapter (Q 1).

5. THE APPLICATION OF THE PROVINCE OF ALL MANKIND AND THE COMMON HERITAGE OF MANKIND PRINCIPLES TO OUTER SPACE ACTIVITIES

For the purpose of my analysis, it is appropriate to divide space activities into three groups, namely: (1) space-created works, the production of which involves use of outer space resources. Generating nuclear power using Helium-3 and manufacturing pharmaceuticals or electronics under zero gravity fall under this category; (2) space-related activities i.e., activities conducted in outer space but which are functionally related to earth, e.g., remote sensing and satellite telecommunication; and (3) non space-related works i.e., any work created in outer space which does not fall in either of the other two categories.

Are all three categories subject to the Common Heritage principle? Are those entities engaging in these space activities required to share any benefit derived from their investment? Do the Province and Common Heritage of Mankind principles override any intellectual property rights of those engaging in space activity? To answer these questions, we need to review the treaties where these two principles appear to find out how these two principles are interpreted. To recap, Article I of the Outer Space Treaty and Article 4(1) of the Moon Agreement state: 'the exploration and use of outer space shall be the province of all mankind', and Article 11(1) of the Moon Agreement further provides that 'the Moon and its natural resources are the common heritage of mankind'. These provisions define the legal status of outer space and its resources as a common heritage of mankind, which no public or private entity can appropriate as their own.

Since the Common Heritage and the Province principles are enunciated to govern the use, exploration and exploitation of outer space and its resources, an essential first step is to interpret the terms 'use', 'exploration' and 'exploitation'.

The term 'use' is considered to be equivalent to 'utilization' and 'exploitation', with the proviso that 'exploitation' seems to involve a commercial characteristic.[110] In addition, taking account of views expressed during negotiations relating to the draft treaty and states' practice prior to and after entry into force of the treaty, it could be concluded that

---

[110]   Reijnen (n 108) 93.

the terms 'use', 'exploration' and 'exploitation' encompass non-exclusive rights of all states to engage in exploitative activities.[111]

Applying this now to the three categories of outer space activities, processing Helium-3 available on the Moon to produce nuclear power can be better justified as 'using' the Moon and its resources, rather than being construed as being a space-created product. This is because the exemplar clearly acquires physical resources from the Moon as part of its process, rather than just taking advantage of weightlessness conditions on the Moon for processing. Furthermore, taking into consideration the potential breath of scope, as indicated above, it is possible that the production of such space-created products under weightlessness conditions may also be determined as falling within the scope of 'use, exploration and exploitation' of outer space, since these products are a result and benefit from space-exploitative activity. The space-related works, remote sensing and satellite telecommunication, might also 'use' outer space resources if applying the same interpretation of 'using', since these satellites have to be stationed in the orbit for their operations. On the other hand, intellectual works created while in outer space, but without any involvement of space resources – for example, writing new software code or a literary work – should fall outside the scope of the principles under consideration.

The next questions are how and to what extent the Province and Common Heritage principles apply to these space-related and space-created activities conducted 'using' space resources and the zero-gravity advantage, and then to consider the intellectual property law implications. In particular, does application of these principles mean that right holders have to relinquish their intellectual property rights by sharing the benefit with others, who have not contributed labor and effort in creation of such works?

I shall first consider remote sensing data. In a typical scenario, the state which is being monitored lacks the technological capability necessary to access any raw data and so would have to purchase processed data about its own territory from the state responsible for the remote sensing activity. Is this requirement to purchase contrary to the Province and Common Heritage principles? Does freedom to access, freedom of use and an equitable sharing mean of space law require the 'sensing' state to provide free use, access and sharing of all remote sensing data in a non-commercial way?

---

[111]   Christol (n 93) 42.

In order to answer these questions, it is necessary to supplement the texts of the space treaties guidance provided in UN Resolution 41/65 on the topic of remote sensing.[112] Although the resolution has no legal force, it has influential weight for possible future legislation.[113] Principle IV of this resolution reaffirms that the remote sensing activities 'shall be conducted in accordance with the principles contained in article I of the Outer Space Treaty' and that such 'activities shall be conducted on the basis of respect for the principle of full and permanent sovereignty of all states and people over their own wealth and natural resources'. Taking this UN principle into account, together with the Outer Space Treaty, one scholar concludes that the commercial practice of selling remote sensing data falls outside the common interests, since the sensed state has to pay for data concerning its own territory.[114]

However, in my view, it would be incorrect to interpret that a free access, free use and an equal sharing of information requirement on remote sensing data has to be on non-commercial basis only. This is because Article I of the Outer Space Treaty refers to the free use, free access of outer space and its celestial bodies. There is nothing in Article I that implicitly refers to the use and access of space technology. Thus, the trading of remote sensing data could not be contrary to the common interest principle in the Outer Space Treaty, because it falls *beyond* the scope of this provision, in my opinion.

Regarding the equitable sharing benefit encompassed in the Common Heritage principle, there are divergent views as to its meaning. One school of thought assumes that the reluctance of space-faring nations to ratify the Moon Agreement is attributable to the fact that these states believe that this rule could (or would) be interpreted in favor of developing states i.e., the benefit derived from space resources must be shared equally among all states regardless of their individual contributions. Thus, space-power nations are unwilling to share the benefits from their labor and investment and insist that such sharing does not apply to the technology in the exploration.

Notwithstanding how equitable sharing should be interpreted, this provision is not applicable to remote sensing data. This is because the

---

[112]   UN General Assembly Resolution 41/65, 3 December 1986, namely, 'Principles on Remote Sensing of the Earth from Space', A/RES/41/65 (hereinafter UN Remote Sensing Principles). Available online at <http://www.unoosa.org/pdf/gares/ARES_41_65E.pdf> (accessed 31 January 2016).

[113]   *Ethiopia v. S.Africa*; *Liberia v. S.Africa* (Second Phase) [1966] ICJ Rep 6 at 50–51, para 98, see also Reijnen (n 108) 90.

[114]   Ibid 91.

Common Heritage principle of Article 11(1) of the Moon Agreement, and the exploration and use of the Moon based on equality as stated in Article 11(4), clearly relate to exploitation of the Moon itself and its resources. Nothing in these provisions refers to exploitation of technology. In addition, the remote sensing data represents data about the earth, not the Moon. Thus, I believe that remote sensing data falls outside the scope of the Province and the Common Heritage principles. In addition, refusing the sensing state an opportunity to obtain a return from its investment would lessen the incentive for those states to develop space technology. This would hinder all states from reaping any indirect benefit of this technological advantage.

As regards satellite telecommunication, similar reference is needed to UN Resolution 37/92 which relates to direct broadcasting satellites. Principle A of this resolution states that direct broadcasting satellites 'should promote the free dissemination and mutual exchange of information and knowledge in cultural and scientific field', and Principle C indicates that 'all states and people are entitled to and should enjoy the benefits from such activities. Access to the technology in this field should be available to all states without discrimination on terms mutually agreed by all concerned'.[115] As a result of this resolution, some scholars believe that the commercial practice of state involvement in direct broadcasting satellites would impede the equal sharing rules as enunciated in space treaties, interpreting this UN resolution in the same way as that relating of remote sensing.[116]

Nevertheless, I believe that neither the freedom of use, freedom of access nor the equal sharing benefit refers to satellite technology for the same reasons discussed in connection with remote sensing. In addition, the condition that access to the technology will be subject to 'mutual agreement' does not preclude an exchange of information on a commercial basis. Thus, I would conclude that the operation of satellite communication in outer space is not opposed to those space law doctrines. In addition, it is necessary to keep in mind that this resolution is not legally binding and only covers direct broadcasting satellites, not *all* satellite telecommunication.

---

[115]   UN General Assembly Resolution 37/92, 10 December 1982, 'Principles Governing the Use by States of Artificial Earth Satellites for International Direct Television Broadcasting', A/RES/37/92 (hereafter UN Direct Broadcasting Satellites Principle) <http://www.unoosa.org/pdf/gares/ARES_37_92E.pdf> (accessed 31 January 2016).

[116]   Reijnen (n 108) 92.

But I draw different conclusions in the case of space-created activities as compared with those in the space-related activities. This is because the former engages in the 'utilization' of space resources both physically (in case of Helium-3) or indirectly (in case of the production of goods under zero gravity). Therefore, it is more likely and justifiable to interpret that all benefits deriving from these particular space activities must be shared equally among states to comply the conditions set forth in space treaties. But as mentioned earlier, allowing all states to access and share benefits from the exploitative activities, without reasonably rewarding the owner of these technology in return, would definitely hinder the development of space technology. As a result of generally reducing the incentives for space investment, this in turn would hamper dissemination of those particular benefits from those space activities which should be available to all mankind.

6. CONCLUSION

In conclusion, none of the principles in the space treaties as discussed explicitly refer to the relinquishment of intellectual property rights in outer space. On the contrary, these rules should be interpreted in the way to support and allow an increase in commercial activities in outer space, because the benefit deriving from the exploitation and use of outer space is without doubt of great advantage and importance for human kind.

The next chapter will focus on the international conventions relating to intellectual property rights, and it will investigate how and to what extent such rights are relevant to outer space activities.

2. International intellectual property rights instruments and their implications for outer space activities

Intellectual property laws protect works created by human intellectual effort. Such works can be categorized in various types which are protected, subject to the conditions required by law, irrespective of the location of their creation.[117] Thus, a work created in outer space is just as eligible for intellectual property protection as those works which are created on earth. Consequently, there are various forms of intellectual property which are relevant to protect space activities, including copyright, patents, trademarks and trade secrets. But, the principal forms which will be discussed in this research are copyright and patents; other intellectual property rights fall beyond the scope of this study.[118]

---

[117] The Convention Establishing the World Intellectual Property Organization (WIPO), concluded in Stockholm on 14 July 1967 (Article 2(viii)) provides that intellectual property shall include rights relating to:

- literary, artistic and scientific works
- performances of performing artists, phonograms and broadcasts,
- inventions in all fields of human endeavor,
- scientific discoveries,
- industrial designs,
- trademarks, service marks and commercial names and designations,
- protection against unfair competition,
- and all other rights resulting from intellectual activity in the industrial, scientific, literary or artistic fields.

[118] WIPO's primary focus for the intellectual property protection in outer space activities is also directed at patents and copyright. See International Bureau of WIPO, 'Intellectual Property and Space Activities' (April 2004) <http://www.wipo.int/export/sites/www/patent-law/en/developments/pdf/ip_space.pdf> (accessed 31 January 2016).

Section 1 of this chapter begins with an overview of the major international intellectual property law instruments, focusing only on those relevant to this research. Section 2 will examine and categorize the forms of intellectual property protection which apply to space activities. Section 3, the main body of this chapter, will examine the implications of the pertinent instruments to space activities, including the difficulties which may arise when applying their principles to space activities. Section 4 assesses the impact of key international principles relating to patent protection to outer space. Section 5 examines obligations to provide enforcement procedures, as applied to outer space activities. Finally, concluding remarks will introduce the analysis contained in the subsequent chapters.

1. INTERNATIONAL INTELLECTUAL PROPERTY RIGHTS INSTRUMENTS

At present, the many international conventions in force relating to intellectual property can be divided into two groups: those international agreements relevant to so-called industrial property rights (i.e., patents, trademarks and industrial designs) and those relating to copyright. This section will briefly summarize those conventions relating to copyright and patents only. In addition, attention will be directed at those conventions primarily concerned with substantive matters. Thus, those addressing procedural matters will be mentioned only briefly.

1.1 Patents

1.1.1 The Paris Convention
The Paris Convention for the Protection of Industrial Property of 1883 (as amended) (hereafter 'the Paris Convention') plays an important role in terms of industrial property protection. This treaty regulates all kinds of industrial property, such as patents, utility models, industrial designs, trademarks, service marks, trade names, matters of unfair competition and trade secrets.[119] The Paris Convention contains a number of core principles to harmonize industrial property protection among signatory states and set minimum levels of protection. The first important principle

---

[119] Article 1 of the Paris Convention. For further details, see Paul Torremans, *Intellectual Property Law* (6th ed., OUP 2010) 29; Annette Kur and Thomas Dreier, *European Intellectual Property Law Text, Cases & Materials* (Edward Elgar 2013) 19–20.

set out in the Paris Convention is that of 'national treatment'. This is enshrined in Article 2 (1) of the Convention and requires member states to afford equal treatment to their nationals and to foreign nationals of other member states alike. Another core principle is the right to claim priority pursuant to Article 4 of the Convention. Having filed a first application in their home state, an applicant may assert their claim to 'priority' in any later equivalent application for protection filed, within a defined time period, in any other member state. All later applications which include a valid priority claim will have an effective filing date, or 'priority date', which corresponds to the filing date of that first application. The Convention also establishes that any priority-claiming applications filed in various countries are independent of each other.[120] This means that a refusal to grant an application in one state has no direct effect on the proceedings of equivalent applications in other member states. Although these three key principles guarantee minimum standards among member states in terms of these procedural matters, the Paris Convention does not attempt to harmonize substantive matters which are left to national legislation.[121]

1.1.2   The Patent Cooperation Treaty (PCT)

The Patent Cooperation Treaty (PCT) aims to address procedural burdens arising from filing equivalent patent applications in multiple countries. This treaty permits the initial filing of a single 'international' patent application designating over 100 possible signatory states. This international application preserves the original priority date for any subsequent national filings derived from the PCT application. The international phase also includes a preliminary search which provides applicants guidance as to the application's likely patentability. Thus, the PCT Treaty mainly deals with procedural process rather than substantive matters.

1.1.3   The Patent Law Treaty (PLT)

The Patent Law Treaty, adopted in 2000, aims to harmonize and streamline national procedures for processing patent applications. The Treaty establishes a standard for the formal requirements for patent applications, including the contents of any international application filed under the PCT.[122]

---

[120]   Article 4bis (1) of the Paris Convention.
[121]   Torremans (n 119) 30.
[122]   Article 6 of the Treaty.

1.2 The International Copyright and Neighboring Rights Conventions

1.2.1 The Berne Convention

The Berne Convention, first adopted in 1886, is applicable to all works in literature, science and the arts.[123] It establishes four key principles. The Berne Convention, like the Paris Convention, establishes a principle of national treatment,[124] such that foreign authors et al. may expect equal treatment as national authors in any member state. Secondly, the Convention precludes any formalities for protection. In other words, protection must arise automatically without any prerequisite registration.[125] The third principle is that of independent protection i.e., enjoyment and exercise of rights granted is independent of the protection of the work in the country of origin.[126] Territoriality is the final key principle: protection extends only in the territory of the protecting state.[127] The Berne Convention also contains provisions regarding the minimum standards of protection in terms of the minimum rights afforded to authors and the length of protection. However, given the era of its original drafting, the scope of the Convention does not explicitly extend to new technological and digital works like computer programs, databases and software-generated works.[128]

1.2.2 The WIPO Copyright Treaty

The WIPO Copyright Treaty (WCT) was adopted in 1996 to supplement the Berne Convention in relation to new technological developments. The WCT is a special agreement within the meaning of Article 20 of the Berne Convention.[129] This means that the level of protection granted in this treaty cannot be interpreted as being lower than that required by the

---

[123]   Article 2 of the Convention.
[124]   Article 5(1) of the Convention.
[125]   Article 5(2) of the Convention.
[126]   Ibid.
[127]   Ibid.
[128]   Hanns Ullrich, 'TRIPS: Adequate Protection, Inadequate Trade, Adequate Competition Policy' (1995) 4 *Pacific Rim Law & Policy Association* 153, 165.
[129]   Article 1(1) of the WCT states 'This Treaty is a special agreement within the meaning of Article 20 of the Berne Convention', and Article 20 of the Berne Convention provides that 'The Government of the countries of the Union reserve the right to enter into special agreements among themselves, in so far as such agreements grant to authors more extensive rights than those granted by the Convention, or contain other provisions not contrary to this Convention'.

Berne Convention. The substantive provisions of this treaty are a response to changes arising from digital technology, especially the internet – the so-called 'digital agenda'. The WCT establishes a right of communication to the public by which authors enjoy the exclusive right to make their works 'available to the public in such a way that members of the public may access the works from a place and at a time individually chosen by them'.[130] Secondly, contracting states must provide 'adequate legal protection and effective legal remedies against the circumvention of effective technological measures used by the authors in connection with the exercise of their rights'.[131] Thirdly, contracting states are obliged to provide adequate legal remedies against third-party interference with any 'rights management information' used.[132]

1.2.3 The Rome Convention

The Rome Convention was adopted in 1961 to provide protection, termed 'neighboring rights', to the entrepreneurial works of performers, producers of sound recordings and broadcasters, which are outside the scope of the Berne Convention. Similar to the Berne Convention, national treatment is the main principle of the Rome Convention. This means the performers, phonogram producers and broadcasters are treated similarly and enjoy the same protection in any contracting parties as is granted to their nationals.[133] The national treatment is granted to any performance taking place in another contracting state, incorporated in a protected phonogram or carried by a protected broadcast.[134] In the case of a sound recording, contracting states shall grant national treatment to producers of phonograms when the producer is a national of another contracting state or when the first fixation is made or first published in another contracting state;[135] and, in the case of a broadcast, when the broadcasting organization is situated in another contracting state, or when the broadcast was transmitted from a contracting state.[136] Additionally, Article 6(2) of the Convention embodies the principle of territoriality in respect of broadcasts: a contracting party is only obliged to protect broadcasts if the headquarters of the broadcasting organization is situated in another contracting state and the broadcast was transmitted from a

---

[130]　Article 8 of the WCT.
[131]　Article 11 of the WCT.
[132]　Article 12 of the WCT.
[133]　Article 2(1) of the Rome Convention.
[134]　Article 4 of the Rome Convention.
[135]　Article 5 of the Rome Convention.
[136]　Article 6 of the Rome Convention.

transmitter situated in that contracting state. The convention provides certain substantive rights to performers, phonogram producers and broadcasters which provide remedies for certain unauthorized acts.[137]

1.2.4 The WIPO Performances and Phonograms Treaty

The WIPO Performances and Phonograms Treaty (WPPT), adopted in 1996, supplements the Rome Convention to extend the rights of performers and phonogram producers (but not broadcasters) from those embodied in the Rome Convention.[138] Importantly, WPPT upgrades protection afforded to performers from 'the possibility of preventing' in the Rome Convention to exclusive rights.[139]

1.2.5 The Brussels Satellites Convention

The Brussels Satellites Convention is considered to be a special agreement under Article 22 of the Rome Convention. This Convention, prompted by the increasing use of satellites in international telecommunications,[140] applies the rights afforded in the Rome Convention to broadcasting organizations.[141] Contracting states are obliged to take measures necessary to prevent the 'distribution of program-carrying signals by any distributor for whom the signals emitted to or passing through the satellite are not intended'.[142] Such protection, however, extends to the signals emitted by the originating organization, but not to the actual content of the program transmitted. Although the obligations set forth in this Convention appear to be a matter of public international law, some commentators have argued that the 'adequate measures' required by Article 2 may include private rights, such as national copyright or neighboring rights laws.[143]

---

[137] Articles 7, 10 and 13 of the Rome Convention.
[138] Articles 7–10 and Articles 11–14 of the Treaty.
[139] Articles 7 and 6 of the Rome Convention and the WPPT, respectively.
[140] WIPO, *WIPO Intellectual Property Handbook* (2nd ed., WIPO 2008) <http://www.wipo.int/edocs/pubdocs/en/intproperty/489/wipo_pub_489.pdf> (accessed 31 January 2016) 321.
[141] It is arguable that 'satellite transmission' is already encompassed under the Rome Convention's definition of 'broadcasting'. See Paul Goldstein et al., *International Copyright Principles, Law and Practice* (3rd ed., OUP 2013) 62.
[142] Article 2 of the Brussels Satellite Convention.
[143] Goldstein et al. (n 141) 63.

1.3   The TRIPs Agreement

The scope of application of the TRIPs Agreement extends to all types of intellectual property, including copyright and patents.[144] As the provisions of both the Paris and Berne Conventions are incorporated into TRIPs, signatories to this agreement are obliged to comply with the provisions of these conventions, discussed above.[145] Protection of performers, producers of phonograms and broadcasting organizations is required under Article 14 of the Agreement. As with the other international intellectual property conventions, the principle of national treatment is also enshrined in TRIPs, and it applies to all industrial property rights and to copyright. In the case of performers, producers of phonograms and broadcasting organizations, the national treatment obligation only applies in respect of the rights provided under this Agreement.[146] Additionally, the TRIPs Agreement requires member states to comply with the 'Most-Favored Nation' principle (MFN). MFN requires any member state which grants a privilege to nationals of any other country to immediately and unconditionally accord the same treatment to nationals of all other member states.[147]

1.4   Relevant EU Directives

As some parts of this book analyze the application of United Kingdom IP legislation to outer space activities, it is necessary to examine the following EU Directives, when relevant.

1.4.1   The EU Satellite and Cable Directive
The EU Satellite and Cable Directive governs the applicability of copyright and related rights to satellite broadcasting and cable retransmission in the European Union.[148] Article 1(2) (b) sets forth the 'emission theory'.[149] This states that the right of satellite communication

---

[144]   Article 1.2 of the TRIPs Agreement.
[145]   Articles 2.1 and 9.1 of the TRIPs Agreement.
[146]   Article 3.1 of the TRIPs Agreement.
[147]   Article 4 of the TRIPs Agreement.
[148]   Council Directive 93/83/EEC of 27 September 1993 on the coordination of certain rules concerning copyright and rights related to copyright applicable to satellite broadcasting and cable retransmission.
[149]   There are a number of theories for the communication to public rights, see Chapters 4 (8.2 case 2) and Chapter 5 (2.4.2 case 2).

can only be exercised in the country of origin or the uplink country.[150] This provision restricts the applicable law in case of an infringement to that single country from which the signals are emitted. This Directive will be reviewed in greater detail in the choice of law section of Chapter 5.[151]

1.4.2 The EU Database Directive

The EU Database Directive obliges all the EU member states to protect databases resulting from a substantial investment under their domestic legislation.[152] This Directive applies both to copyright and a *sui generis* database right, and it will be reviewed when discussing the protection of remote sensing data in Chapter 4 of this book.[153]

1.4.3 The EU Software Directive

The EU Software Directive requires member states to protect computer programs as literary works under a copyright regime,[154] although the directive does not define a 'computer program'.[155] This Directive will be relevant where the choice of law rule leads to the application of any EU member national laws on the legal protection of computer programs.[156]

1.4.4 The EU Information Society (InfoSoc) Directive

The InfoSoc Directive aims to harmonize aspects of copyright and related rights,[157] including the right to communicate works to the public and the right to make works available to the public,[158] distribution rights[159] and

---

[150] Article 1(2)(b) of the EU Satellite and Cable Directive states 'The act of communication to the public by satellite occurs solely in the Member State where, under the control and responsibility of broadcasting organization, the programme-carrying signals are introduced into an uninterrupted chain of communication leading to the satellite and down towards the earth'.

[151] See Chapter 5, hypothetical case no. 1 under the choice of law section.

[152] Directive 96/9/EC of the European Parliament and of the Council of 11 March 1996 on the legal protection of databases.

[153] See Chapter 4 in the section on subject matter.

[154] Article 1(1) of Directive 2009/24/EC of the European Parliament and of the Council of 23 April 2009 on the legal protection of computer programs.

[155] Ibid. The Directive states that a program includes preparatory design work.

[156] See case 8.3 in Chapter 4.

[157] Directive 2001/29/EC of the European Parliament and of the Council of 22 May 2001 on the harmonization of certain aspects of copyright and related rights in the information society.

[158] Article 3 of the Directive.

the limitations and exceptions to the exclusive rights.[160] This Directive will be reviewed later in this book, when it becomes pertinent.

2. THE APPLICATION OF INTELLECTUAL PROPERTY RIGHTS TO SPACE ACTIVITIES

As previously mentioned,[161] space activities require intellectual and financial investment, such that any intellectual works created as a result deserve protection as much as works created on earth. Space activities may be eligible for protection under a number of intellectual property rights, including: (1) the copyright and related rights protection of satellite broadcasts and remote sensing data; (2) the protection of technical innovations and inventions by patents; and (3) the protection of a space project's name or a space company's name as a trademark to strengthen the image. Nevertheless, this book will focus only on patents and copyright[162] because these two IP rights are most likely to be applicable to most current space activities. However, should space tourism become more commercialized and sustainable in the future, the protection of trademarks in outer space may also become an important issue for consideration, not only in respect of corporate trademarks mentioned above, but also having regard to the potential for selling trademarked souvenirs in outer space.

2.1 Copyright and Neighboring Rights

Owing to their highly complex nature, the application of copyright law to satellite broadcasts and remote sensing data raises a number of important legal issues. Since copyright applies to literary and artistic works, including databases and computer programs, satellite broadcasts and remote sensing data fall within the category of copyright-protected works.

Satellite broadcasts fall within the subject matter category of 'broadcasts' which are eligible for protection either under copyright law or under neighboring rights protection. This is because the Berne Convention does not include broadcasts as the subject matter of copyright, although broadcasts are identified as 'neighboring rights' in the Rome

---

[159]   Article 4 of the Directive.
[160]   Article 5 of the Directive.
[161]   See the Introduction, pp.1–4.
[162]   (n 118).

Convention. Nevertheless, some national legislation protects the subject matter of 'neighboring rights' under copyright law and such is the case with broadcasts under the UK Copyright, Designs and Patents Act of 1988.[163] The protection of satellite broadcasts will be discussed in detail in Chapter 4. In addition, because the transmission of any satellite communication is comprised of two legs – an uplink and a downlink leg – which are governed by the national law of different countries, this leads to issues surrounding the appropriate choice of law. This will be discussed in Chapter 5.[164]

Regarding works created by remote sensing, so-called Earth Observation Data (EOD), it is more complicated to determine whether these are eligible or not for copyright protection. EOD are divided into three distinct categories determined by the degree of processing which has taken place, namely: primary (or raw) data, processing data and analyzed information.[165] The processing data and analyzed information are more likely to gain copyright protection since these are the result of a technically sophisticated process requiring human intellectual input.[166] The primary data, however, is collected by an automated computer operating a program.[167] It is doubtful whether such raw data are protected by copyright, although it is arguable that raw data might gain copyright protection under the umbrella subject matter category which is the 'selection and arrangement of data'.[168] Does selection and arrangement of raw data give rise to the protection as set forth in Article 10(2) of the Agreement on Trade-Related Aspects of Intellectual Property Rights (the 'TRIPs Agreement')?[169] And if such raw data falls outside the scope of copyright protection, does it qualify as a database eligible for protection

---

[163] See Chapter 4 section 1.1.3.

[164] See Chapter 5, the hypothetical case no. 1 in choice-of-law section.

[165] UN Remote Sensing Principles (n 112).

[166] Catherine Doldirina, 'The Impact of Copyright Protection and Public Sector' in Ray Purdy and Denise Leung (eds), *Evidence from Earth Observation Satellites* (Martinus Nijhoff 2013) 298.

[167] Ibid.

[168] Catherine Doldirina, 'A Rightly Balanced Intellectual Property Rights Regime as A Mechanism to Enhance Commercial Earth Observation Activities' in Corinne M. Jorgenson (ed.) *Proceedings of the International Institute of Space Law: 52nd Colloquium on the Law of Outer Space* (American Institute of Aeronautics and Astronautics 2009) 304–306.

[169] S.G. Sreejith, 'The Pertinent Law for Outer Space Related Intellectual Property Issues: An Odyssey into TRIPs' (2005) 45 *Indian Journal of International Law* 180, 189.

as a *sui generis* under another legal regime ancillary to copyright protection? These questions will be addressed in detail in Chapter 4.[170]

Apart from specific space-related activities, a general intellectual work created in outer space might also be copyrightable, provided it meets all the relevant legal requirements. However, questions pertinent to determining its protection may arise. For example, how is 'publication' to be interpreted for works created in outer space? Could distribution of copies among an astronaut team in outer space be interpreted as publication? We will examine these issues later in Chapter 5.[171]

Additionally, Canadian astronaut Chris Hadfield's recent, and much publicized, rendition of David Bowie's song 'Space Oddity' serves as a good example for the purpose of discussion,[172] since this song is protected as a copyright work. Therefore, its unauthorized performance might constitute an infringement. While fortunately in this case, Hadfield had obtained David Bowie's permission, this case still stands as a good study, in term of some legal aspects. For example, if Hadfield's performance was an infringing act, which law would be applicable since the performance took place on the International Space Station, and not on the earth? Does the territorial scope of copyright protection preclude the right holder from entitlement to any remedy? Might the infringement be deemed to have occurred in the territory of the state of registry of that space module, such that application of that state's domestic law would be appropriate? Would the outcome be different if the infringing performance takes place outside the International Space Station, for instance, on the Moon's surface? What if an astronaut performs a song which he has created himself while he is in outer space? Is such a song copyrighted? If so, will the uploading and downloading of his performance on the internet by unauthorized third parties constitute an infringement? And which national law would be applicable in this case?

Whether and to what extent works created in outer space are copyrightable, and issues of applicable law will be examined in detail in Chapters 4 and 5 of this book.[173]

---

170   See Chapter 4, section 1.1.1.
171   See the hypothetical case no. 3 in the choice-of-law section in Chapter 5.
172   Mark Whittington, 'Chris Hadfield, "Space Oddity," and Copyright Law in Space', *Examiner* (23 May 2013) <http://www.examiner.com/article/chris-hadfield-space-oddity-and-copyright-law-space> (accessed 31 January 2016).
173   See case 4 section 8.4 in Chapter 4 and hypothetical case no. 3 in section 2.4 in Chapter 5.

2.2 Patent

Pursuant to the TRIPs Agreement, an invention is eligible for patent protection regardless of the location of its invention.[174] Thus, an invention created in outer space may be patented, provided that it fulfills the substantive requirements of patentability. Therefore, the first issue to be addressed is patentability. Article 27(1) of the TRIPs Agreement states that any invention, whether a product or a process, in any field of technology is potentially patentable.[175] There are some ambiguities in determining the patentable subject matter in certain space activities. One example is the orbit in which telecommunication satellites are placed. Some confusion arises as to the issue of its patentability. The cases of *Hughes Aircraft Company v. United States*[176] and *TRW v. ICO*[177] are two well-known US cases on orbit patents, and they will be discussed in Chapter 3 to explain how the patentability requirements relate to satellite orbits.[178]

In addition, some space-created work, such as the process for generating nuclear power using Helium-3 on the Moon, and pharmaceutical or electronics products (which could be created on earth, but are more cost-effective to manufacture in outer space), deserve special attention in terms of the requirement for novelty. It is questionable whether such inventions would meet the novelty requirement, since prior art might already exist on earth. Which prior art is relevant is another issue which deserves special consideration within the context of space technology. This is because astronauts and scientists may purposefully, or serendipitously, create an invention during a scientific exploration in outer space and may use such invention for experimental purposes. Would such use of this technology constitute a public disclosure which would affect the

---

[174] Article 27.1 of the TRIPs Agreement stipulates that 'patents shall be available and patent rights enjoyable without discriminations as to the place of invention'.

[175] Article 27.1 of the TRIPs Agreement states, 'patents shall be available for any inventions, whether products or processes, in all fields of technology, provided that they are new, involve an inventive step and are capable of industrial application'.

[176] *Hughes Aircraft Company v. United States* 29 Fed Cl. 197 (1993).

[177] *TRW v. ICO*, cited in Bradford Smith et al., 'Problems and Realities in Applying the Provisions of the Outer Space Treaty to Intellectual Property Issues' in *Proceedings of the 40th Colloquium on the Law of Outer Space* (International Institute of Space Law of the International Astronautical Federation, 1997) 172–173.

[178] Section 1.1.1 in Chapter 3.

patentability when later filing an application for protection? Or is such use excluded from the prior art by analogy to the experiments carried in a closed laboratory on the earth?[179] Might newly invented space technology fall into the public domain if it is disclosed to public unintentionally during a satellite broadcast which depicts the interior of spacecraft?[180] Does any disclosure in outer space constitute prior art, bearing in mind that definitions of relevant disclosure making up the prior art is generally articulated in territorial terms, which do not make reference to outer space? In the case of pharmaceutical products which are cost-effectively produced in outer space, does the process for production lack novelty as a result of prior use on earth? Since a process comprises a number of factors, one of which is the atmosphere in which the process is carried out, is a process conducted in outer space novel, when the fact that it is performed in a different environment is taken into consideration?[181] These legal issues will be examined thoroughly in Chapter 3.[182]

It seems that such inventions which, although invented in outer space, may be used either in outer space or on earth, would be patentable under selected national jurisdictions on earth, provided the particular invention passes all the requirements for registration. However, another category of inventions are those which can only be invented and used in outer space. I doubt whether such category would raise the issue of patentability and infringement since it falls outside the scope of any jurisdiction.[183] Another question arises regarding the patentability of an invention created in outer space. For instance, one possible scenario is where a space experiment designed and tested successfully in outer space cannot be replicated on earth because of the difference in environmental conditions. How would this affect the patentability of the invention when filing a patent application? Is a special patent regime for outer space justified by its different environment? These legal issues will be analyzed in Chapter 3.

---

[179]   Albert Tramposch, 'International Aspects of Protection for Inventions Made or Used in Outer Space' (ESA Workshop on Intellectual Property Rights & Space Activities, Paris, December 1994) 187, 195.

[180]   Ibid.

[181]   Sreejith (n 169) 194.

[182]   See Section 1.2.1 in Chapter 3.

[183]   See more in Section 1.2.3 in Chapter 3.

3. IMPLICATIONS OF THE FUNDAMENTAL PRINCIPLES IN INTERNATIONAL INTELLECTUAL PROPERTY RIGHTS INSTRUMENTS FOR OUTER SPACE ACTIVITIES

As identified in Section 1, there are three principles contained in the international intellectual property instruments which have the potential to create constraints when applied to outer space activities. These principles – territoriality, national treatment and most-favored nation – will now be examined in turn.

3.1 The Principle of Territoriality

The territoriality principle defines the intellectual property right as territorial in scope. In other words, the protection afforded to a work protected by an intellectual right is limited within the boundary of the country where that right has been granted.[184] Thus, the exclusive rights granted to the owner of the intellectual property work cannot be exploited beyond the territory of the granting state. Consequently, any allegedly infringing acts must occur within the territory of the country where the protection has been obtained.

The exclusive rights granted to right holders are defined in the domestic laws of each country, and equivalent rights in different jurisdictions are independent from each other, as stated in the international intellectual property conventions. Article 5(2) of the Berne Convention provides that 'the enjoyment and the exercise of these rights ... shall be independent ... governed exclusively by the laws of the country where protection is claimed'.[185] Similar provisions are also included in Article 4bis(1) of the Paris Convention,[186] Articles 4 through 6 of the Rome Convention and Articles 3(1) and 3(2) of the TRIPS Agreement. The territorial scope of IP rights has also been recognized in national

---

[184] Eugen Ulmer, 'Territorial Limitation of Intellectual Property Rights', *International Encyclopedia of Comparative Law: Copyright*, vol. 14 (2007), 5. There are a number of studies on the territoriality principle of IP, for example, Ullrich (n 128) 158–159.

[185] The full text of the Berne Convention is available at <http://www.wipo.int/treaties/en/ip/berne/trtdocs_wo001.html> (accessed 31 January 2016).

[186] The full text of the Paris Convention is available at <http://www.wipo.int/treaties/en/ip/paris/trtdocs_wo020.html#P147_20484> (accessed 31 January 2016).

jurisdictions, as reiterated, for instance, by the US Supreme Court in *Brown v. Duchesne* in connection with the territorial scope of patents.[187]

However, a strict application of this territoriality principle has been heavily criticized as inappropriate when applied to cross-border or multi-territorial IP cases.[188] Nevertheless, courts in some jurisdictions have applied domestic IPR law, exceptionally and extraterritorially, to an infringing act which occurred in another jurisdiction. For example, in *NTP v. RIM*, the US court applied US patent law to an infringing act committed abroad, relying on the principle of substantial test and localization.[189] Also in *Steele v. Bulova Watch Co.,* the US court found that the defendant was liable for infringement of the plaintiff's trademark which was registered in the United States, even though the defendant affixed the infringing mark and sold the products in Mexico. In this case, the court found infringement since the defendant was a US citizen and his infringing act had effects in the United States.[190]

Although such examples illustrate deviation from the territorial principle in intellectual property rights in the United States, it is uncertain whether every country would have common understanding and adopt the same approach on this matter. In addition, the extraterritorial application of IP law in those cases concerns other jurisdictions on earth, not outer space – an area which belongs to no state. It is doubtful whether the territorial scope of national intellectual property law would be extended to outer space in the same way as in a case of a cross-border jurisdiction.

---

[187]   *Brown v. Duchesne* 60 US 183 (1856) 195. The US Supreme Court in this case ruled that 'The patent laws are authorized by that article in the Constitution which provides that Congress shall have power to promote the progress of science and useful arts by securing for limited times to authors and inventors the exclusive right to their respective writings and discoveries. The power thus granted is domestic in its character, and necessarily confined within the limits of the United States'.

[188]   Paulius Jurcys, 'The Role of the Territoriality Principle in Modern Intellectual Property Regimes: Institutional Lessons from Japan' (New Spaces, New Actors and the Institutional Turn in Contemporary Intellectual Property Law Conference, Kyushu, February 2010) 1–6 <http://www.law.kyushu-u.ac.jp/programsinenglish/conference2010/draft15.pdf> (accessed 31 January 2016).

[189]   *NTP v. RIM*, 418 F.3d 1282 (2005). Under the principle of substantial test and localization, the patent holder has to prove that the accused device would substantially infringe the system and method claims of his US patent. And there must be an attempt to appropriate the invention with some connection to the US either commercial or physical. See Timothy R. Holbrook, 'Extraterritoriality in US Patent Law' (2008) 49 *William & Mary Law Review* 2119, 2170–2171.

[190]   *Steele v. Bulova Watch Co.* 344 U.S. 280 (1952).

In this regard, the distinction has to be made between 'an object launched into outer space' and 'outer space, as such'. Pursuant to Article VIII of the Outer Space Treaty, when an object is launched into outer space, the flag state retains jurisdiction and control over that object. At present, the United States is the only country which has enacted law to extend its jurisdiction to invention in outer space, by virtue of Section 105 of 35 U.S.C. (Invention in Outer Space) ('US Patent in Space Act').[191,192] In addition, the Intergovernmental Agreement of 1998 ('IGA'), signed by the state partners of the International Space Station, provides quasi-territorial effect to the state of registry on the element of its registration.[193,194] Thus, the US Patent in Space Act and the IGA are examples where states have extended the scope of their domestic patent law to extraterritorial areas, based upon the so-called flagship principle. This principle grants authority to the state of registration to adjudicate cases occurring on board its spacecraft by determining such spacecraft could be deemed as its territory.[195]

Some scholars believe that extraterritorial application of national IP law in outer space is permitted since Article 1(1) of the TRIPs Agreement grants the flexibility for member states to extend their domestic law to outer space.[196] Thus, it is possible to postulate that the national intellectual property law of the relevant launching country might be applicable in the case of an object launched into outer space. However, such extraterritorial applicability of national intellectual property law seems to be less firmly founded unless it is explicitly stated in a statutory provision, such as that of the US law. Hence, it is necessary to examine whether a spacecraft or space station could be deemed as part of the territory of a state by application of the flagship principle in cases where there is no explicit provision under relevant domestic law. Alternatively, it may simply be the case that no remedy is available if a relevant state makes

---

[191]   35 U.S.C. Section 105(a).

[192]   More discussion of this legislation can be found in Chapter 3 under section 4. Infringement.

[193]   Article 21.2 of the IGA.

[194]   The International Space Station will be addressed later in section 6 in Chapter 3.

[195]   This issue will be discussed again in Chapter 3 under section 4. Infringement.

[196]   Article 1(1) of the TRIPs Agreement states, 'Members shall be free to determine the appropriate method of implementing the provisions of this Agreement within their own legal system and practice.' See Ruwantissa Abeyrantne, 'The Application of Intellectual Property Rights to Outer Space Activities' (2003) 29 *Journal of Space Law* 1, 15.

no provision in its domestic legislation to specifically deem any activities in outer space to have taken place within its territory.[197] Problems of determining jurisdiction also arise when multiple states are involved in the launching of a space station. This matter will be given full attention in Chapter 5.[198]

The situation might be even more problematic in the case of an activity taking place, not in any spacecraft or vehicle, but in outer space itself. For example, does an individual in outer space require authorization to copy or download a copyright work? Will such an act constitute an infringement and, if so, which national jurisdiction provides the legal basis for such a determination, taking the strict application of the territoriality rule into consideration. As previously mentioned, extending the reach of domestic intellectual property rights to activities beyond the territorial scope seems problematic, without abandoning the territorial confinement of national IP law. This difficulty will be discussed again, in detail, in Chapter 5.[199]

3.2   The National Treatment Principle

National treatment is another important principle enshrined in inter-national intellectual property conventions, as outlined previously. For example, the principle is set out in articles 2(1), 5(3), 4 and 3(1) of the Paris Convention, the Berne Convention, the Rome Convention and the TRIPS Agreement, respectively. National treatment requires each member state to treat nationals of other member states and its own nationals alike, in terms of granting and enforcing intellectual property rights. The principle of national treatment does not really lead to a conflict of law problem because this principle does not directly ascribe application of the law of any particular country. On the contrary, this non-discrimination principle allows the member states to apply their own laws both to their nationals and to non-nationals, supplemented by the system of minimum rights under the international conventions.[200]

---

[197]   Sa'íd Mosteshar, 'Intellectual Property Issues in Space Activities' in Sa'íd Mosteshar (ed.) *Research and Invention in Outer Space Liability and Intellectual Property Rights* (Martinus Nijhoff 1995) 196.

[198]   See Chapter 5 in jurisdiction in outer space (quasi-territorial juris-diction).

[199]   See Sections 2.3 and 2.4 in Chapter 5.

[200]   Ulrich Loewenheim, 'The Principle of National Treatment in the International Conventions Protecting Intellectual Property' in Martin J. Adelmann

However, in certain situations, national treatment cannot be properly implemented in respect of outer space activities. Taking account of the fact that outer space is not the territory of any state, 'outer space' is not eligible to become a member party to any international intellectual property convention. As a result, an individual who benefits from intellectual property protection in one state may not benefit from national treatment elsewhere according to the principle, if the first fixation of the work, the habitual residence of author, and the work's first publication all take place in outer space. In other words, creation of a work in outer space may indirectly prevent the national treatment principle from being operative. This may be best illustrated by reference to the following hypothetical case studies.

3.2.1 Case 1

Citizen A is a national of country A and Citizen B is a national of country B. Country B has not signed the Paris Convention. Citizen A and Citizen B each invent a new product separately during a prolonged stay in a module of a space station. The space station is registered by country C, which is a member of the Paris Convention. Upon his return to the earth, there is no doubt that Citizen A can file a patent application for his product in any Paris member state, subject to satisfaction of the usual conditions. However, what about the case of Citizen B? Can Citizen B file a patent application in country A? Is country A obliged to accord Citizen B the same treatment as accorded to Citizen A, its own national? Given that Citizen B is a national of a country outside the Paris Union,[201] Article 3 of the Paris Convention requires him to be domiciled in the territory of one of the countries of the Paris Union in order to receive the same treatment as nationals of Paris Convention countries. However, Citizen B is not domiciled in any country in the Paris Union, and thus he does not gain national treatment pursuant to Article 3 of the Convention. Country A therefore has no obligation to grant the same quality and quantity protection to Citizen B as it grants to Citizen A, its own national. For example, Citizen B might be granted a shorter patent term than what granted to Citizen A for the same invention.

Might Citizen B benefit from the national treatment principle based upon his long stay in the International Space Station? Can this be deemed to be as a domicile, since the ISS is not a country? Can we apply the

---

et al. (eds), *Patents and Technological Progress in a Globalized World* (Springer 2009) 593.

[201] The Paris Union countries are those countries which have signed the Paris Convention.

'quasi-territory' principle to this case and legitimately interpret that Citizen B is domiciled in country C by virtue of his stay in the module which is the registered element of country C in that space station, and in this way will Citizen B benefit from national treatment when filing application in country A?[202] The answers to the above questions seem to be uncertain and controversial. These problems can be solved to a certain aspect under the private international law regime which will be examined in Chapter 5.[203]

3.2.2   Case 2

A and B are astronauts and nationals of countries A and B, respectively. While walking on the Moon's surface, they spontaneously devise a new song and dance. All the other members of the astronauts' team witness their performance, and one of them, Astronaut C, records it using his smartphone. After returning to the earth, Astronaut C once more fixes this performance without obtaining consent from either Astronaut A or Astronaut B. Will the location of the performance in outer space preclude the applicability of the national treatment principle? And can Astronauts A and B sue Astronaut C for infringing their performance rights?[204]

Suppose that country B is not a party to the Rome Convention. Under Article 4(a) of the Rome Convention, each contracting state is obliged to accord non-national performers the same treatment as it accords to its nationals, provided their performance takes place in another contracting state. The fact that the performance in question took place in outer space seems to deny Astronaut B from the benefit of national treatment,[205]

---

[202]   The quasi-territory principle is 'the power of state in respect of ships, aircraft and spacecraft having its nationality. A state exercises this power over its flag vessels when an incident occurs beyond its territory. The quasi-territorial jurisdiction extends not only to the vehicle but also to all personnel on board irrespective of their nationality'. See Cheng (n 26) 79 and Gbenga Oduntan, *Sovereignty and Jurisdiction in the Airspace and Outer Space: Legal Criteria for Spatial Delimitation* (Routledge 2012) 36.

[203]   See hypothetical case no. 3 in jurisdiction section in Chapter 5.

[204]   Some additional legal questions arise from this hypothetical case. For instance, whether the record of such performance by a smartphone in outer space is a fixation? Whether such performance in outer space is protected and which law would be applicable? And if C has also made copies of such performance and distributed to other member of the group in outer space, whether his act would be constituted as an infringement since there is no copyright law in outer space? These questions will be discussed later in case 4 under the choice of law section in Chapter 5.

[205]   See Articles 2(1) and Article 4(1) of the Rome Convention.

whereas Astronaut A enjoys protection from the same performance since he is a national of country A.[206] The situation in this case is therefore different from the previous case because the work was created in outer space and not in the ISS, where we might adopt the quasi-territory principle as another alternative solution. Thus, the national treatment principle is meaningless to some extent when applied to works created in outer space.

Other differences arise from the fact that the performance is a work created by Astronauts A and B. Copyright may subsist in such work, a literary (a song) and dramatic work (dance) if there is a fixation.[207] However, the national treatment rule seems to be inapplicable to this case if country B is not a party to the Berne Convention and Astronaut B is not domiciled in any Berne country pursuant to Article 3 of the Berne Convention.

3.3 The Most-Favored Nation (MFN)

The most-favored nation (MFN) principle has been established in the TRIPs Agreement. This principle obliges member states to accord immediately and unconditionally the same treatment granted to the nationals of any other country to nationals of all other member states.[208] In other words, a member state is not able to grant any special advantage, privilege or immunity to nationals of any one particular country, without granting the same terms to nationals of all member states. Similar to the National Treatment principle, the MFN principle does not pose any problem when applied to works created by nationals of any member state in outer space, but the scope does not extend to the situation where a work is created by a national of a non-member state. This is because a work created by the nationals of non-member states is not obliged to receive the same treatment as those works created by the nationals of member states owing to the technical limitation elaborated previously in the hypothetical cases under the National Treatment section. These hypothetical cases are analogous to examples in this case, and so need not to be repeated here.

---

[206] Subject to the law of the performer's rights protection in country A.

[207] The record of such work by a smartphone can be considered as fixation. The fact that such recording is made by a third party (C) without the author's consent are irrelevant. See Lionel Bently et al., *Intellectual Property Law* (4th ed., OUP 2014) 92.

[208] Article 4 of the TRIPs Agreement.

4. THE IMPACT OF SOME INTERNATIONAL PRINCIPLES ON PATENT PROTECTION IN OUTER SPACE

4.1 Priority Rights

Patents are different than copyright in the sense that protection does not arise automatically, but rather it is necessary to file an application for registration, and protection arises upon registration. The priority rights granted under the Paris Convention which aim to preserve the novelty of an invention for a fixed period may prove to be problematic in case of inventions made in outer space. This is because the priority right arises only in the territory of the Paris Union country where the applicant files the first application disclosing the invention.[209] As there is definitely no patent office in outer space, and even if it were possible to establish one, it would still be doubtful whether a priority right would be operative, given that outer space is not considered as a territory of any country including, of course, any Union country. No issue regarding the priority right will arise if the inventor is able to arrange for an application to be filed for their invention on earth through a communication channel available while he is in outer space. However, if the inventor has to wait until he returns to earth in order to file a patent application, then he risks losing the benefit of priority for as long as he is unable to file for protection in a Union country on earth.[210] The same problem arises if the inventor's patent lawyer files a patent application on his behalf in a non-member state. Does this mean that any disclosure made by an inventor to other colleagues during their stay in outer space may affect the patentability of the invention claimed in a later-filed application? In other words, does an inventor enjoy a 'grace period' while he remains in outer space? These issues will be examined in Chapter 3.[211]

---

[209] Article 4A (1) of the Paris Convention states, 'Any person who has duly filed an application for a patent, or for the registration of a utility model, or of an industrial design, or of a trademark, in one of the countries of the Union, or his successor in title, shall enjoy, for the purpose of filing in the other countries, a right of priority during the periods hereinafter fixed'.

[210] This is the case only if details of the invention have been disclosed while he is in outer space. Otherwise, the only risk from the delay is that someone else will file an application for the same invention before he gets to lodge his own application.

[211] See Chapter 3 section 1.2.1.

4.2   Independence of Patents

Article 4bis of the Paris Convention establishes the principle of the independence of patents. This principle means each equivalent patent, granted individually by each respective national patent office, is independent from each other, irrespective of whether these patents share a common priority claim. This enshrines the concept of property rights which excludes others from exploiting or making use of the patentee's invention without authorization. The independence principle of patents therefore appears in conflict with the public benefit principle set forth in Article 12 of the Outer Space Treaty and Article 15 of the Moon Agreement.[212] Article 12 of the Outer Space Treaty requires all member states to open unconditionally all stations, equipment and vehicles stationed in outer space to other nations to visit at their request.[213] Article 15 of the Moon Agreement also obligates member states to open their facilities on the Moon upon request to any visitors.[214] It might be argued that an inventor or patentee in outer space loses his right to exclude by virtue of these requirements to make available to third party by these provisions in the space treaties. For example, on land, a company can decide whether and who enters their research laboratories. If they are working on new research, they would not allow third parties in to see what they were doing. If they did so, they might reasonably expect them to sign a confidentiality agreement, which would maintain the novelty of their later-filed application. If space law entitles anyone else the right to visit a space lab, and cannot oblige them to treat what they see as confidential, then any later patent application would lack novelty.

Hence, the questions remain: (1) should the public benefit concept contained within the space treaties outweigh the IP property rights granted to an inventor? (2) Is it fair to force an inventor to make available any activity carried out in outer space to all third parties who claim the

---

[212]   David Irimis, 'Promoting Space Ventures by Creating an International Space IPR Framework' (2011) 33 *European Intellectual Property Review* 35, 40.

[213]   Article 12 of the Outer Space Treaty states, 'All stations, installations, equipment and space vehicles on the Moon and other celestial bodies shall be open to representatives of other States Parties to the Treaty on a basis of reciprocity. Such representatives shall give reasonable advance notice of a projected visit, in order that appropriate consultations may be held and that maximum precautions may be taken to assure safety and to avoid interference with normal operations in the facility to be visited'.

[214]   Article 15(1) of the Moon Agreement provides 'all space vehicles, equipment, facilities, stations and installations on the Moon shall be open to other States Parties'.

public benefit rights provided in the space treaties? These questions will be discussed in Chapter 3.[215]

4.3 The Temporary Presence

The temporary presence principle is set forth in Article 5ter of the Paris Convention. This principle exempts any Union member from liability of infringement if they happen to use devices patented by another Union member while they are temporarily or accidentally present on board vessels, aircraft or land vehicles in that territory.[216] The question arises whether this principle also governs any space object. On a first reading of the text as it appears, it seems obvious that a space object is excluded. Thus, if elements of a space station are temporarily present (e.g., for the purpose of launching or return to earth) in a foreign country, any use of third party patented technology will not be automatically exempted from the exclusive rights of the patentee and, accordingly, would be considered an infringement, if patent protection is in place in that foreign country.[217] This issue seems to be problematic for outer space activities which will be discussed in detail later in Chapter 3.[218]

5. THE IMPACT OF ENFORCEMENT PROCEDURES OBLIGATIONS IN OUTER SPACE ACTIVITIES

Article 41 of the TRIPs Agreement obliges member states to provide enforcement procedures which permit effective action against any act of infringement of intellectual property rights covered by the Agreement. In the context of the current research, the question arises whether these

---

[215] See section 1.2.1 in Chapter 3.

[216] An example of the implementation of this principle can be found in *Brown* (n 187) in which the US Supreme Court ruled that 'The rights of property and exclusive use granted to a patentee do not extend to a foreign vessel lawfully entering one of our ports and the use of such improvement in the construction, fitting out, or equipment of such vessel while she is coming into or going out of a port of the United States, is not an infringement of the rights of an American patentee, provided it was placed upon her in a foreign port, and authorized by the laws of the country to which she belongs'.

[217] International Bureau, WIPO, 'Meeting of Consultants On Inventions Made or Used in Outer Space' (Geneva, 6–7 March 1997) at para 56–60 <http://www.wipo.int/export/sites/www/patent-law/en/developments/pdf/inventions_space.pdf> (accessed 31 January 2016).

[218] See Section 5.1 temporary presence in Chapter 3.

obligations extend to any acts of infringement which take place in outer space. Before this question can be answered, it must first be determined whether an unauthorized use of protected work constitutes 'infringement' owing to the territorial scope of IP law. Taking into account both the territorial scope of IP law and the lack of specific IP law in outer space, it is unlikely that most use occurring in this spatial area would be infringing. Nevertheless, situations might arise where domestic IP law is enforceable by the application of flagship theory and private international law principles. For instance, in cases where patented technology is used without authorization in a spacecraft and where such use is treated as if it had occurred within the territory of the state of registry of the spacecraft, then if patent protection is in force in that territory, then the same level of enforcement should be available to the patentee irrespective of whether an infringement took place in outer space. Therefore, the obligation under this article is applicable as long as the unauthorized act is constituted as an infringement regardless of the location where it takes place.

6. CONCLUSION

For the reasons outlined above, it seems that the territorial scope of intellectual property laws may not fit well with the protection of intellectual property created and used in outer space, since national law, in principle, applies only to the territory of a country, and not to outer space. The applicability of national IP law therefore poses some limitations when applying to works and inventions created or devised in outer space. Though an extraterritorial application of IP law might serve as a solution in these circumstances, whether this alternative is appropriate seems uncertain, and it might not be widely accepted among states. Moreover, the special characteristics of outer space technically prevents non-member states of the international intellectual property conventions from obtaining similar benefits under the National Treatment and Most-Favored Nation Principles as those member states. In other words, those fundamental principles cannot be implemented effectively owing to the limitations of outer space, as examined above. In addition, there are still some legal issues, such as determining what constitutes relevant prior art, and the temporary presence exception to infringement which may arise when applying domestic intellectual property law to works created in outer space. The following chapters will investigate whether these legal problems can be resolved under the present international regime or whether it is necessary to implement a special legal regime for intellectual property created or used in outer space.

3.   Patents in outer space

A patent provides exclusive rights to protect an invention. These rights are awarded in exchange for the disclosure of the invention to the public. Normally, patent protection is territorial. This means a patent's protection only extends to the territory of the country of grant. Therefore, an invention made, used or infringed in outer space may not always be protected under any particular patent regime. In addition, it appears questionable whether an invention devised in outer space, or which is only exploitable in outer space, is eligible for patent protection on earth. If this actually proves to be the case, then it may well reduce any incentive for investment in inventions in outer space. Nevertheless, the huge potential benefits, such as microgravity works in outer space, has led to increasing efforts to bring inventions in outer space under the umbrella of patent protection. It is therefore necessary to be able to effectively patent not only for innovation technologies which can be used exclusively in outer space, but also for those which are usable either on earth or in outer space.

A search of the United States Patent and Trademark Office patent database using the keywords 'outer space' and 'zero gravity' identifies 175 patents that refer to these terms. The results of this exercise supports the potential for an increasing number of space activities,[219] as well as indicating that outer space activities have the potential to be patentable. However, owing to the distinct environment of outer space, potential problems with IP protection are foreseeable.[220] In the case of unauthorized use of protected technology in outer space, it is the territorial nature of patents and territorial limits of the scope of protection which appear

---

[219] USPTO Patent Full-Text and Image Database, <http://patft.uspto.gov/ netacgi/nph-Parser?Sect1=PTO2&Sect2=HITOFF&p=1&u=%2Fnetahtml%2FPT O%2Fsearch-bool.html&r=0&f=S&l=50&TERM1=outer+space&FIELD1=&co1 =AND&TERM2=zero+gravity&FIELD2=&d=PTXT> (search conducted on 31 January 2016).

[220] Gabriella Catalano Sgrosso, 'Applicable Jurisdiction Conflicts in the International Space Station' (Proceedings of 43rd Colloquium on the Law of Outer Space, Rio De Janeiro, October 2000) 183.

problematic, whereas practical and technical problems may arise when assessing patentability.

Since the issue of patentability of a space invention has specific and distinct legal issues from conventional inventions on earth, this chapter aims to address issues regarding patents and outer space by reviewing the following sub-topics: (1) patentable subject matter; (2) novelty; (3) inventive step; (4) industrial application; (5) ownership; (6) joint invention; (7) infringement and (8) exceptions. The specific issues raised by the International Space Station (ISS) will be examined at the end of this chapter, only where issues are separate from the normal scope of national patent law.

In this regard, the national legislation in the United Kingdom and United States have been selected for comparative discussion. The European Patent Convention and Community Patent Regulation will also be reviewed in parallel with UK legislation, when relevant, since these two pieces of legislation play a vital role for patent protection in European countries, including the UK.[221] Of the jurisdictions under consideration, at present, only the United States has enacted patent legislation which deals specifically with outer space. US law will therefore feature in some parts of this chapter as the only relevant legislation in force.

1. PATENTABILITY

The first issue to be addressed is whether an invention in outer space is patentable.[222] Neither the national patent legislation in the jurisdictions under consideration nor any international instrument appears to prevent any such invention from being patented. Article 27(1) of TRIPs states that: 'patents shall be available for any inventions, whether products or processes, in all fields of technology, provided that they are new, involve an inventive step and are capable of industrial application'. As this provision indicates that patents will be granted to *any* invention which meets the substantive requirements, there is nothing in TRIPs which explicitly precludes inventions in outer space from patent protection. In addition, the international community seems to accept the idea of

---

[221]   At present, the Community Patent Regulation is not yet in force. See <https://www.epo.org/news-issues/news/2015/20151215.html> (accessed 5 January 2016).

[222]   An invention in outer space for discussion in this chapter covers both one devised in outer space and one which can be exploited only in outer space.

protection for space-related inventions. For examples, the United States has enacted its legislation to give effect to inventions in outer space.[223] The European Union has reached agreement on the text of the Community Patent Regulation,[224] which applies equally to inventions made or used on earth as to those created or used in outer space.[225]

This legislation means that once an invention has been devised, it is eligible for patent protection provided that it fulfills all requirements of patentability under national legislation. In other words, the place of invention is irrelevant. However, there are some features of intellectual creations made in outer space which require particular consideration when considering patentable subject matter.

1.1   Patentable Subject Matter

None of the relevant international conventions discussed in Chapter 2 define what patentable subject matter is.[226] However (and in addition to the provisions of Article 27(1) outlined above), Articles 27(2) and 27(3) of TRIPs provide some guidance as to what subject matter member countries may *exclude* from patentability in their national legislation.[227] This issue is left to be determined by national legislation and practice. In general, any intellectual creation or human discovery can be made the subject of a patent application. For example, the US Supreme Court has held that 'anything under the sun that is made by a man' is potentially patentable under US law.[228] The US Patent Act provides for four categories of invention which may be patented: a process, an apparatus, a method of manufacture and a composition of matter.[229] In contrast, the UK Patent Act of 1977 ('UK Patent Act') neither categorizes the subject

---

[223]   35 U.S.C. 105.

[224]   The Regulation entered into force on 20 January 2013 but will be applicable from the date of the entry into force of the Agreement on a Unified Patent Court, see <https://www.epo.org/news-issues/news/2015/20151215.html> (accessed 5 January 2016). However, this Regulation is not yet in force; see (n 221).

[225]   Article 3(2) of the Community Patent Regulation states 'this Regulation shall apply to inventions created or used in outer space, including on celestial bodies or on spacecraft, which are under the jurisdiction and control of one or more Member States in accordance with international law.'

[226]   See Section 1.1 patents in Chapter 2.

[227]   For example, Articles 27(2) excludes an invention which is contrary to public order from patentability.

[228]   *Diamond v. Chakrabarty* 447 U.S. 303, 309 (1980).

[229]   35 U.S.C. § 101.

matter of a patentable invention, nor even defines what is meant by the term 'invention'. Instead, the legislation only states that any invention which meets the requirements under the law shall be patentable.[230] However, Section 1(2) provides a non-exhaustive list of particular subject matter which falls outside the scope of an 'invention'.[231] Thus, by virtue of Sections 1(2) and 60(1) of the UK Patent Act, inventions are either products or processes.[232] Articles 52(1) and (2) of the European Patent Convention (EPC 2000) share similar provision on patentable inventions as those stated in Section 1(1) (2) of the UK Patent Act.

In sum, any invention, whether it is a product or process, is eligible for patent protection and will be patentable, provided it meets the patentability requirements and does not fall within a specific exclusion (such as may be enacted for subject matter which is contrary to public order, morality, health or welfare).[233] In addition, the laws of nature, abstract ideas, naturally occurring substances and mathematical formula are disqualified as patentable subject matter.[234]

Questions arise as to how these requirements for patentability are applied to certain inventions created in outer space and their end products. These will be explored using the examples of a method of operating telecommunication by using an orbital slot; a method of generating nuclear energy by using Helium-3 on the Moon; and processes for creating certain pharmaceutical and electronic materials in a zero-gravity environment. The question of whether and to what extent these inventions are patentable subject matters will be examined below.

1.1.1 A method of operating telecommunication by using an orbital slot

In the satellite telecommunication industry, it is essential to send satellite constellations into proper orbital positions so as to achieve the most efficient and successful operation. This requires use of methods which

---

[230] Section 1(1) of the UK Patent Act.
[231] For example, a discovery, rule or method for playing a game or a program is listed as the non-inventions under the said provision. See also Article 52(2) of the EPC 2000 which also provides for a non-exhaustive list of excluded subject matter.
[232] R. Miller et al. *Terrell on the Law of Patents* (17th ed., Sweet and Maxwell, 2011) 35.
[233] For example, see Section 1(3) of the UK Patent Act, Article 53(a) of the EPC 2000.
[234] S.W. Halpern et al., *Fundamentals of United States Intellectual Property Law: Copyright, Patent and Trademark* (4th ed., Wolters Kluwer Law International 2012) at 154 and 191; J.M. Mueller, *Patent Law* (3rd ed., Aspen Publishers 2009) at 285–286.

calculate an appropriate velocity and orientation. This section aims to investigate which aspects of this technological area may represent patentable subject-matter. Orbits *per se* (in terms of a physical locality) are not, of course, patentable since these, like other natural resources, are not inventions and so do not qualify as patentable subject matter.[235] However, orbits may be part of a technological process for sending a satellite into an appropriate position.[236] The question to be resolved is whether a process in which an orbit (itself, non-patentable matter) forms part of the invention would meet the requirements for patentability.

In the United States, the USPTO has already granted a number of patents in respect of methods for locating telecommunication satellites in orbital slots in outer space. In these methods, an orbit is part of a process of achieving a telecommunication service. As discussed above, Section 101 of the US Patent Act identifies four possible statutory categories of patentable subject matter.[237] The telecommunication methods under consideration are properly classified in the 'process' category.[238] Even though orbits feature as part of the patented process, or as one step in a method claim, the overall process of satellite orbiting is not itself a pure product of nature, since it includes additional subject matter which does feature human intellectual intervention and, therefore, the process as a whole falls within the scope of Section 101. Examples of granted patents in this field include methods for storing spare satellites in orbit,[239] as well as satellite cellular telephone and data communication systems[240] in

---

[235] Bently (n 207) 379–380 explained that a patent is a limited monopoly which is granted to an inventor in return for the disclosure of technical information. See also the discussion of orbit under the section of non-appropriation in Chapter 1 of this book.

[236] Andrew Rush, 'Patenting Orbits? It's All Part of the Process', *IP in Space* (12 September 2012) <http://ipinspace.com/2012/09/12/patenting-orbits-its-all-part-of-the-process/> (accessed 31 January 2016).

[237] 35 U.S.C. 101 Invention patentable states, 'Whoever invents or discovers any new and useful process, machine, manufacture, or composition of matter, or any new and useful improvement thereof, may obtain a patent therefor, subject to the conditions and requirements of this title'.

[238] Janice Mueller (n 234) 255 explained in her book that 'a process in patent is synonymous with a method and is merely a series of steps for carrying out a given task'.

[239] US 3995801 A, <http://www.patentgenius.com/patent/3995801.html> and <http://www.patentstorm.us/patents/3995801/claims.html> (accessed 31 January 2016).

[240] US 5410728 A, <http://www.patentstorm.us/patents/5410728.html> and <http://www.patentbuddy.com/Patent/5410728> (accessed 31 January 2016).

which satellites are required to maintain and switch positions between particular orbits. The two US court decisions which are landmark cases in terms of space patents infringement, namely *Hughes Aircraft v. the United States*[241] and *TRW v. ICO Global Communications*,[242] both concerned methods involving satellite orbits.[243] The first case concerned a patent for a method of obtaining and maintaining a satellite's position in orbit, and the second case related to a patent for a mobile satellite communications system comprising a number of satellites placed in orbits at particular attitudes.[244] Thus, these decided cases confirm that methods of satellite orbiting which feature an orbit as part of the process are patentable subject-matter under US law.[245]

However, it might be argued that the subject of TRW's patent claim was not in fact eligible subject matter for a patent.[246] Although TRW did not claim its 'invention' as use of a particular earth orbit, 'as such' (but rather a combination of orbits and a plurality of satellites functioning in a particular manner[247]), the scope of the patent's claims was so broad as to make it almost impossible for third parties to avoid infringement if using a similar satellite system in a medium earth orbit.[248] In other words, it is arguable that the real 'innovation' was the particular choice of orbit, but the patent claim was drafted to disguise this fact, by combining it with other claimed features which, while necessary, were essentially conventional.

---

[241] *Hughes Aircraft* (n 176).

[242] This case was settled out of court. TRW's suit was dismissed by the court in April 1997 (order of dismissal of 31 March 1997 in case number 96–3381KMW (MCX), US District of California), see more in Nandasiri Jasentuliyara, *International Space Law and the United Nations* (Kluwer Law International 1999) 311. More discussion on this case can be found at Smith (n 177) 193–194; Rene Oosterlinck, 'Tangible and Intangible Property in Outer Space' (Proceedings of 39th Colloquium on the Law of Outer Space, Beijing, October 1996) 280–281.

[243] These two cases will be discussed later under the infringement section.

[244] More discussions on these two cases can be found, for instance, in Bradford Lee Smith (n 177) and Carl Q. Chistol, 'Persistence Pays Off: The Case of Hughes Aircraft Company v. USA, 1976–1999' (Proceedings of the 42nd Colloquium on the Law of Outer Space, Amsterdam, October 1999) 190–198 and 199–207, respectively.

[245] The use of certain orbits or trajectories might be contrary to the non-appropriation principle in space law, see Section 4.2 in Chapter 1.

[246] Oosterlinck, 'Tangible and Intangible Property in Outer Space' (n 242) 281.

[247] Ibid.

[248] Ibid.

As discussed previously, the UK Patent Act lacks a definition of what qualifies as an 'invention' and statutory categories of patentable subject matter. Subject matter will be patentable if it does not fall within the scope of excluded-subject matter under Section 1(2) of the Act, provided that it meets the other requirements for patentability. The question to be considered is whether a method of operating a global telecommunication system in which orbits feature as part of the process is appropriate subject matter for a UK patent. Again, under the UK law, orbits are natural resources, and therefore are non-patentable subject matter. With no case law which relates directly to orbits, analysis of case law which has applied Section 1(2) of the UK Patent Act to exclude other subject matter will be made.

In *Genentech*,[249] the House of Lords considered the scope of Section 1(2) of the UK Patent Act in relation to use of known DNA technology to produce t-PA, a valuable activator to prevent blood clots. While some of the patent's claims were found to be 'pure discoveries' and so unpatentable subject matter, the Court held that 'a claim to a method embracing a discovery ... may well be an invention' which is patentable.[250] In the same way, since the subject matter of the telecommunications method under consideration in question is not for orbit *as such*, but for a technological process, it would therefore be patentable under the UK law, by analogy to the case law above.

1.1.2 Nuclear power using Helium-3 on the Moon

As discussed in Chapter 1, nuclear power can be generated more cost-effectively than on earth by using Helium-3 which is available on the Moon.[251] Nuclear power production is a potentially vast and beneficial source of energy for humankind, but it is a process which does not naturally occur, either on earth or on the Moon, without human intellectual intervention.[252] Pertinent issues arise whether and to what extent an invention of a process for generating nuclear power can be protected and which aspects are appropriate subject matter for patent protection. It seems reasonable to accept that a method of producing nuclear power in outer space would be eligible subject matter for a patent. Such a method is a technological process which should qualify as an invention because it

---

[249]   [1989] R.P.C. 147 (C.A.).
[250]   Ibid 208. This case is also discussed in Torremans (n 119) 85–86.
[251]   See section 4.2 in Chapter 1.
[252]   Keith Veronese, 'Could Helium-3 Really Solve Earth's Energy Problems?' IO9 (11 May 2012) <http://io9.gizmodo.com/5908499/could-helium-3-really-solve-earths-energy-problems> (accessed 31 January 2016).

is devised using human intellect. Under the current practice, there are a number of methods of producing nuclear power which have been patented in many countries, including the US and in EU member states.[253] Nevertheless, any particular method of nuclear power generation may then fail to be patentable on other grounds. For example, the process may lack novelty, or be obvious – if it can be demonstrated that the claimed process makes no significant contribution to the state of the art.[254]

However, while a particular process and/or apparatus for generating nuclear power might be patentable, nuclear power *per se* would be excluded from patentability since it is neither a product nor a process but the power used to generate heat and electricity. Therefore, it is a type of energy, not a patentable subject matter. Only the method of generating energy will be eligible for patentability, although any energy produced by a patented method may be considered to be a 'patented product'.[255]

1.1.3 Pharmaceuticals and electronics produced in zero gravity

Pharmaceutical and electronic products produced in zero gravity would be eligible subject matter for patent protection (both in respect of the products per se and to the method of production), since such inventions result from human intellectual input. However, they might fail to satisfy the other requirements of patentability. For example, the patent claim may lack novelty if the particular product at issue is already available on earth. Therefore, the one remaining question is whether a process of producing such products would be patentable if the only point of novelty is the use of a zero-gravity environment. Is use of the same method under different atmospheric conditions considered as relevant prior art? This question will be looked at further in the following section.

---

[253] Francois Leveque, 'Innovation Trends in Nuclear Power Generation' EU Energy Policy Blog (9 May 2010) <http://www.energypolicyblog.com/2010/05/09/innovation-trends-in-nuclear-power-generation/> (accessed 31 January 2016). U.S. Patent No. 8.529.713 on system and method for annealing nuclear fission reactor materials and U.S. Patent No. 3.564.302 are examples of patents concerning nuclear power.

[254] A valid patent might also be granted for a novel and inventive set of apparatus used for generating nuclear power.

[255] Some patents which include claim 1 as 'a method for making X comprising …' also include a claim which says 'X made by the method according to claim 1'. In both cases, X itself may be an existing product (i.e., lacking novelty & inventive step, but the patent affords protection to X when made by process Y). See Section 60(1)(c) PA77.

In addition, as a result of experimentation on the ISS, new materials might be created or isolated in its weightless environment which cannot be isolated on earth.[256] It is questionable whether such materials would be considered to be 'naturally occurring' and therefore barred from patent protection as ineligible discoveries.[257] In that event, however, the particular process of making that new material in a weightless environment would appear to be potentially patentable subject matter, since it would result from human intellectual intervention.[258]

1.1.4   Satellite navigation signals

A satellite navigation service is definitely beneficial for a satellite navigation system and requires a significant financial investment. Thus, attempts to patent such technology to secure a return on investment is justifiable.[259] However, it is necessary to clarify at this stage that any protectable subject matter in this case would not be the signal itself, but rather it would be a method or system of processing navigation satellites signals which qualified as an eligible subject matter for patent protection.[260, 261]

1.2   Requirements for Patentability

Normally, there are three basic criteria for patentability. These are novelty, inventive step and industrial application. For example, Section 1(1) of the UK Patent Act states:

---

[256]   C. Heather Walker, 'Potential Patent Problem on the ISS' (Proceedings of the 42nd Colloquium on the Law of Outer Space, Amsterdam, October 1999) 64. However, the author did not mention what the new material was.

[257]   Ibid.

[258]   Ibid.

[259]   The Ministry of Defence's attempt to patent satellite signals is reported in <http://www.wired.co.uk/news/archive/2012–07/10/british-mod-patent-gps> (accessed 31 January 2016).

[260]   US Patent no. US 847 1763 B2 on processing of satellite navigation system signals and related receive-signal verification is an example of patenting satellites signals which obviously states that the patentable subject matter in this case is a process not a signal. For information about this US patent, see <http://www.google.com/patents/US8471763?dq=US+patent+on+a+navigation+satellite+signal+processing+system&hl=th&sa=X&ei=8Dk3UvE6yqqEB6Kqg MAG&ved=0CDgQ6AEwAA> (accessed 31 January 2016).

[261]   The USPTO guideline for patentable subject matter excludes signal per se as a subject matter of patentability. See training paper of the USPTO <http://www.uspto.gov/patents/law/exam/101_training_aug2012.pdf> (accessed 31 January 2016).

A patent may be granted only for an invention in respect of which the following conditions are satisfied, that is to say –

(a) the invention is new;
(b) it involves an inventive step;
(c) it is capable of industrial application;
(d) the grant of a patent for it is not excluded by subsections (2) and (3) below;

and reference in this Act to a patentable invention shall be construed accordingly.

Equivalent requirements are also enshrined in the US Patent Act[262] and in any other national legislation[263] in compliance with Article 25(1) of TRIPs. In the next part, we shall examine whether a space invention faces any particular hurdles before it can pass these three core criteria of patentability.[264]

1.2.1 Novelty

The first requirement for an invention to be patentable is that it must be new.[265] It is understood that an invention is considered to be new if it does not form part of the state of the art.[266]

To date, a number of inventions have been devised aboard the ISS.[267] The purpose of this section is to examine two particular questions: (1) whether any disclosure of an invention in the ISS forms part of the state of the art which destroys the novelty of any later-filed patent application for that invention; and (2) whether an invention created under a zero-gravity environment is novel and, if so, for which types of patent claims i.e., product, process or product-by-process.

---

[262]   35 U.S.C. 101–103.
[263]   See for examples, Article 52(1) of the EPC 2000, Section 5 of the Thai Patent Act B.E. 2522 (1979) as subsequently amended ('Thai Patent Act') and Section 18(1) of the Australian Patent Act (1990).
[264]   In this chapter, a space invention refers to all three types of space invention which are the space-created invention, space-related invention and general invention created in outer space. See section 1 in Chapter 1.
[265]   Section 1(1)(a) of the UK Patent Act; EPC 2000 Article 52(1); Section 102 of the US Patent Act and Section 5(1) of the Thai Patent Act.
[266]   For example, see section 6 of the Thai Patent Act.
[267]   Mark L. Uhram, 'Microgravity-Related Patent History' <http://www.iss-casis.org/portals/0/docs/2012%20patent%20history.pdf> (accessed 31 January 2016).

In order to assess the novelty of an invention, it is necessary to study how the 'state of art' is determined. Section 2(2) of the UK Patent Act defines the term 'the state of art' as follows:

> The state of the art in the case of an invention shall be taken to comprise all matter (whether a product, a process, information about either, or anything else) which has at any time before the priority date of that invention been made available to the public (whether in the United Kingdom or elsewhere) by written or oral description, by use or in any other way.

Article 54(2) of the EPC 2000 provides a similar definition of the state of the art. In essence, an invention is not new if it was previously disclosed to public or was the subject of an earlier patent application filed before the date of application for the invention under consideration.

US patent law does not provide the definition of the state of the art, but it sets out conditions for novelty by stating that an invention is unpatentable if 'the claimed invention was patented, described in a printed publication, or in public use, on sale or otherwise available to the public before the effective filing date of the claimed invention'.[268]

Under the UK Patent regime, the novelty of an invention is assessed at the priority date of the invention. However, the US patent law sets different dates for judging the novelty of an invention. This is because the US Patent Act has a narrower state of the art compared with that in UK legislation, since it excludes earlier public disclosures of the same invention made by the inventor within a particular time frame. This provides a limited 'grace period' in which the inventor is free to publicly disclose his invention without prejudicing the novelty of any later US patent application.[269] Although the US patent system recently changed from a 'first-to-invent' regime to a 'first-to-file' regime, the grace period has still been retained.[270]

Some scholars claim that the new US patent system is not a true 'first-to-file' system, as operational in other countries, but is better described as a 'first-to-disclose' system. This moniker recognizes the

---

[268]   35 U.S.C. 102 (a)(1) (The full text is available online at <http://www.uspto.gov/web/offices/pac/mpep/consolidated_laws.pdf> (accessed 31 January 2016).

[269]   An inventor relying upon a US grace period may, however, prejudice the novelty of any later patent applications filed in other jurisdictions, such as the UK, which do not recognize grace periods, irrespective of whether priority is claimed under the Paris Convention.

[270]   See 35 U.S.C. 102 (b) conditions for patentability, novelty and 35 U.S.C. 102 (b) (pre-AIA) for comparison.

inventor's ability to publicly disclose his invention within the one-year period before filing a patent application, without jeopardizing the novelty of his own invention.[271] In other words, inventors are able to practice their inventions for one year prior to filing their patent applications in the United States. The grace period is not limited to disclosures made only by the inventor or joint inventor, but also 'by another who obtained the subject matter disclosed directly or indirectly from the inventor or joint inventor'.[272] Thus, in the United States, the novelty of an invention will be assessed either from the date of first public disclosure or the priority date as the case may be, rather than only the priority date as in other countries.

Since the state of the art for the purposes of novelty is assessed at the priority date of the invention in question, it worth recapping briefly here what the priority date is. The right of priority provided in the Paris Convention[273] (and outlined in Chapter 2) entitles a patent applicant up to 12 months from the date of filing of their first patent application in one Paris Union country (the 'priority date') to file equivalent applications for the same invention in other Union countries. Any later applications made with a valid priority claim have an effective filing date in terms of novelty as of the original priority date. This affords the applicant 'priority' over any third-party applications filed for the same invention during the period between the priority date and the actual filing date.[274] Furthermore, the rights of priority will cover for any act that might occur during the priority period which would otherwise jeopardize the novel status of the invention, such as any disclosure of the invention e.g., by sale.[275] The function of the right of priority is to secure the first applicant's right within the Paris Union.[276] Therefore, the ability to rely upon an earlier priority date plays an important role when an applicant is deciding when and whether to file patent applications in multiple countries. Hence, the priority date for any invention normally is either the

---

[271] 35 U.S.C. 102 (b) of the Leahy-Smith America Invents Act (2011) (effective from 16 March 2013). See comments on this new law in L. Kravets, 'First-To-File Patent Law Is Imminent, But What Will It Mean?' and Jason A. Engel and James E. Fajkowski, 'Major Patent Law Changes: First-To-File Provisions' <http://techcrunch.com/2013/02/16/first-to-file-a-primer/> and <http://www.klgates.com/major-patent-law-changes-first-to-file-provisions-effective-march-16-2013-12-18-2012/> respectively (accessed 31 January 2016).

[272] New 35 U.S.C. 102 (b)(1)(A).

[273] Article 4 A(1) of the Paris Convention.

[274] Article 4 C(1) of the Paris Convention.

[275] Article 4 (B) of the Paris Convention.

[276] Tramposch (n 179) 190.

date on which the application is filed or up to 12 months earlier, if the
first application for the same invention was filed in another Paris
Convention country.[277]

In principle, an invention is new if it has not been disclosed to the
public prior to the priority date. However, most national patent laws,
including the EPC 2000,[278] lack a provision which is equivalent to the
'grace period' as stated in the US Patent Law which protects the novelty
of an invention based upon the applicant's own prior public disclosure up
to one year prior to its filing date.[279] In other words, aside from the
United States, most countries generally adopt an 'absolute' novelty
regime, without a pre-filing grace period, except in very limited situations.[280] For example, Article 55 EPC 2000 provides for two scenarios
where the making available to public of an invention would not jeopardize the novelty of a later filed patent application. The first is display at an
official exhibition, and the second is 'an evident abuse in relation to the
applicant or his legal predecessor'.[281] Section 2(4) of the UK Patent Act
also provide a limited grace period for certain circumstances as an
exception for the disclosure to public.

When considering the novelty of an invention, there is no geographical
limitation as to where relevant prior art has been disclosed.[282] This means
that the public knowledge or use anywhere in the world are treated as
prior art. Nonetheless, under the previous first-to-invent system, US
legislation limited prior art based upon public knowledge or use to
knowledge or use within the United States.[283] Thus (excluding the
specific exceptions discussed above), according to the definition and
practice of nations, the 'state of the art' refers to all matter which is

---

[277]   Bently (n 207) 467.
[278]   The European Patent Convention (EPC) of 1973 as revised by the Act
Revising Article 63 EPC of 17 December 1991 and the Act revising the EPC of
20 November 2000 <http://www.cpo.org/law.practice/legal-texts/html/epc/2010/e/
mal.html> (accessed 31 January 2016).
[279]   Brian Derby, 'Industrial Property Rights and Space Activity: An EPO
Perspective' (Proceedings of an ESA Workshop on Intellectual Property Rights &
Space Activities, Paris, December 1994) 176.
[280]   Mueller (n 234) 159.
[281]   EPC 2000, Article 55 (1)(a)(b).
[282]   Section 2(2) of the UK Patent Act, Article 54(2) of the EPC 2000,
Section 6 of the Thai Patent Act and new 35 U.S.C. 102 (a)(1).
[283]   35 U.S.C. 102 precludes a patent from issuing if an invention was
'known or used in this country'.

publically available anywhere in the world before the priority date of invention.[284]

The question of whether an invention has been prior disclosed or 'made available to the public' is a factual one, and to obtain a clearer understanding of the requirements, it is necessary to examine judicial holdings.

The UK House of Lords, in *Synthon BV v SmithKline Beecham*, held that an invention is made available to the public if there has been an 'enabling disclosure'. Thus making available consists of two separate requirements: 'prior disclosure' and 'enablement'.[285] Therefore, prior availability is not sufficient alone to destroy novelty, the disclosure must be of the type which would enable the invention to be put into effect.[286] The EPO Technical Board has indicated that it is sufficient for the disclosure in question to have been placed on a shelf in the library one day before the priority date to be effective prior art. It is the making available which is pertinent, irrespective of whether any members of the public are actually aware of it.[287] The US court held that an invention was known or used when such invention was publically accessible.[288] In summary, an invention is deemed to be disclosed such that it lacks novelty, if the invention has been made available in a manner which enables it to be put into practice by a person with an appropriate level skill in the relevant art.[289]

Regarding an invention created in outer space, the first question to consider is whether any disclosure of an invention made in the ISS forms part of the state of the art. This seems to be problematic. For example, consider the case where an astronaut devises an invention while in a spacecraft. If the invention is known to other astronauts and scientists in that spacecraft, is this deemed to be a disclosure to the public?[290] Taking the judicial decisions into account, if the subject matter contained in the relevant patent claim is clearly evident, then the disclosure would appear to be an enabling one. Therefore, assuming the disclosure is deemed to

---

[284] Bently (n 207) 531.

[285] *Synthon BV v. SmithKline Beecham* [2006] RPC (10).

[286] Bently (n 207) 537.

[287] T 381.87 OJ EPO 1990, 213, see also Catherine Seville, *EU Intellectual Property Law and Policy* (Edward Elgar 2009) 15.

[288] *Gayler v. Wilder*, 51 U.S. (10 How.) 477, 498 (1850).

[289] Halpern (n 234) 161. In Europe, the notional person is the 'person skilled in the art', whereas in the US it is the 'person with ordinary skills in the art'.

[290] Walker (n 256) 62.

be 'available to the public', then the claimed invention in any later patent application filed on earth would not be novel, unless the disclosure falls within one of the specific exceptions, as provided by law. In this case, disclosure would not appear to fall within any such exclusion. This is because the disclosure of invention at issue does not amount either to an international exhibition or official exhibition.[291] However, an applicant may take advantage of the grace period allowed under the US law to avoid novelty issues, provided that any US patent application is filed within one year of this public release. However in other countries, including the UK, where there is no equivalent grace period, any disclosure of the invention to other astronauts and scientists on the spacecraft would invalidate any later patent application filed on the basis of lack of novelty.

A related question is whether the invention is novel in countries other than the United States where there is no grace period. How is novelty affected if the inventor/astronaut's work is being observed remotely and broadcast back to earth via satellites? Given that an invention is not patentable in most countries if it is prior disclosed to public, it appears that there is no special exception for space-related activities to preserve an invention's novelty, outside the grace period provision in the US Patent Act. This would lead to confusion among the interested parties in this field since it would effectively prevent any space inventions from being patentable in the majority of states where no grace period for self-disclosure is provided.

Therefore, a crucial factor is the extent to which disclosures of the kind outlined above would be considered as being 'available to the public'. Is it possible that these novelty issues may be avoided by use of confidentiality agreements by which parties having information regarding the invention agree not to disseminate details they have received? Would such an agreement be sufficient to protect the novelty of invention? The answer to this question seems to be in the affirmative, at least in some jurisdictions. The EPO Board of Appeal, for example, has ruled that 'if access to a document is deliberately restricted to certain persons it is by that token not available to the public even if the group of persons able to gain knowledge of the content of the document is large'.[292]

---

[291]   See Article 11 of the Paris Convention, Section 2(4)(a)(b)(c) of the UK Patent Act, 35 U.S.C. 102 (b), AIA, 35 U.S.C. 102(b)(1)-(2), Article 55 (1)(a)(b) EPC 2000.

[292]   T 300/86 28 August 1989.

As yet, there are currently no judicial opinions available which address disclosure in outer space. However, the novelty requirement is a qualitative criterion, which aims to prevent the patenting of an invention which is already available or known to the public. Taking this fact into consideration, in my view it is not justifiable to equate *any* disclosure of an invention in the ISS to one which makes it available to the public. This is because any disclosure of the invention takes place in a *particular* module of the space station. This is an environment which is arguably analogous to work on an invention which is carried in a closed laboratory on earth in circumstances where details of the invention are known only by a limited number of people who would be deemed to treat this information as confidential.[293] The EPO Guidelines also clarify that use of an invention on private property (giving examples of factories and barracks) is not considered as public use, if it is only made available to, for example, company employees or soldiers who are bound by confidentiality in their contracts of employment.[294] Also, while there is uncertainty as to whether a module in the ISS would be treated as a private laboratory, pending a judicial precedence, this issue was long foreseen by the partners of the Intergovernmental Agreement (IGA). A Code of Conduct for the International Space Station Crew was adopted by partners of the IGA, and strict confidentiality rules are included as part of the code.[295] These rules specifically bind astronauts and scientists working in the ISS to maintain all information regarding any research and development work conducted in the ISS confidential, and any disclosure requires prior written approval. Thus, at present, the main measure available to preserve the novelty of any space invention is the strict confidentiality rules in the ISS Crew Code of Conduct. Nonetheless, while such rules aim to prevent technology created in the ISS from being released to a third party, it still remains to be seen whether these measures are considered sufficient by a court, and it is still possible that information relating to an invention which is known and used in the ISS could still be considered as valid prior art.

---

[293] This same opinion also expressed by Tramposch (n 179) 195.

[294] EPO Guidelines as of June 2012, Part G Chapter IV at 7.2.3 <http://documents.epo.org/projects/babylon/eponet.nsf/0/6c9c0ec38c2d48dfc1257a21004930f4/$FILE/guidelines_for_examination_2012_en.pdf> (accessed 31 January 2016).

[295] 14 CFR 1214.403 Code of Conduct for the International Space Station Crew <http://www.law.cornell.edu/cfr/text/14/1214.403> (accessed 31 January 2016).

However, the confidentiality rules only bind those covered by the ISS Crew Code of Conduct or other employees. Therefore, the novelty of an invention could be destroyed if any third parties visit the ISS in reliance of the benefit rights afforded in the space treaties. In this regard, a confidentiality agreement with that third party would serve as a tool for protecting the novelty of that invention.[296] It should be noted that if an employee, third party or astronaut discloses details in breach of their agreement, then this would be exactly the type of non-prejudicial disclosure which would be caught by the limited exceptions in some legislation such as in Article 55 of the EPC and Section 2(4) of the UK Patent Act. In such case, the novelty of an invention in dispute is still valid.[297] In addition, in case of the broadcast of research conducted in the ISS, the novelty of any invention can also be preserved through a confidentiality agreement providing that the transmission is only viewed by those bound by confidentiality (and assuming that steps were taken to ensure that the signal was encrypted).

We now turn to the next question regarding pharmaceutical drugs and electronic devices which would be cost effective if produced in outer space in a zero-gravity environment, since it is questionable whether such a product would qualify for patent protection, having regard to prior art already available on earth. A method of producing such zero-gravity drugs and devices might satisfy the novelty requirement, because a zero-gravity environment may introduce a new integer in the process which has not been disclosed before. However, a claim to the product itself would not be patentable because the end product itself lacks novelty. The very purpose of the novelty requirement is to prevent subject matter in the prior art from being re-patented.[298]

Nevertheless, in some cases it is possible to identify applications for zero-gravity drugs and electronics which would potentially be eligible for both product and process claims. Take, for instance, a process of producing a known drug for curing cancer which is available on earth, and which comprise a purified protein distracted under zero gravity in outer space. Again, this process may be novel if a zero-gravity environment is a significant part of the process. Then it could be argued that the

---

[296]   See section 4.2 the independence of patents in Chapter 2.

[297]   However, in the US, a third party disclosure can be covered by the grace period if the third party obtained the subject matter disclosed directly or indirectly from the inventor. There is no such exception for disclosures against the will of right holders as in the case of the UK. See AIA, 35 U.S.C. 102(b)(1)-(2).

[298]   Bently (n 207) 529.

process of making the drug is different from the process used on the earth because it requires different environmental conditions.[299] In this example, however, a claim to the product itself may also satisfy the novelty requirement, if the level of purity of the protein is such that it simply cannot be obtained on earth,[300] assuming the protein to be an essential component of the drug. Even if the purified protein is not an essential ingredient of the drug, the drug itself might be eligible for patent protection nevertheless, provided the process itself was novel, and the drug was claimed in a 'product-by-process' claim in the UK. This would be analogous to the UK Court of Appeal holding in *Kirin-Amgen* case. Here the court stated that there was 'no reason why the limitation of claims to products produced by a process could not impart novelty ... if a person invents a new method of extracting gold from rock, he can obtain a claim to the process and ... he can also monopolize the gold when produced directly by the process'.[301] However, this route appears to have been closed off, because the House of Lords overturned the Court of Appeal decision, finding instead that where a product was already known, a product-by-process would not be patentable (even if the process was new), as its novelty had already been destroyed.[302]

As we can see from these examples, the novelty of space invention needs a special standard of assessment, which is different from earthly invention. For example, where an invention is made or used in the ISS before a patent application is filed, if such use is considered as a 'public disclosure', the invention at issue may be unpatentable owing to lack of novelty. In addition, it is uncertain whether zero-gravity conditions in outer space could render an invention produced in this environment novel. In each case, the outcome depends upon the courts and respective patent officers to decide on a case-by-case basis, and such decisions might differ from country to country.

Even if a space invention passes the novelty requirement, there remain two further requirements which must also be satisfied to obtain patent protection. The following section will address the issue of inventive step in reference to space inventions.

---

[299] Mosteshar (n 197) 193.

[300] If the purity level of the product in suit is distinguishable from the prior art, it would be novel and met the novelty requirement. See *Eli Lilly v. Generics Drug Sales*, 460 F 2d 1096,174 USPQ 65 (5th Cir 1972), see more in Mosteshar (n 197) 192.

[301] *Kirin-Amgen Inc. v. Hoechst Marion Roussel* [2003] RPC 31, para 33.

[302] *Kirin-Amgen Inc. v. Hoechst Marion Roussel* [2005] RPC 9.

1.2.2 Inventive step

An invention is considered to meet the inventive step criteria if, to a person skilled in the art, it represents more than an obvious advance in the state of the art.[303] Hence, even if an invention is new, it may not be considered different enough from the prior art to possess an 'inventive step' and so satisfy the non-obviousness requirement.[304] The term 'inventive step' is used interchangeably with the term 'non-obviousness'.[305]

Section 3 of the United Kingdom Act provides:

> An invention shall be taken to involve an inventive step if it is not obvious to a person skilled in the art, having regard to any matter which forms part of the state of the art.

Thus, an invention would not be patentable if it is obvious to a person skilled in the art. A person skilled in the art is a notional practitioner, aware of common knowledge in the art available to him on that date.[306] But whether any particular invention is obvious or not requires careful consideration. Assessment of any claimed inventive step is a difficult and problematic task, which is a qualitative matter to be decided on a case-by-case basis.[307] For this reason, study of case law affords significant guidance, and, generally, evidence from experts in the relevant field will be determinative when assessing obviousness. The inventive step requirement ensures that only sufficiently creative technology which makes a contribution to the state of the arts and thus warrants exclusive protection receives patent protection.[308]

Courts in the UK used to adapt a four-step test for assessing an inventive step.[309] First, the Court makes an assessment as to the normal

---

[303]   Section 3 of the UK Patent Act, Article 56 of the EPC 2000 and 35 U.S.C. 103.

[304]   35 U.S.C. 103 and see also Halpern (n 234) 183.

[305]   Sheldon W. Halpern (n 234) 488. The term 'inventive step' tends to be used more frequently in Europe, since the EPC defines patentability using this term, and likewise 'non-obviousness' is used more frequently in the United States.

[306]   Seville (n 287) 112 and Halpern (n 234) 187.

[307]   Bently (n 207) 554–555.

[308]   Ibid 464.

[309]   The reformulation of approaches which were ruled in *Windsurfing International Inc. v. Tabur Marine (Great Britain) Ltd* [1985] RPC 59 (CA) and *Pozzoli v. BDMD SA & Anor* [2007] FSR 37 (CA), [2007] EWCA Civ 588 (22 June 2007). See more on these two cases in Torremans (n 119) 68 and Bently (n 207) 557–558.

knowledge of a person skilled in the art as of the priority date.[310] The second step is to identify the inventive concept or concepts claimed. This may be done by identifying the problem which the invention addresses, and the particular solution which each inventive concept proposes, in terms of a particular claimed combination of features. The third stage is to identify the differences between what is known from the prior art and the claimed concept.[311] The final step is an assessment as to the significance of the technical differences between the prior art and the claimed features.[312] Evidence whether the invention is obvious from a commercial perspective, or appeared obvious to the actual inventor, is irrelevant to an inventive step.[313] As was the case in *Pozzoli SPA v. BDMD SA & Anor*,[314] any patent granted which is later found to be obvious to the person skilled in the art is invalid. This is because an inventive step requires some degree of invention.

When considering inventive step or non-obviousness, the prior art's teaching has to be assessed as a whole.[315] This means that while a determination of lack of novelty may only be based upon a *single* piece of prior art, inventive step can be challenged on the basis of teaching derived from a number of different sources.[316] Similarly, while a claim may be found to be novel based solely upon the presence in a claim of a non-technical feature, when examining whether an invention possesses inventive step, only its technical features are relevant.[317] Typically, each piece of prior art includes only some of the features of the claimed invention, so the question to be addressed is whether it is obvious, or not, to combine various features from different prior art sources, to arrive at the claimed invention.

The EPO suggests that in assessing inventive step, the relevant question to ask is not whether it is obvious that a skilled person 'could' combine the prior art teachings, but rather whether the skilled person 'would' adopt that particular approach.[318] Again, at the EPO,

[310]   Torremans (n 119) 69.
[311]   Ibid.
[312]   Ibid.
[313]   Ibid.
[314]   *Pozzoli SPA* (n 309).
[315]   *Therasense v. Becton, Dickinson & Co.*, 593 F.3d 1289, 1297 (Fed. Cir. 2010).
[316]   Halpern (n 234) 185, see also Bently (n 207) 561.
[317]   Section 1(2) of the UK Patent Act and Article 52(1) of the EPC 2000, see more explanation in Bently (n 207) 564–565.
[318]   Torremans (n 119) 76.

commercial success of the claimed invention alone is irrelevant to prove its inventiveness.[319]

Similar to the EPO's 'would and not could' approach, the US courts have developed a test for determining obviousness based upon 'reasonable expectation of success'. This is an assessment as to whether a person of ordinary skill in the art, looking to solve the particular problem addressed by the invention and faced with the closest piece of prior art, would modify it as required by the patent claim, with a reasonable expectation of success. If so, the claimed invention is obvious.[320] In addition, the US courts also look for evidence of 'simultaneous invention' to support a finding that the invention in question is obvious.[321] Under this approach, if any third party has independently made the same invention within a short period of time after the priority date, it is more likely that the claimed invention 'was the product only of ordinary mechanical or engineering skill'.[322]

Thus, the inventive step criteria requires not only that any invention at stake is new, but it has to be new enough in its particular field that it would not be anticipated by a person skilled in the art. For example, for a method for producing a zero-gravity drug to have inventive step, the fact that such drug is made in a zero-gravity environment is not likely to be sufficient,[323] but rather, other aspects of the method employed during its manufacture must be sufficiently distinct to render its non-obvious.

Therefore, in case of space-related activities, known for use of advanced technology, the question remains whether and to what extent those technologies can be considered as non-obvious. Should the benchmark for inventive step for space inventions be set at the same standard as for inventions on earth?

Taking into account that the purpose of the inventive step requirement is to ensure that a claimed invention represents an advance in its particular field which would not result simply from routine adaptation of existing available technology, it appears to me that the same assessment of non-obviousness is appropriate, irrespective of whether it is a space invention or one on earth. This second requirement therefore seems to be less problematic than the first requirement of novelty. Whether an

---

[319]   Ibid.
[320]   In re *Dow Chemical Co.*, 837 F.2d 469, 473 (Fed. Cir. 1988).
[321]   *Geo. M. Martin Co. v. Alliance Machine Systems International LLC.* 618 F.3d 1294, 1305 (Fed. Cir. 2010).
[322]   Ibid.
[323]   Since, for example, it is generally known in the pharmaceutical field that zero-gravity conditions are known to produce higher yields or higher purity.

invention is inventive or not is a matter of fact, which needs to be considered on an individual basis. However, having regard to the complexity of space technologies, it might prove to be more difficult to apply the non-obviousness criteria as a practical matter, since determining what would be known by the notional 'person skilled in the art' might require expert evidence from specialists in a number of different fields.

1.2.3 Industrial application

The third requirement for patentability requires that the claimed object is capable of 'industrial application'. In other words, it must be possible to foresee a practical use of the invention.[324] If an invention is still at only a high-level theoretical stage, then it would be premature to file a patent application.[325]

Unlike the novelty and non-obviousness requirements, the threshold for satisfying this utility requirement is low.[326] Hence, only a relatively small number of inventions are rejected as lacking industrial application.[327]

Section 4(1) of the UK Patent Act provides that 'an invention shall be capable of industrial application if it can be made or used in any kind of industry, including agriculture'. The equivalent requirement enshrined in Article 57 EPC 2000 states: 'An invention shall be considered as susceptible of industrial application if it can be made or used in any kind of industry, including agriculture'. The utility rule is also required under US patent law.[328] However, it is not necessary to prove actual use of the invention: only a potential for use is expected under this requirement.[329] Since none of the statutory provisions offer guidance how industrial applicability is determined, case law analysis is needed to explain this matter.

The utility requirement seems to be most easily met in case of mechanical or electrical inventions, since the practical application of such inventions are clearly evident from the drawings or diagrams which form

---

[324] Torremans (n 119) 81. In *Brenner v. Manson*, the U.S. Supreme Court ruled that the claimed invention in question which concerned about a new process for making a known steroid was still an unpredictable art and was at a too primarily stage to merit a patent. 388 U.S. 519 (1966) cited in Mueller (n 234) 239–240.
[325] Mueller (n 234) 239–240.
[326] Ibid 235.
[327] Ibid.
[328] 35 U.S.C. 101 also requires that patentable inventions are useful.
[329] Seville (n 287) 117.

part of the patent application.[330] It is more difficult to prove in case of a pharmaceutical or biological invention whether the actual invention claim would actually exhibit the intended pharmacological activity, since these types of inventions possess an evolving utility.[331] Thus, a spectrum of utility has been developed for assessing of their industrial applicability,[332] which is satisfied provided the claimed invention lies on this spectrum.[333]

Case law shows that courts seem to require that an invention needs to be potentially practical in order to pass the test of utility,[334] such that a patent claim is rejected on the ground of industrial application if any use of the invention is based only on a predicted, and not actual, function.[335] In the case of space-based activities, a patentee might be expected to show that their outer space invention is capable of industrial application using the same criteria as those of earth inventions. Whether any claimed invention meets the utility requirement is another factual matter which needs to be assessed on a case-by-case basis. Hence, a space invention should satisfy the utility requirement, provided it is likely to find a practical application and is actually operable for this particular industry.

But what remains to be determined is whether an invention which can only be used in outer space would be eligible for patent protection under national legislation on earth? Would an invention satisfy the industrial application criteria if it would only be workable under zero gravity in outer space? What is the interpretation of sufficient utilization or potential use? Do national provisions require the invention to be capable of industrial application within that territory covered by the patent grant? How does a patent examiner assess the practical utilization of an invention during the patent application process? Would it be sufficient to satisfy the industrial application requirement that an invention has potential utility in outer space?

The purpose of the industrial application requirement is to ensure that an invention has a potentially useful purpose in industry. Taking this into account, it seems reasonable to conclude that any space invention which can only be used in outer space should satisfy this requirement, provided the invention serves some useful function for mankind, regardless of the actual location where utilization of the invention takes place. Consider

---

[330] Halpern (n 234) 181.
[331] Ibid 182.
[332] Ibid 181.
[333] Ibid.
[334] *Eli Lilly v. Human Genome Sciences* [2008] RPC 29 confirmed on appeal [2010] EWCA CSU 33.
[335] ICOS Corporation/Seven transmembrane receptor [2002] 6 OJEPO 293.

the following example. Fluids in space do not flow in the same way as they do on earth. For this reason, a conventional coffee cup cannot be used in space. The USPTO has recently accepted a patent application for a coffee cup specifically adapted for zero-gravity conditions, which was devised by scientists during an earlier mission in the ISS.[336] This 'zero-gravity' coffee cup clearly has utility in a weightless environment, and the acceptance of this patent seems to demonstrate that at least the USPTO considers utility in terms of usefulness for the stated purpose, irrespective of the place where such utility would be realized. Thus, the method of how to prove its utility is a practical question and provided an inventor can convince the patent office that an invention is useful, then the utility requirement is met.[337]

Therefore, the industrial application requirement appears a less problematic assessment compared with the requirements of novelty and inventive step. This is at least partly because this determination is generally more straightforward and is based upon consideration of the invention itself, without requiring any comparison between the invention and the state of the art, and without needing to assume the mantle of a person skilled in the art.

Even though a space invention might meet the requirements of novelty, non-obviousness and industrial application, it might still be excluded from patentability if the nature of the invention falls under a specific exclusion provided in national legislation. For example, in the UK, methods of medical treatment are not patentable, whereas medical and surgical procedures are patentable in the US.[338] The specific exclusions contained in national legislation vary between jurisdictions, but typical

---

[336] 'The Zero Gravity Coffee Cup' NASA Science News (15 July 2013) <http://science.nasa.gov/science-news/science-at-nasa/2013/15jul_coffeecup/> (accessed 31 January 2016).

[337] In my view, there are a number of ways to test its utility which can either be conducted on earth by creating a zero gravity environment or an inventor can send a video tape of its utilization in outer space as evidence.

[338] See section 4A of the UK Patent Act, Article 53(c) of the EPC 2000 and 35 U.S.C. 101. A method of making self-sealing episcleral incision, U.S. Patent No. 5,080,111 is cited as an example in Mueller (n 234) 286. Notwithstanding that medical and surgical procedures are patentable as processes under 35 U.S.C. 101, a patent on certain medical or surgical procedures is unenforceable by virtue of 35 U.S.C. 287(c). This means the patentee is deprived of any remedy for infringement available under the provisions of 35 U.S.C. 281 (civil action for infringement), 35 U.S.C. 283 (injunction), 35 U.S.C. 284 (damages) and 35 U.S.C. 285 (attorney fees).

exclusions include plant varieties and animal varieties,[339, 340] as well as exclusions based upon *ordre public* and morality[341] grounds.

In summary, an invention in outer space is patentable provided it passes all the requirements of patentability without falling within a category of excluded subject matter.[342]

2. OWNERSHIP

This section will consider questions surrounding ownership of an invention and the distinction between inventorship and ownership, since the inventor of the subject matter claimed is not always deemed to be the owner of the invention.[343] Ownership of a patent may be legally transferred by whomever has legal title to the invention, irrespective of whether the actual inventor consents to such onward transfer or not.[344] The rights to grant licenses, to assign a share in a patent and to sue for patent infringement all vest with the owner, not the actual inventor.[345] However, inventors have certain rights too. It is therefore necessary and important to identify the proper owner and inventor of any patent rights. In contrast to the patentability issues discussed previously, ownership does not pose any specific issue for outer space inventions. Therefore, the standards for determination are the same as those inventions created on the earth.[346]

Generally, an invention belongs to its inventor, unless the invention arises during the course of their employment; in which the employer is the first owner of the patent.[347] US patent law (35 USC 101) does not specifically identify the owner of an invention as such, but rather indicates who is entitled to a patent for that invention, namely: that 'Whoever invents or discovers any new and useful process, machine,

---

[339] Paragraph 3(f) Schedule A2 of the UK Patent Act and Article 53(b) of the EPC 2000.

[340] See Exclusions from Patentable Subject Matter and Exceptions and Limitation to the Rights in WIPO Standing Committee on the Law of Patents (13th session, Geneva, 23 to 27 March, 2009) SCP/13/3 p. 12.

[341] Section 1(3) of the UK Patent Act and Article 53(a) of the EPC 2000.

[342] See for example, Sections 1(2)(3), 4A of the UK Patent Act, and Article 53 of the EPC 2000 concerning exceptions to patentability.

[343] Halpern (n 234) 215.

[344] *Sewall v. Walters*, 21 F.3d 411, 417 (Fed. Cir. 1994).

[345] *Rite-Hite Corp v. Kelly Co.*, 56 F.3d 1538, 1551–1552 (Fed. Cir 1995).

[346] Tramposch (n 179) 196.

[347] For example, see Section 39 of the UK Patent Act.

manufacture, or composition of matter, or any new and useful improvement thereof, may obtain a patent therefor'. However, US contracts of employment typically include terms which identify the employer as the owner of employee-derived inventions and require inventors to assign patent rights in the event that a patent application is filed.

Additionally, the United States has specific federal legislation which states that any invention made in performance of work under contract with National Aeronautics and Space Administration (NASA) is the exclusive property of the United States, regardless of whether or not the inventor was employed or assigned to perform the work.[348] This legislation undoubtedly discouraged the private sector from taking part in space activities. Therefore, a further agreement, the Space Act Agreement, was adopted.[349] Under this new arrangement, NASA has rights to any invention made solely by the partner,[350] such that legal title to such invention remains with the respective investing party, although NASA has an option to seek a license to use any such invention.[351] Similar practice regarding ownership of intellectual property rights are found in European Space Agency (ESA) contracts. Under clause 37 of the General Provisions on Intellectual Property Right in the ESA General Clauses and Conditions,[352] ownership of any patents filed remains with the contractor under the contract with ESA who has developed the underlying inventions.[353]

---

[348] Section 305(a) 1–2 of the 1958 National Aeronautics and Space Act as amended (the full text of this act is available online at <http://history.nasa.gov/spaceact-legishistory.pdf>) (accessed 31 January 2016), see more discussion on this matter in Yun Zhao, 'Patent Protection in Outer Space, with Particular Reference to the Patent Regime in Hong Kong', (2006) 14 *Asia Pacific Law Review* 161, 165–167.

[349] The NASA Space Act Agreement guide available online at <http://nodis3.gsfc.nasa.gov/NPD_attachments/NAII_1050_1B.pdf> (accessed 31 January 2016).

[350] See clause 2.2.10.3.2 of the NASA Space Act Agreement guide.

[351] See more discussion on this topic in Zhao (n 108) 21–22.

[352] ESA/C/290, rev 5, available at <http://emits.sso.esa.int/emits-doc/reference/docrefe.pdf> (accessed 1 October 2013).

[353] Clause 37.1 of the General Provision states, 'The Contractor shall be the owner of any invention made in the course of or resulting from work undertaken for the purpose of the contract and shall be entitled to protect such invention by patent or other form of industrial property right in accordance with applicable laws'.

Thus, the ownership of patents in space activities belongs either to the inventor, or to their employer in the case of an invention created under an employment contract, subject to any agreement to the contrary.

3. JOINT INVENTION

In the case of joint invention for space activities, the issue is dealt with in the same way as with joint inventions on earth. US patent law provides that 'in the absence of any agreement to the contrary, each of the joint owners of a patent may make, use, offer, or sell the patented invention ... without the consent of and without an accounting to the other owners'.[354] In other words, each co-owner has full and undivided rights and as such is free to fully exploit the invention without recourse to any co-applicant or co-owner.[355] The UK Patent Act includes a similar provision, in which co-owners have an equal undivided share in the patent.[356]

4. INFRINGEMENT

Normally, national patent laws are enforceable on a territorial basis. Thus, for a patent to be infringed, the patented invention must be used, made or sold within the territory of the state which has granted that patent.[357] This territorial nature gives rise to questions of whether any particular national law is applicable if a potentially infringing act occurs in outer space. How and to what extent is a patent granted by any one country applicable in outer space? Can any act be unlawful or constitute an infringement if no state law is applicable in outer space? Is the position different if the alleged infringement occurs in the ISS, since each module of this manned spacecraft is deemed to be the territory of the registration state?[358]

---

[354]   35 U.S.C. 262.

[355]   Zhao (n 108) 22–23.

[356]   Section 36(1) of the UK Patent Act.

[357]   See for example, *Deepsouth Packing Co. v. Laitram Corp.,* 406 U.S. 518, 532 (1972), Marta Pertegas Sender, *Cross-Border Enforcement of Patent Rights* (OUP, 2002) 1, T.U. Ro et al., 'Patent Infringement in Outer Space In Light of 35 U.S.C. 105: Following The White Rabbit Down The Rabbit Loophole' <http://128.197.26.36/law/central/jd/organizations/journals/scitech/volume172/documents/Kleiman_Web.pdf> 4 (accessed 31 January 2016).

[358]   See more discussion on this issue in Chapter 5, in which three hypothetical situations will be taken into account in detail.

In order to answer these questions, let us begin by examining state jurisdiction. State jurisdiction can be categorized as either a prescriptive jurisdiction or an enforcement jurisdiction. The former is concerned with the ability of a state to declare any particular conduct subject to its laws, whereas the latter is the ability of a state to enforce its law against individuals.[359] Lack of territorial jurisdiction resulted in efforts to introduce a principle of 'flag-state' jurisdiction in case of outer space activities.[360] Under the flag-state principle, a registering State exercises its jurisdiction over any vessel registered of its nationality, whenever such a vessel is in a common area where no state claims national sovereignty, such as on the high sea.[361] Similarly, space law also recognizes that a State of registry retains jurisdiction and control over objects which it sends into outer space. This principle is enshrined in Article VIII of the Outer Space Treaty.[362] The 'State of registry' is defined as a 'launching state',[363] which is either the country which launches a space object, the country which procures the launching of a space object or the country from whose territory or facility a space object is launched.[364] And in cases where there are two or more launching states in respect of a space object, they shall jointly determine which one of them shall register that space object.[365] Thus, it is likely that jurisdiction and applicable law lie with the national law of the State of registry.[366] However, due to the limitation of territoriality scope of patent law, it is uncertain for states to apply their national patent laws to activities in their registered space crafts without also extending the reach of their patent laws to their registered space objects.

Therefore, some countries, such as the United States, have extended their extraterritorial jurisdiction to govern an invention in outer space.[367]

---

[359] Tim Smith, 'A Phantom Menace? Patents and the Commercial Status of Space' (2003) 34 *Victoria University Wellington Law Review* 545, 549.

[360] Ibid 551.

[361] Ibid.

[362] Article VIII of the 1967 Outer Space Treaty states, 'A State Party to the Treaty on whose registry an object launched into outer space is carried shall retain jurisdiction and control over such object, and over a personnel thereof, while in outer space or on a celestial body'.

[363] Article 1(c) of the Registration Convention.

[364] Article 1(a) of the Registration Convention.

[365] Article 2 (2) of the Registration Convention.

[366] See jurisdiction in outer space (quasi-territorial jurisdiction) section in Chapter 5.

[367] Anna Maria Balsano et al., 'The Community Patent and Space-Related Inventions' (2004) 30 *Journal of Space Law* 1, 3.

Section 105 of the US Patent Act provides that 'any invention made, used or sold in outer space on board a spacecraft under the jurisdiction and control of the United States is deemed to be made, used or sold on the United States territory unless agreed by an international agreement'.[368] Germany is another country that amended its patent law to give extra-territorial effect to inventions on board a European Space Agency (ESA)-registered element.[369] The same action was taken in case of European Space Agency-registered element in the International Space Station where the Intergovernmental Agreement (IGA) allows for the extension of any ESA partner states to apply their national intellectual property law to their registered elements in any ESA state.[370]

Issues remain, however, in circumstances where a particular national patent law does not give specific effect to extraterritorial infringement. In this case, it is clearly more complicated if a space invention is patented, but any granting State fails to apply its patent law to any infringing activity which occurs in outer space.

The territoriality principle can be decisive regarding the question of applicable law. In the absence of statutory law empowering the reach of a particular domestic patent law to govern inventions in outer space, it remains uncertain whether states would extraterritorially extend national law to space objects which are registered in that jurisdiction and which have been launched into outer space. Judicial opinion on the extra-territorial application of patent law may differ from country to country, as exemplified below in a dispute which arose in the United States.

Before the US Patent Act in Space came into force, US court rulings on the extraterritoriality of the US patent law gave rise to several concerns. In *Deepsouth Packing Co. v. Laitram Corp.*, the United States

---

[368]   35 U.S.C. 105 established the applicability of US patent law to an invention on board a spacecraft under the jurisdiction or control of the United States which deviated from the use of terminology jurisdiction and control in Article VIII of the 1967 Outer Space Treaty. Such deviation has been explained that the United States has no intention to assert the applicability of its patent law to space objects which the US may control but has no jurisdiction. The word 'or' does not intend to apply the US patent law to foreign-registered space objects but only to any non-registered space objects under US control. See P. Meredith, 'Status of the "Patents in Space" Legislation in Congress – October 1989' (1989) 17 *Journal of Space Law* 163, 166; Arnold Vahrenwald, 'Intellectual Property on the Space Station "Freedom"' (1993) 9 *European Intellectual Property Review* 318, 319.

[369]   Balsano et al. (n 367) 3.

[370]   Article 21(2) of the IGA.

Supreme Court held in 1972 that US patent law had no extraterritorial effect and was not intended to apply to activities taking place beyond the territorial limit of the United States.[371] This differed from earlier decisions reached in *Gardiner v. Howe* (1865)[372] and in *Marconi Wireless Telco. v. USA* (1942),[373] in which US courts ruled that US patent laws did apply on board US vessels operating on the high seas.[374] Hence, use of inventions patented in the United States on board US-registered vessels on the high seas without authorization did constitute patent infringement.

Another interesting case dealt directly with the applicability of patent law in spacecraft. In *Ex Parte McKay*,[375] it was ruled that granting a patent to an invention exploitable in outer space under national US legislation was legitimate, providing that the state of registry retained its jurisdiction over such spacecraft.[376] In this case, it was argued by the USPTO Examiner that a process for obtaining oxygen from extra-territorial materials was not patentable since US patent law did not apply to inventions exploited in outer space.[377] However, the USPTO Appeal Board took a different view, taking account in their decision of Article VIII of the Outer Space Treaty. It ruled that:

> It is clear from Article VIII of the said Treaty that jurisdiction of the United States in personam over any person is present if the object launched into outer space is of United States registry ... A patent grant under 35 U.S.C. 154 by the United States for a process to be carried out on the Moon by personnel subject to its jurisdiction is thus not inimical and at variance with [US patent law].[378]

Uncertainty on the extraterritorial reach of the US patent law was resolved with the enactment of the US 1990 Patent Act in Space. Section 105 of that Act empowers the extraterritorial application of US patent law

---

371 *Deepsouth Packing Co.* (n 357).
372 9 Feb Cases 1157 (Federal Case no. 5,219).
373 53 USPQ 246, 259, 81 CCI 671.
374 Alejandro Piera, 'Intellectual Property in Space Activities: An Analysis of the United States Patent Regime' (2004) 29 *Air and Space Law* 42, 70.
375 *Ex Parte McKay* (1975) 200 USPQ (BNA) 324 (PTO BA), cited in Smith (n 359) 551–552.
376 Ibid.
377 Ibid 552.
378 Ibid.

in the case of outer space activity.[379] This Section 105 has since been interpreted in *Hughes Aircraft Co. v. United States*. This case concerned the infringement of a US patent used in the launch of several space objects. The patent in suit related to technology used to control the attitude of spin-stabilized space objects, and the case examined whether use of such a device in various space objects infringed this US patent. In the case of the first space object, an ARIEL 5 satellite, it was found that the US patent was not infringed. The satellite never entered US territory; even though certain control steps were undertaken from NASA's Goddard Space Center in Maryland, ARIEL 5 was built and primarily controlled from a center in the United Kingdom.[380] Therefore, it was held that any use of patented invention in the ARIEL 5 was insufficient to be considered as use within US territory. Any infringement therefore occurred outside the United States, and US patent law did not apply.[381] However, in case of the HELIOS A and HELIOS B, both non-registered US spacecraft, the same court found that the use of the same patented technology fell within the US border, since both spacecraft were launched from Cape Canaveral in Florida. (Another spacecraft, AMPIE UKS, entered the US once, for the purpose of its launch, but this use escaped infringement by virtue of Section 272 of the US Patent Act, which is discussed further below.[382])

---

[379]   35 U.S.C. 105 (1990) states '(a) Any invention made, used, or sold in outer space on a space object or component thereof under the jurisdiction or control of the United States shall be considered to be made, used or sold within the United States for the purposes of this title, except with respect to any space object or component thereof that is specifically identified and otherwise provided for by an international agreement to which the United States is a party, or with respect to any space object or component thereof that is carried on the registry of a foreign state in accordance with the Convention on Registration of Objects Launched into Outer Space.
(b) Any invention made, used, or sold in outer space on a space object or component thereof that is carried on the registry of a foreign state in accordance with the Convention on Registration of Objects Launched into Outer Space, shall be considered to be made, used, or sold within the United States for the purposes of this title if specially so agreed in an international agreement between the United States and the state of registry'.

[380]   *Hughes Aircraft Co.* (n 176).

[381]   In *Hughes*, NASA asserted that the US Court lacked jurisdiction on non-US registered crafts. See more of this discussion in Carl Q. Christol, 'Judicial Protection of Intellectual Property: Hughes Aircraft vs. US' (Proceedings of 37th Colloquium on the Law of Outer Space, Jerusalem, 1994) 150 and Smith (n 359) 553.

[382]   See more in Section 5.1. on temporary presence.

The extraterritorial applicability of US patent law does not only apply for the purpose of protection against patent infringement but, also to the acquisition of patent rights. The case of *Rosen v. NASA* concerned an invention of method and apparatus for orienting a satellite, and it considered when the invention, as claimed, had been 'reduced to practice'[383] under US patent laws. Since the control stations as described in the patent specification were shown to be located on board a US satellite, it was held that the required 'reduction to practice' had been achieved within US territory.[384]

Another example of extending the reach of national patent law to outer space can be found in the proposed Community Patent Regulation. Article 3(2) states that the Regulation will be applicable to 'inventions created or used in outer space including on celestial bodies or on spacecraft which are under the jurisdiction and control of one or more Member States in accordance with international law'.[385]

As the Community Patent Regulation has been drafted to create a unified patent throughout EU, as well as establishing a unitary EU-wide court system, it is expected that once in force, this Regulation will alleviate any problems arising from the enforceability of intellectual property laws in outer space under Article 21(4) and (5) of IGA.[386]

From the foregoing analysis, it appears that the international community seems to accept that a state of registration may assert its jurisdiction and its patent law to its own space-registered objects. Thus, if

---

[383] There are two types of reduction to practice: constructive and actual. The constructive reduction to practice means a patent application is filed with the USPTO in which the applicant never built or tested the invention provided that such application satisfies the disclosure requirements of 35 U.S.C. 112. Whereas the actual reduction to practice involves the construction of the invention and the test to prove that it works for the intended purpose. See Mueller (n 234) 102–103 and Halpern (n 234) 171–172.

[384] *Rosen v. NASA* 152 USPQ 757, 768 (1966). For more on the extra-territorial reach of the US patent law, see Daniel P. Homiller, 'From Deepsouth to the Great White North: The Extraterritorial Reach of United States Patent Law after Research in Motion' (2005) 17 *Duke Law and Technology Review* 1, 5–6, <http://scholarship.law.duke.edu/cgi/viewcontent.cgi?article=1137&context=dltr> (accessed 31 January 2016).

[385] Proposal for a Council Regulation on the Community Patents (2000/C 337 E/43) <http://eur-lex.europa.eu/legal-content/EN/TXT/PDF/?uri=CELEX: 52000PC0412&from=EN> (accessed 5 January 2016).

[386] A.M. Balsano, et al., 'The IGA and ESA: Protecting Intellectual Property Rights in the Context of ISS Activities' in F.G. von der Dunk et al. (eds), *The International Space Station* (Martinus Nijhoff Publishers 2006), 71.

an alleged infringement is committed on board the ISS, the state of registry of the module where such infringement occurs would appear to have jurisdiction over the case and be able to apply its own national patent law.

Nonetheless, the 'flag-state' does not seem to solve issues arising from the territorial limitation of patents entirely. If infringement of a German patent occurs within the US-registered module, does such conduct actually constitute an infringement since it might be expected that the German patent protection could extraterritorially extend only to activity within the German (ESA) module, and not in the US module? In other words, the extension of the flag-state principle is not applicable to a foreign-registry, its applicability is still limited to the territory of the granting state and only in the area deemed to be within its territory.[387] It is noted that the infringement of any European Partner states of the ESA which takes place in an ESA-registered module will be enforceable under the national law of each concerned party by virtue of Article 21 of the IGA. Issues related to the ISS will be discussed in Section 6 in this chapter.[388]

Similar questions also arise in case of infringement in the area outside the ISS, such as on the surface of the Moon. Thus, if a US patent is infringed on the Moon (or other celestial bodies), rather than inside the station, would such conduct still be considered an infringement? This scenario deals not only with the territoriality principle of patents, but also the unavailability of any applicable national patent law, since there is no national law in force in outer space. These questions will be reviewed later in Chapter 5, since it is an issue of private international law.[389]

---

[387]   It is arguable that the US courts may establish its jurisdiction over patent infringement cases which occur in a foreign-registry spacecraft in certain situations where the act of offer to sell and importation is committed on board the foreign-registry spacecraft. This is because Section 105 only applies to 'any invention made, used, or sold in outer space' but not to the acts of 'offering to sell' or 'importing'. Compare this to the provision of 35 U.S.C. 271 (a) which states that the unauthorized making, using, offering to sell, or selling any patented invention within the US and importing any patented invention into the US is considered to be infringement. Thus, the offer to sell and import patented inventions in a foreign-registry spacecraft does not fall under the exception as stated in Section 105; therefore the US courts may establish their jurisdiction over those cases accordingly. See Ro (n 357) 27.

[388]   See Section 6 below.

[389]   See hypothetical cases no. 2 and 3 in the choice of law section in Chapter 5.

5. EXCEPTIONS TO INFRINGEMENT

Patent law includes a number of specific exceptions which provide a defense to allegations of patent infringement in the case of certain unauthorized acts. Most jurisdictions share a similar set of defenses. These include exceptions for a temporary presence within the jurisdiction, private and non-commercial uses, experimental uses, private prior use and repair. The temporary presence exception has the most relevance to outer space activities. When examining these exceptions below, attention will be paid primarily to the temporary presence defense; others will be only briefly addressed.

Any defense to patent infringement will only be taken into account once the alleged act is actually deemed to constitute patent infringement. In certain situations, it remains arguable whether patent infringement is possible in outer space if national patent laws do not apply there.[390]

5.1 Temporary Presence

'Temporary Presence' within a territory is, in certain circumstances, a defense to patent infringement. This principle features in the Paris Convention. Article 5ter of the Paris Convention provides:

> In any country of the Union the following shall not be considered as infringements of the rights of a patentee:
>
> 1. the use on board vessels of other countries of the Union of devices forming the subject of his patent in the body of the vessel, in the machinery, tackle, gear and other accessories, when such vessels temporarily or accidentally enter the water of the said country, provided that such devices are used there exclusively for the needs of the vessel;
> 2. the use of devices forming the subject of the patent in the construction or operation of aircraft or land vehicles of other countries of the Union, or of accessories of such aircraft or land vehicles, when those aircraft or land vehicles temporarily or accidentally enter the said country.

After the adoption of the temporary presence in Article 5ter of the Paris Convention, this defense has been statutorily established in many countries, including the United States[391] and the United Kingdom.[392]

---

[390] Ibid.

[391] Section 272 of the US Patent Act provides, 'The use of any invention in any vessel, aircraft or vehicle of any country which affords similar privileges to vessels, aircraft, or vehicles of the United States, entering the United States temporarily or accidentally, shall not constitute infringement of any patent, if the

It appears that the temporary presence principle does not apply to use of patented inventions in spacecraft. This is because the first paragraph of Article 5ter specifically refers to the use of patented inventions on ships, whereas the second paragraph applies to use on aircraft and land vehicles, respectively. However, US patent law has adopted a broader definition. Section 272 of the US Patent Act applies the principle of temporary presence to spacecraft, since it makes reference to the temporary presence of a 'vehicle', terminology which is broad enough to include spacecraft.[393] This interpretation has been confirmed by the court in the case of *Hughes Aircraft Co. v. United States.* In that case, the Court held that launch of a spacecraft which incorporated US patented technology fell within the temporary presence defense of Section 272, and as such was excluded from patent infringement.[394]

The UK Patent Act, does not make explicitly reference to 'spacecraft' in the provisions relating to the temporary presence. Nonetheless, in the UK, the temporary presence defense might also apply to spacecraft, since (like the US patent statute) the UK Patent Act does not explicitly exclude spacecraft from this defense, and it also uses the term 'vehicle' in its provision. This term could be interpreted broadly to include any kind of registered vehicle,[395] and thus a registered spacecraft could fail within its

---

invention is used exclusively for the needs of the vessel, aircraft, or vehicle and is not offered for sale or sold in or used for the manufacture of anything to be sold in or exported from the United States'.

[392]   Section 60(5) of the UK Patent Act reads 'An act which apart from this subsection, would constitute an infringement of a patent for an invention shall not do so if –

(a) it consists of the use of a product or process in the body or operation of a relevant aircraft, hovercraft or vehicle which has temporarily or accidentally entered or is crossing the United Kingdom (including the air space above it and its territorial waters) or the use of accessories for such a relevant aircraft, hovercraft or vehicle;'

[393]   42 U.S.C. 2457(k) reads 'Any object intended for launch, launched, or assembled in outer space shall be considered a vehicle for the purpose of section 272 of Title 35'.

[394]   *Hughes Aircraft Co.* (n 176) 231–233, 240–241; Ted L. Field, 'The Planes, Trains, and Automobiles Defense to Patent Infringement for Today's Global Economy: Section 272 of the Patent Act' (2006) 12 *Boston University Journal of Science & Technology Law* 26, 50.

[395]   Section 60(7) of the UK Patent Act states: '"relevant ship" and "relevant aircraft", hovercraft or vehicle mean respectively a ship and an aircraft, hovercraft or vehicle registered in, or belonging to, any country, other than the United Kingdom, which is a party to the Convention for the Protection of Industrial

remit.[396] However, if a narrow interpretation of the word 'vehicle' is adopted, a foreign-registered spacecraft accidentally entering the territory of UK would not be able to avoid infringement by relying on this defense.

The exclusion of spacecraft in the temporary presence defense in some countries, but not others, leads to problems when considering the application of patent laws to space activities. For example, the use of a US-patented device in the French spacecraft which is launched or landed in the United States will not infringe US patent by virtue of Section 272 of the US Patent Code, whereas the same use of such device, if also patented in the UK, if the same spacecraft were to take off or land in the UK might constitute an infringement, since this jurisdiction could rule that use in a spacecraft is not included in their temporary presence defense. However, the position regarding use of any patented technology on the ISS is clear, since Article 21.6 of the IGA sets out a temporary presence defense when transporting any patented technology between any place on earth and any flight element of the Space Station.[397]

Therefore, an amendment to explicitly include spacecraft in this exception, as in US law, is suggested. However, use of the 'spacecraft' might lead to debate as to whether or not this term should be interpreted to include satellites. In my view, the temporary presence defense should also apply to satellites and cover a situation where a foreign satellite is brought into a particular territory for launch. Therefore, in order to avoid misinterpretation, it is suggested that the term 'space object', which appears in the 1975 Registration Convention is used instead of the term 'spacecraft'.[398] Alternatively, states might consider defining the term 'vehicle' in the same way as that in the US legislation.[399]

Property signed at Paris on 20th March 1883 or which is a member of the World Trade Organization.'

[396] The *Manual of Patent Practice* (UK Intellectual Property Office, October 2013) provides no guidance on how this exception be interpreted <http://www.ipo.gov.uk/practice-sec-060.pdf> (accessed 31 January 2016).

[397] See more in Section 6 of this chapter.

[398] Article I (b) of the Registration Convention defines the term 'space object' to include 'component parts of a space object as well as its launch vehicle and parts thereof;'.

[399] 42 U.S.C. 2457(k).

5.2 Repair

Repair is a further defense which avoids infringement liability. This defense is considered as an implied license, such that an authorized purchaser of any patented product is permitted to repair or replace worn or damaged parts of the product as necessary for continued use.[400] However, the concept of a 'repair' does not extend to what would be considered as a re-making or reconstruction of the product, and such would give rise to patent infringement.[401] Thus, an astronaut on the ISS is free to repair any patented product without liability for infringement, provided such a repair is not so extensive to amount to making a new product, and provided that the repair defense is operative in the national patent law of that particular module of the ISS.[402] In other words, an alleged infringement is conducted within the territory of the protecting state (the state whose patent was granted).[403]

5.3 Other Exceptions

There are a number of unauthorized acts which are not considered to constitute patent infringement. These are experimental uses,[404] private

---

[400]   *Wilson v. Simpson*, 50 U.S. 109 (1850); *Aro Mfg Co. v. Convertible Top Replacement Co.*, 365 U.S. 338, 342–346 (1961); *Wilbur-Ellis Co. v. Kuther* 377 U.S. 422, 424–425 (1964) cited in Mineko Mohri, 'Repair and Recycle as Direct Patent Infringement?' in Christopher Heath et al. (eds), *Spares, Repairs and Intellectual Property Rights* (Wolters Kluwer 2009) 62; Halpern et al. (n 234) 228.

[401]   *United Wire Limited v. Screen Repair Service Ltd* [2001] RPC 439, [2001] FSR 24 cited in Mohri (n 400) 62; *American Cotton-Tie Co. v. Simmons* 106 U.S. (16 Otto.) 89 (1882) cited in Halpern et al. (n 234) 228.

[402]   See Article 21(2) of the IGA.

[403]   Section 60(5)(D) of the UK Patent Act. There is no explicit provision on the repair defense neither in the US Patent Code nor the Thai Patent Act. But such defense was first explained by the US Supreme Court in 1850 in Wilson case (n 400). See also Mueller (n 234) 407.

[404]   For example, Section 60(5)(b) of the UK Patent Act. This exception does not exist in the US statute; however, the US courts have recognized experimental use as an exception to infringement. See *Sawin v. Guild*, 21 F Cas 554, 555 (C.C.D. Mass 1813) (No. 12,391) reported in S.T. Michel, 'The Experimental Use Exception to Infringement Applied to Federal Funded Inventions' <file:///F:/juf/doc%20for%20thesis/articles/Patent%20exception%20in%20US%20law.pdf> (accessed 31 January 2016).

non-commercial uses[405] and prior use.[406] These exceptions may be applicable once an alleged infringing act is committed, irrespective of the location where such infringement takes place. However, it is arguable whether an unauthorized act committed in outer space constitutes infringement. Since outer space is claimed to be a land of no law, any unauthorized use of a patented product or process arguably falls outside the scope of any granted patent protection.[407]

What is termed the 'prior use defense' may be relevant to activities in outer space. Under this defense, a person has rights to continue any act which he did, or prepared to do, before the priority date of a patent, which would otherwise be an infringement of a patent for the invention. While any public prior use by a third party would invalidate any later filed patent application, this is not the case where any prior use has taken place in private. The prior use defense therefore covers any such 'secret' prior use.

The prior use exception is applicable only to any previous act which has taken place within the country where the patent is granted. This raises the question of whether this defense is available where the prior use occurred within the ISS. For example, Scientist A, a member of the US research team, develops a device in the US module of the International Space Station. The same device is later developed independently and patented by another person in the United States. Can A continue to use his device in the US, relying upon his prior use in the ISS as a defense to patent infringement? Taking into account that the US module is deemed to be the United States territory by virtue of Article 21(2) of the IGA, in my view such a defense should be applicable to this case.

6.   INTERNATIONAL SPACE STATION

It is vital to specifically consider operation of the ISS in this chapter, since of all intellectual works created in this permanently manned space station, the major focus of attention is undoubtedly on inventions and

---

[405]   For example, Section 60(5)(a) of the UK Patent Act. This exception does not exist in US law.

[406]   For example, Section 64(1) of the UK Patent Act and 35 U.S.C. 273. See also Article 4(B) of the Paris Convention, which leaves the issue of implementation to the discretion of member states.

[407]   See Chapter 5 regarding applying the *lex loci protectionis* rule in outer space section.

patent protection,[408] taking into consideration a large number of patents granted for inventions devised in the ISS, it appears to warrant special attention.[409] However, the discussion under this section will be limited to those particular issues which are specifically distinguished from the normal patent rules owing to its contractual characteristics. These are choice of law and jurisdiction.

The International Space Station (ISS) operates through cooperation among five partners: Canada, the European Space Agency (ESA), Japan, the Russian Federation and the United States.[410] ESA, which is an intergovernmental organization comprised of 20 European member States, acts as one partner to the ISS.[411] The legal basis of the ISS is the Intergovernmental Agreement (IGA) and four related Memoranda of Understanding among Partners for regulating operation and utilization of the ISS.[412] Each Partner shall register the flight elements which it provides as space objects[413] and own the elements it provides.[414]

As previously identified, questions arise when infringement occurs in outer space since national patent legislation is not generally applicable. Nevertheless, it is widely accepted that in respect of objects, including spacecraft and satellites launched into space the patent law of that state which retains jurisdiction and control of that object while in outer space will be applicable.[415] The International Space Station is potentially more complicated, since legislation of several nationals is in theory enforceable. However, recognizing this issue, the IGA contains provisions which specifically relate to intellectual property, which will now be reviewed.

While the principles agreed under the IGA are applicable only to agreed parties, and third-party states are not bound by the scope of this agreement, it is still worth studying since it exemplifies how many of the

---

[408]   Rene Oosterlinck, 'The Intergovernmental Space Station Agreement and Intellectual Property Rights' (1989) 17 *Journal of Space Law* 23, 26.

[409]   <http://www.nasa.gov/mission_pages/station/research/news/microgravity_research.html> and <http://www.iss-casis.org/portals/0/docs/2012%20patent%20history.pdf> (accessed 31 January 2016).

[410]   <http://www.esa.int/Our_Activities/Human_Spaceflight/International_Space_Station/About_the_International_Space_Station> and <http://www.esa.int/Our_Activities/Human_Spaceflight/International_Space_Station/International_Space_Station_legal_framework> (accessed 31 January 2016).

[411]   <http://www.esa.int/About_Us/Welcome_to_ESA/What_is_ESA> (accessed 31 January 2016).

[412]   Balsano et al. (n 386) 63–64.

[413]   Article 5(1) of the IGA.

[414]   Article 6(1) of the IGA.

[415]   Balsano et al. (n 386) 66.

major space-faring states believe issues of intellectual property rights in outer space should be addressed.

Article 5 of the IGA recognizes the jurisdiction and control of the state of registry and confirms that the national law of the flag state will be applicable. Thus, in cases of intellectual property matters arising in the ISS, the applicable law would be the law of the state of registration of the relevant element.[416] For example, if an alleged infringement takes place within the US element, then US law will be applicable. In the case of the ESA, questions arise in respect to exercise of jurisdiction and control over its module in the ISS, since ESA is an international organization not a state.[417] This matter will be addressed in Chapter 5, when jurisdiction is specifically reviewed.[418]

Article 21 of the IGA is devoted entirely to intellectual property. Article 21.1 defines the term 'intellectual property' within this Agreement as being the same as stated in Article 2 of the Convention Establishing the World Intellectual Property Organization done at Stockholm on 14 July 1967. While Article 21 governs all kinds of intellectual property rights, only patent matters will be addressed here.

Article 21.2 establishes the principle of quasi-territoriality to the ISS by stating that 'an activity occurring in or on a Space Station flight element shall be deemed to have occurred in the territory of the Partner State of that element's registry, except that for ESA-registered elements any European Partner State may deem the activity to have occurred within its territory'.[419] Hence, any patent infringement occurring in the Japanese element is deemed to occur in Japan. However, in light of the territorial scope of a patent, patent infringement can only take place in the protecting state. Thus, a Japanese patent is infringed only if used

---

[416]   Article 5(1) states, 'In accordance with Article II of the Registration Convention, each Partner shall register as space objects the flight elements listed in the Annex which it provides, the European Partner having delegated responsibility to ESA, acting in its name and on its behalf'. Article 5(2) provides that 'Pursuant to Article VIII of the Outer Space Treaty and Article II of the Registration Convention, each Partner shall retain jurisdiction and control over the elements it registers in accordance with paragraph 1 above and over personnel in or on the Space Station who are its nationals. The exercise of such jurisdiction and control shall be subject to any relevant provisions of this Agreement, the MOUs, and implementing arrangements, including relevant procedural mechanisms established therein'.

[417]   Vahrenwald (n 368) 320.

[418]   See jurisdiction in outer space (quasi-territorial jurisdiction) section in Chapter 5.

[419]   Ibid.

without authorization within the Japanese module, but not in the US module. Only if an equivalent US patent has been obtained will unauthorized use of the same technology within the US module amount to patent infringement.

The position is unclear regarding use of patented technology within the ESA element, since Article 21.2 provides that any activity occurring within this element is deemed to have occurred in the territory of each European partner. In other words, use within the ESA element is deemed to be use simultaneously in all 20 European countries. It has been proposed that the ESA element in the ISS should be considered instead as a single territory.[420] Would this mean that if a French patent is infringed in the ESA element, infringement is deemed to occur not only in France, but in the other European partner territories too, even if the same patent is not registered in other European partners? In other words, would securing patent protection in France effectively give automatic patent protection in other European Partner States of ESA without registration, at least where activity within the ISS is concerned?

Owing to the territorial scope of patent, this outcome seems unlikely since a patent cannot be infringed anywhere beyond the territory of the granting state, but this question will be examined in Chapter 5.[421]

By establishing the quasi-territoriality principle, some states have enacted patent law which gives extraterritorial effect in their registered space objects.[422] Only two of the 20 European Partners of ESA, namely Germany and Italy, have implemented the provisions of the IGA into their national legislations and so ensure that their national intellectual property laws would apply to inventions created on ESA-registered elements.[423] Problems may therefore arise in case of the remaining European Partners, where domestic patent law is not specifically applicable to use of patented inventions on board their registered spacecraft. For instance, an unauthorized use of subject matter covered by a French patent in the ESA module may not be an infringement, since French patent law may be held inapplicable, since the territorial reach of French patent law has not been specifically extended to French-registered spacecraft or the ESA element of the ISS.[424]

---

[420]   Vahrenwald (n 368) 322.
[421]   See Chapter 5, hypothetical case no. 1 in choice of law section.
[422]   35 U.S.C. 105.
[423]   Balsano et al. (n 367) 67.
[424]   This is based on the fact that such invention is registered for protection only in France.

As the result of states' concern about national security, and in particular about sensitive information which might be disclosed before or during the patent application procedure, many countries require that the first patent application for any invention must be filed in the country in which the invention was made or in the country where the inventor resides.[425] Filing foreign patent applications before this security screening has taken place in the 'home' territory is generally forbidden. Article 21.3 of the IGA further provides that

> in respect of an invention made in or on any Space Station flight element by a person who is not its national or resident, a Partner State shall not apply its laws concerning secrecy of inventions so as to prevent the filing of a patent application in any of her Partner State that provides for the protection of the secrecy of a patent applications contacting information which is classified or protected for national security purposes.[426]

In essence, this provision ensures that national laws concerning secrecy of inventions are not applicable in the case of an invention created in the ISS.[427] Thus, an inventor on the ISS is free to select where to file a patent application first[428] and is only then subjected to the national laws concerning secrecy of the state of first filing.[429] In fact, it has been claimed that this provision was intended to avoid the sanctions of the U.S. Inventions Secrecy Act.[430]

Article 21.4 avoids liability for multiple damages accruing from any single act of infringement, where patent protection is in place in more than one European Partner State of the space station. This provision states that an owner of the patented invention cannot recover from his patent infringement in more than one European Partner State. However, since the ESA module in the space station considered to be a single jurisdiction, the patent holder is free to elect the forum for his infringement claim.[431] This might lead to problems with forum shopping, since

---

[425] Vahrenwald (n 368) 322.
[426] Zhao (n 348) 170.
[427] Vahrenwald (n 368) 322.
[428] Ibid.
[429] Ibid.
[430] 35 U.S.C. 181–188. See J.B. Gantt, 'Space Station Intellectual Property Rights and U.S. Patent Law' (Proceedings of an International Colloquium on the Manned Space Stations – Legal Issues, Paris, November 1989) 109.
[431] Article 21.4 states, 'Where a person or entity owns intellectual property which is protected in more than one European Partner State, that person or entity may not recover in more than one such State for the same act of infringement of

any rights holder normally would elect to bring his suit to the court with the highest potential compensation. This might create legal uncertainty and unfairness among concerned parties.[432]

In addition, multiple infringement actions could arise for the same act of infringement, because the patent rights may be owned by different entities in different ESA jurisdictions. In recognition of this, Article 21.4 provides that once infringement proceedings have been instigated in any one ESA state, any court in a later-filed case may grant a temporary stay pending the outcome of the first-filed case.[433] Again, this provision was drafted to protect defendants for being subjected to multiple actions based upon same allegedly infringing act.

Article 21.5 deals with the licensing of intellectual property rights, and states that receive a license to use any intellectual property right granted in any European Partner State will extend to any use of in the ESA element of a space station. For example, by virtue of the provision, a license to use technology protected by a French patent and used in the ESA element will not only be considered as authorized use under the French patent but also authorized use under any patents registered in any other European Partner State.[434] In other words, the grant of a license in one of the European Partner states is equivalent to an implied license in the remaining European Partner States of ESA, when exploiting the license in the ESA element space station.

Article 21.6 established the principle of temporary presence[435] to exclude from infringement any articles in transit through any Partner

---

the same rights in such intellectual property which occurs in or on an ESA-registered element'.

[432]   Balsano et al. (n 367) 68.

[433]   Article 21.4 states. 'Where the same act of infringement in or on an ESA-registered element gives rise to actions by different intellectual property owners by virtue of more than one European Partner State's deeming the activity to have occurred in its territory, a court may grant a temporary stay of proceeding in a later-filed action pending the outcome of an earlier-filed action'.

[434]   Article 21.5 states, 'With respect to an activity occurring in or on an ESA registered-element, no European Partner State shall refuse to recognize a license for the exercise of any intellectual property rights if that license is enforceable under the laws of any European Partner State, and compliance with the provisions of such license shall also bar recovery for infringement in any European Partner State'.

[435]   Article 21.6 states, 'The temporary presence in the territory of a Partner State of any articles, including the components of a flight element, in transit between any place on earth and any flight element of the Space Station

State. In other words, transport of patented articles between any of the partner states on earth and any element of the ISS registered by another partner will not infringe any patent rights registered in the latter state. This provision mirrors the provisions of Section 272 of the US Patent Act and Article 5ter of the Paris Convention.

Article 16 of the IGA is also potentially relevant to the intellectual property rights in the ISS. This provision allows each Partner State to agree to a cross-waiver of liability in which each Partner State waives all claims against any of the entities or person on damages arising from space operation. However, a cross-wavier liability will not be applicable to IP claims.[436]

Although the IGA seems to resolve certain problems regarding patent rights and creation or exploitation of technology in the ISS, its provisions are only applicable to Parties of the IGA, and are not binding on third parties. Thus, issues still remain unresolved regarding inventions in outer space involving entities from multiple states, especially when non-participating partners of the IGA are involved. Whether non-IGA States will adopt the same rules as the IGA partners is still a problem awaiting a solution.

7. CONCLUSION

There are still areas of uncertainty surrounding patent protection to outer space inventions. The fact that an invention has been made in outer space does not change the basic requirements for patentability: novelty, inventive step and industrial application.[437] However, due to the special nature of space invention, in particular the test of its novelty, it is questionable whether the patentability requirements should be determined under the same standards as applied to inventions made on earth. Does any use of a space invention in the International Space Station before a patent application has been filed on earth destroy its novelty? It would appear that current confidentiality rules are sufficient to cope with this problem. Is a zero-gravity environment alone a sufficient difference from equivalent 'earthly' prior art to render a space invention non-obvious? This remains an issue which would need to be resolved on a case-by-case basis. Does an invention which can only be worked in outer space meet

registered by another Partner State or ESA shall not in itself form the basis for any proceedings in the first Partner State for patent infringement'.

[436] Article 16 (3)(d)(4) of the IGA.
[437] Balsano et al. (n 367) 7.

the requirement of industrial application? It would seem that since it is possible to re-create zero-gravity conditions in a closed laboratory on earth, this should be sufficient to satisfy this requirement, since any such invention would have the potential to be worked on earth.

While space objects can be brought within the jurisdiction of national patent laws, much activity in outer space appears to be beyond the scope of national patent laws. However, in the absence of a provision similar to Section 105 of the US Patent Act which specifically extends the scope of national patent law to any nationally registered space object, it remains to be resolved whether or not national courts would consider that national patent law applies to space objects, including activity which takes place within the International Space Station. It seems likely, but by no means certain, that 'flag-state' jurisdiction might be commonly acceptable.

Those areas of uncertainty remain open for further study and debate. In the meantime, this lack of clarity as to the extent of protection which space invention may receive put the development of these areas of technologies at risk. There is a real need to these legal problems be resolved, and owing to its complicated and special nature, a new and specific legal regime of patent in space has been proposed.[438]

---

[438]   See, for example, Oosterlinck (n 408) 36; Tramposch (n 179) 197; Ro, et al. (n 357) 33.

4. The application of copyright law to outer space activities

In Chapter 3, the discussion focused on how and to what extent patent law is applicable to outer space activities. This chapter focuses upon copyright, another form of intellectual property right which protects, *inter alia*, literary and artistic work.[439] As with other areas of intellectual property law, the scope of copyright protection is territorially limited. In light of the increasing number of activities taking place in outer space, it is legitimate to question how this territoriality impacts upon subsistence of copyright protection and infringement of any protected rights in outer space.

Copyright subsistence is dependent upon either the nationality or domicile of the author or the place of the first publication of the work.[440] Therefore, the place of creation is irrelevant. Thus, a work created in outer space is eligible for copyright protection, provided that it meets the statutory requirements for protection. The purpose of this chapter is to analyze the application of copyright law in outer space activities. The discussion in this chapter will cover the following areas: (1) subject matter; (2) originality; (3) fixation; (4) authorship of work; (5) joint authorship; (6) ownership; (7) qualifying conditions; (8) duration; (9) infringement; and (10) exceptions. In this regard, the copyright law of the two jurisdictions considered previously in respect of patent law, namely the United Kingdom and the United States, as well as the relevant international copyright conventions will be examined to determine which jurisdiction provides the best fit for space activities. The potential for problems arising from the application of copyright law to outer space activities will be explored using four hypothetical cases, which will form the basis of discussion in the infringement section of this chapter.

---

[439]   Torremans (n 119) 179.
[440]   See below, Section 6.

1. SUBJECT MATTER

For copyright to subsist in a work, the work must first fall within one of
the categories specified in the legislation. Under the Berne Convention,[441]
literary and artistic works are the subject of protection. Article 2(1) of the
Berne Convention provides an expansive definition of 'literary and
artistic works' as including 'every production in the literary, scientific
and artistic domain, whatever may be the mode or form of its expression'. With such an expansive and non-exhaustive definition, the Berne
Convention leaves room for member countries to include other works
within the scope of copyright protection, at their discretion.[442] Thus, the
subject matter of copyright varies from country to country. Some
jurisdictions have enacted legislation containing an exhaustive list of
protectable subject matter, whereas others (like the Berne Convention)
define potentially protectable works in open-ended terms.[443]

The UK's Copyright, Designs and Patents Act 1988 ('CDPA 88')
stipulates that only eight types of works qualify for copyright protection.[444] In contrast, US copyright legislation provides an open-ended type
of protectable works. Section 102 of the US Copyright Act states that
'copyright protection subsists, in accordance with this title, in original
works of authorship fixed in any tangible medium of expression; works
of authorship include the following categories ...' Here, use of the term
'include' signifies that protectable works are not limited to those specifically categorized in the legislation; rather, any original work fixed in a
tangible medium of expression is eligible for copyright protection under
US copyright law.

Thus, to learn whether copyright is pertinent to space activities, we
must first determine whether those works created in outer space are of
the type protected under copyright law or not. To do this, I will divide

---

[441]   See discussion on the Berne Convention Section 1.2.1 in Chapter 2.

[442]   Goldstein et al. (n 141) 188.

[443]   Bently et al. (n 207) 60. See also, for example, Section 6 of the Thai
Copyright Act, which identifies work which is protectable by copyright in an
open-ended way by identifying the subject matter of copyright as any 'literary,
dramatic, artistic, musical, audiovisual, cinematographic, sound recording, sound
and video broadcasting work or any other work in the literary, scientific or
artistic domain whatever may be the mode or form of its expression'.

[444]   Article 1(1) UK CDPA 88.

those works created in outer space into two general groups: space-related works and general (i.e., not specifically space-related) works.[445]

1.1   Space-related Works

There are various activities in outer space which may attract copyright. Space-related works are those which deal directly with space technology. The works which will be considered in this book arise from remote sensing satellites, the Hubble Space Telescope and satellite broadcasting. The status of data and satellite imagery as eligible subject matter will be considered in the cases of remote sensing and the Hubble Space Telescope. The works under consideration in the case of satellite broadcasting are the signals transmitted as well as the content of the programme broadcast. In each case, we shall consider whether the work would be categorized as protectable subject matter in the legislation of each of the two countries under consideration.

1.1.1   Remote sensing

Remote sensing is a tool for observing the earth. As the name suggests, remote sensing uses technology located within a satellite in orbit in outer space, and thus enabling the collection of data at a distance, and which is controlled on earth.[446] Remote sensing technology is therefore of great value to the world community in terms of acquiring information which can only be obtained at a distance, or which relates to areas on earth which are inaccessible or difficult to access. Geospatial data[447] acquired from remote sensing activities are used in many applications, such as national disaster monitoring, military exercises, weather forecasting and land-use management.[448] The UN Remote Sensing Principles defines

---

[445]   In Chapter 1, space activities are categorized into three groups: (1) space-created work, (2) space-related work and (3) non space-related work. As space-created works involve the use of outer space resources, they are most likely to fall under the umbrella of patent protection. Therefore, this section relating to copyright will focus upon two other forms of space activities. See Chapter 1, Section 5, the application of the province of all mankind and the common heritage of mankind principles to outer space activities section.

[446]   Cheng (n 26) 572.

[447]   Geospatial data are 'data files that are comprised of geographically-referenced features (i.e., land cover or soils [sic] types) that are described by geographic positions and attributes in a digital format'. See Julie D. Cromer, 'How on Earth Terrestrial Laws Can Protect Geospatial Data' (2006) 32 *Journal of Space Law* 253, 257.

[448]   Ibid.

'remote sensing' as 'the sensing of the Earth's surface from space by making use of the properties of electromagnetic waves emitted, reflected or diffracted by the sensed objects, for the purpose of improving natural resources management, land use and the protection of the environment'.[449] The data acquired from remote sensing activities are considered to be a sub-category of spatial or geographic data.[450] Sensors on board an orbiting satellite scan a target area on earth to obtain data, which is then sent directly to a monitoring station on earth.[451] The US Land Remote Sensing Policy Act of 1992 defines the term 'land remote sensing' as 'the collection of data which can be processed into imagery of surface features of the Earth'.[452,453]

According to the UN resolution, geospatial data are classified as three remote sensing products: 'primary data', 'processed data' and 'analyzed information'.[454] To determine whether copyright protects remote sensing data it is first necessary to examine whether primary data, processed data or analyzed information falls within a category of copyright protected works.

Primary data, also known as 'raw data', are defined as 'the raw data that are acquired by remote sensor borne by a space object and that are transmitted or delivered to the ground from space by telemetry in the form of electromagnetic signals, by photographic film, magnetic tape or any other mean'.[455] Raw data comprises numbers, images or characters in a digital form (or, historically, in an analogue form) that is not directly usable without further processing and analysis.[456] The US Code Federal

---

[449]   Principle 1 (a) of the UN Remote Sensing Resolution (n 112).

[450]   Lesley Jane Smith and Catherine Doldirina, 'Remote Sensing: A Case for Moving Space Data towards the Public Good' (2008) 24 *Space Policy* 22, 23 <www.sciencedirect.com> (accessed 22 February 2016).

[451]   Patrick A. Salin, 'Proprietary Aspects of Commercial Remote-Sensing Imagery' (1992) 13 *Northwestern Journal of International Law and Business* 349, 349.

[452]   15 U.S.C. 82, Sec. 5602 (5) <http://law.justia.com/codes/us/1999/title15/chap82/sec5602> (accessed 22 February 2016).

[453]   There is no specific legislation on remote sensing available in the UK law.

[454]   UN Remote Sensing Resolution (n 112).

[455]   Principle 1(b) of the UN Remote Sensing Resolution (n 112).

[456]   Smith and Doldirina (n 450) 23; also see the interview with Dr. Sompong Liangrocapart, Lecturer, Department of Physics, Mahanakorn University of Technology (Bangkok, Thailand 3 January 2012).

Regulation[457] gives a similar definition of 'unenhanced data', which was adopted pursuant to the US Land Remote Sensing Policy Act of 1992:

> Remote sensing signals or imagery products that are unprocessed or subject only to data pre-processing. Data pre-processing may include rectification of systems and sensor distortions in remote data as it is received directly from the satellite; registration of such data with respect to features of the Earth; and calibration of spectral response with respect to such data. It does not include conclusions, manipulations, or calculations derived from such data, or a combination of such data with other data. It also excludes phase history data for synthetic aperture radar systems or other space-based radar system.[458]

The Canadian Remote Sensing Space Systems Act of 2005 defines raw data as 'sensor data from a remote sensing satellite, and any auxiliary data required to produce remote sensing products from the sensor data that have not been transformed into a remote sensing product'.[459]

Raw data has also been likened, by analogy, to an undeveloped negative for a photograph.[460] Once the raw data is detected by the sensor in the remote sensing satellite, it is transmitted back to the ground station for processing. It is this processing on earth which makes the raw data usable.[461] The processing stage may involve use of a wide range of techniques, such as improving contrast ratios on the image, spatial filtering, mosaicking adjacent images and enhancing edges in the data.[462] This processing gives rise to a further data set, the 'processing data', which is analogous to a developed photograph. At this stage, human analysts select which of the processing data will undergo the further analysis and interpretation necessary to extract the required information. Following such further analysis, the selected subset of processing data becomes 'analyzed information'.[463]

---

[457]   15 C.F.R. Part 960.3 <http://www.gpo.gov/fdsys/pkg/CFR-2011-title15-vol3/pdf/CFR-2011-title15-vol3-part960.pdf> (accessed 22 February 2016).

[458]   15 U.S.C. 5602 <http://stage.tksc.jaxa.jp/spacelaw/country/america/date/c_1_rimosen_seisakuhou(eng).pdf > (accessed 22 February 2016).

[459]   Section 2 of the Canadian Remote Sensing Space Systems Act, S.C. 2005 <http://laws-lois.justice.gc.ca/PDF/R-5.4.pdf> (accessed 22 February 2016).

[460]   Interview with Dr. Sompong Liangrocapart (n 456).

[461]   Emilio Chuvieco and Alfredo Huete, *Fundamentals of Satellite Remote Sensing* (Taylor & Francis 2010) 2–3; Doldirina (n 168) 305; see also <http://www.crisp.nus.edu.sg/~research/tutorial/process.htm> and <http://research.utep.edu/Default.aspx?tabid=38185> (accessed 22 February 2016).

[462]   Ibid.

[463]   Ibid.

Considering the nature of these three types of remote sensing data, which are the result of a technological process and generated by visible light or other electromagnetic radiation, the most appropriate copyright category for remote sensing data to consider first would appear to be that of 'photograph'.

According to the UK CDPA 88, a photograph is defined as 'a recording of light or other radiation on any medium on which an image is produced or from which an image may by any means be produced, and which is not part of a film'. Thus, geospatial data are an appropriate fit with this definition, and so it would appear to be appropriate subject matter for UK copyright protection as a photograph.

However, it is possible that remote sensing data might also fall within the definition of a database under the UK copyright law. UK CDPA 88 defines a database as 'a collection of independent works, data or other materials which (a) are arranged in a systematic or methodical way, and are individually accessible by electronic or other means'. However, although remote sensing data are transmitted to the ground station as a collection of data in a digital format, the data received are not arranged in a systematic way and are not individually accessible. Therefore, the geospatial data from remote sensing cannot be properly categorized as database under the UK law.[464]

As identified previously, the United States Copyright Act does not categorize copyright subject matter exhaustively, as in the UK. Instead, the US Act lists eight exemplary categories of protectable works. Therefore, the US Copyright Act has a wider reach than the UK Act, since subject matter not specifically listed is still eligible for protection, provided that it is 'original' and is 'fixed in any tangible medium of expression'. Thus, it is not dispositive whether a remote sensing product fits within any of the specific categories listed in the Act. Nevertheless, having considered the subject matter listed, the most appropriate category for geospatial data from remote sensing is a 'pictorial work' since this is defined as including photographs (and maps).[465] Although the US statute does not include a specific definition of the term photograph, since geospatial data falls with a general understanding of the term (as well as the specific legal definitions under UK law), it seems reasonable to assume that it would also be considered a photograph under US copyright law.

---

[464] In this regard, the EU Database Directive is not relevant and is omitted for review in this chapter. See the EU Database Directive in Section 1.4.2 in Chapter 2.

[465] Section 101 of the US Copyright Act.

Notwithstanding this analysis, some scholars consider geospatial data to be better categorized as a database or as a map under US law.[466] Since the geospatial data detected by remote sensing satellite are transmitted to the ground station in a form of spatial data collection, it could be considered a database, as in the case of the UK. However, in the US, there is no special legislation on databases as in the UK. As those geospatial data are collected in a digital format, it might be a 'compilation' under the US law – i.e., a work 'formed by the collection and assembling of pre-existing materials or of data that are selected, coordinated, or arranged in such a way that the resulting work as a whole constitutes an original work of authorship.'[467] In *Feist Publications Inc. v. Rural Telephone Serv. Corp.,*[468] the US Supreme Court interpreted the contents of a telephone directory to be a work of compilation, since the information it collated about each subscriber of the telephone service was pre-existing data.

However, to me it is questionable whether remote sensing data would be a compilation work, since the definition requires 'the collection and assembling of *pre-existing* data'. Remote sensing data arguably is not 'pre-existing', since data collection is in real-time, collected at that moment when the satellite sensor captures it. So, for this reason, I consider that it is unlikely that remote sensing data are properly classified as compilation works.

Similar reasoning applies to whether remote sensing data should be classified as a 'map'. Again, there is no specific definition of map in the US copyright statute, and so it would be construed taking the general meaning of the terminology into account. A map is reasonably defined as 'the representation on a flat surface of the whole or a part of an area or a representation of the celestial sphere or a part of'.[469] Even if remote sensing data is a representation of the earth's surface, it does not provide other referencing details that are normally included on a map, such as location of places, distances between places, roads, parks, and recreational areas. Therefore, I do not believe that remote sensing data would be construed to be a map, as this term is generally understood.

Dennis Karjala considers the meaning of the term 'maps' and concludes that 'today's comprehensive geographic information systems may

---

[466] Cromer (n 447) 269.
[467] Section 101 of the US Copyright Act.
[468] 499 U.S. 340 (1991).
[469] See <http://www.merriam-webster.com/dictionary/map> (accessed 22 February 2016).

simply constitute electronically stored collection of spatial and non-spatial data, which under traditional copyright law are more naturally classified as "compilations" rather than "maps"'.[470] However, irrespective of whether spatial data resulting from remote sensing is better regarded as a 'compilation', a 'map' or a 'photograph', there seems to be agreement that it is certainly subject matter which may be categorized as either a database or an artistic work under the US law. Thus, remote sensing data is a subject matter eligible for copyright protection in the United States.

1.1.2 Hubble Space Telescope

The Hubble Space Telescope, located on a spacecraft orbiting the earth, provides another forum for activity in outer space. An automatic camera located on board the spacecraft is pre-programmed to take pictures at specified locations in outer space.[471] The operation of the Hubble Space Telescope may be explained as follows:

> Hubble's science instruments serve as astronomers' eyes on the universe. Once the telescope observes its celestial object, its onboard computers convert the data into long strings of numbers that are beamed down to earth via communications satellites. The data are then translated into information and pictures, which scientists study. Hubble is equipped with spectrographs and cameras sensitive to ultraviolet, visible, and infrared light.[472]

The product of the Hubble Space Telescope's activities, and the data derived therefrom, is comparable to that of remote sensing – comprising unenhanced data and enhanced data. Thus works created from the Hubble Space Telescope will be categorized, from a copyright perspective, in the same manner as those from remote sensing, and are categorized as satellite images.[473]

---

[470] Dennis S. Karjala, 'Copyright in Electronic Maps', (1994–1995) 35 *Jurimetrics Journal* 395, 396; also see Cromer (n 447) 271.

[471] See <http://hubblesite.org/the_telescope/hubble_essentials/ and http://teachspacescience.org/graphics/pdf/10000870.pdf> (accessed 22 February 2016). See also Elizabeth A. Kessler, *Picturing the Cosmos Hubble Telescope Images and the Astronomical Subline* (University of Minnesota Press, 2012) 69–70.

[472] See 'The Hubble Space Telescope' NASA <https://amazing-space.stsci.edu/resources/print/lithos/hst_litho.pdf> (accessed 22 February 2016). See also Kessler (n 471) 139–140.

[473] Both remote sensing data and the Hubble Space Telescope will be discussed in terms of their originality below.

1.1.3 Satellite broadcasting

Satellite broadcasts enable TV programmes to be broadcast clearly over a wide area. A broadcast station on earth converts TV content into data signals, which are transmitted to satellites in geosynchronous orbits. On receiving the signals, the satellites rebroadcast them to earth to be picked up by viewers' satellite dishes. A viewer's receiver box processes the signal from their dish, which enables the original programme content to be viewed on a TV set.[474]

There are two kinds of work that result from satellite broadcasting. These are the transmission signals and the content of the transmitted programme. Obviously, the programme content itself is merely 'conventional' copyright works and categorized as dramatic works, musical works, sound recordings, films or whatever the case may be. In case of satellite transmission, the most plausible category of work for such transmission would be a broadcast. Section 6(1) of UK CDPA 88 defines a broadcast 'as an electronic transmission of visual images, sounds, or other information which (a) is transmitted for simultaneous reception by members of the public and is capable of being lawfully received by them, or (b) is transmitted at a time determined solely by the person making the transmission for presentation to members of the public.' Thus, this part of the Act protects the transmission or signals, not the content or the work that is carried by it.[475,476] Considering this definition, satellite transmission falls within the broadcast category of work under UK law.

Since the US Copyright Act provides a non-exhaustive list of copyright subject matter, it does not matter that satellite broadcast does not obviously fit in any of the example works listed in Section 102. Satellite broadcasts still merit copyright protection (provided they are original) because they are arguably fixed in a tangible medium of expression.[477]

In term of international instruments related to broadcasts, the scope of the term 'broadcast' is still not clear. Article 3(f) of the Rome Convention defines 'broadcasting' as 'the transmission by wireless means for public reception of sounds or of images and sounds' whereas in Article 2(f) of the WIPO Performances and Phonograms Treaty (WPPT) the term

---

[474]   Jorge Matos Gomez, *Satellite Broadcasting Systems Engineering* (Artech House 2002) 2–3; Levente Tatley, *Intellectual Property Law in Hungary* (Kluwer Law International 2010) 93.

[475]   Kevin Garnett et al., *Copinger and Skone James on Copyright*, vol. 1 (16th edn, Thomson Reuters Limited, 2011) 126.

[476]   Laddie Prescott and Mary Vitoria, *The Modern Law of Copyright and Designs*, vol. 1 (4th ed., LexisNexis, 2011) 460.

[477]   Section 102 of the US Copyright Act.

'broadcasting' means 'the transmission by wireless means for public reception of sounds or of images and sounds or the representations thereof; such transmission by satellite is also "broadcasting"; transmission of encrypted signals is "broadcasting" where the means for decrypting are provided to the public by the broadcasting organization or with its consent.'

It is arguable whether a satellite signal is protected under the Rome Convention, whereas the WPPT makes explicit that satellite signals are included. The 'transmission by wireless means for public reception of sounds or of images and sounds' relate to the signal itself, and it can only be interpreted to be the format, or the means of delivery, of those programs embodied in the broadcast. But some scholars believe that the Rome Convention does grant protection to the signals, since the Convention's definition implicitly protects the broadcaster's technical contributions in term of assembly, production and transmission of contents embodied in the broadcast.[478] In fact, the Rome Convention grants specific rights to broadcasting organizations in terms of controlling signal distribution during the time of the signal's transmission. These are the rights to authorize or prohibit rebroadcasting, fixation and reproduction as stated in Article 13 of the Convention.[479] This lack of clarity has, in any event, been resolved by the Brussels Satellite Convention,[480] which explicitly applies to satellite signals and not the content carried by such signals.[481]

The Berne Convention only relates to copyright, and not to 'neighboring' rights, such as broadcasts. However, this Convention does grant exclusive rights to authors of literary and artistic works to authorize the broadcasting or any other communication of their work to the public.[482]

---

[478]   Goldstein (n 141) 237.

[479]   Matthew D. Asbell, 'Progress on the WIPO Broadcasting and Webcasting Treaty' (2006) 24 *Cardozo Arts & Entertainment* 349, 356.

[480]   Article 2(1) of the Brussels Satellite Convention 1974 states, 'Each Contracting State undertakes to take adequate measures to prevent the distribution on or from its territory of any programme-carrying signal by any distribution for whom the signal emitted to or passing through the satellite is not intended. This obligation shall apply where the originating organization is a national of another Contracting State and where the signal distributed is a derived signal'.

[481]   Nancy Lowe Henry, 'The Convention Relating to the Distribution of Programme-Carrying Signals Transmitted by Satellite: A Potshot at Poaching' (1974) 7 *NYU Journal of International Law and Politics* 575, 584.

[482]   Article 11bis of the Berne Convention. A new treaty protecting broadcasting organizations is currently being negotiated. See <http://www.wipo.int/pressroom/en/briefs/broadcasting.html and http://www.ip-watch.org/2013/

1.2   General (not space-related) Works

It is possible that an astronaut in outer space might create a new work which is eligible for copyright protection, provided it falls within one of the subject matter categories, as provided by law. An astronaut may create a literary work, such as a novel, poem or song lyrics, or perhaps an artistic work, music, film or sound recording, while in outer space. Such work would qualify for copyright protection provided it meets all other requirements, and the work 'qualifies' for copyright protection according to the astronaut's nationality or place of first publication of the work. Thus, it is simply a factual matter of whether 'general works' created in outer space are eligible for copyright protection under the relevant national legislation.

1.3   Excluded Work

Each national copyright law excludes certain works, which otherwise satisfy the protection requirements. Issues may arise in cases where a work is excluded from copyright protection in one country and yet merits copyright in another country.[483] For example, works produced by a government employee are excluded from copyright protection in the United States,[484] whereas such works are eligible for copyright protection in the UK.[485]

2.   REQUIREMENTS

Once any intellectual creation is found to fall within a recognized category of protectable 'work', and so be suitable subject matter for copyright protection, it is then necessary to demonstrate that the work satisfies the remaining requirements before it benefits from copyright protection. The exact requirements depend upon the particular type of work. Thus, we have to consider those works created in outer space by their types of work. In this section, three space-related works (remote

---

12/22/broadcasting-treaty-moving-at-wipo-library-copyright-exceptions-slower/> (accessed 22 February 2016).

[483]   J.A.L. Sterling, 'Space Copyright Law: The New Dimension: A Preliminary Survey and Proposals', <http://www.law.qmul.ac.uk/docs/staff/ccls/sterling/121968.pdf> (accessed 22 February 2016) 12.

[484]   Section 105 of the US Copyright Act.

[485]   See more discussion on this matter below in Section 4.

sensing, Hubble Space Telescope images and satellite telecommunications) will be examined. Any general works created in outer space undergo the same assessment as equivalent works created on earth, and so do not raise any issues relevant to the particular enquiry of this book. Remote sensing data and Hubble telescope image data will be examined together, since we have determined that these works share similar characteristics.

2.1 Originality

Neither the Berne Convention nor the TRIPs Agreement specifies 'originality' as a condition for copyright protection. However, since the purpose of the Berne Convention is to protect the human intellectual *creation*, anything 'created' must result from an individual's own effort. Thus, it is generally accepted that the requirement of originality is implicitly mandated by Berne.[486]

The originality requirement is, in any event, generally accepted as a key condition which must be fulfilled in order to obtain copyright protection.[487] Originality of a work is normally a prerequisite for copyright protection under national laws. Pursuant to Section 1(1) (a) of the UK CDPA 88, copyright only subsists in *original* literary, dramatic, musical and artistic works. In contrast, originality is not required for so-called 'entrepreneurial' works (i.e., sound recordings, films, broadcasts and typographical arrangements), where copyright subsists to the extent that such works are not copied from previous works of the same sort. US copyright law also requires works of authorship to be original to attract copyright protection. Section 102 of the US Copyright Act states that 'Copyright protection subsists … in original works of authorship fixed in any tangible medium of expression'. Unlike in the UK, the US originality requirement extends to all types of work, including sound recordings, motion pictures and other audio-visual works.[488]

Thus, a work is required to be original to warrant copyright protection in the UK and US. However, while originality is required in all types of work under the US law, in the UK this requirement only applies to literary, dramatic, musical or artistic works.

While the test of originality varies from country to country, originality generally requires that a work is one which originates from the author in

---

[486] Garnett et al. (n 475) 138.
[487] J.A.L. Sterling, *World Copyright Law*, vol. 1 (3rd ed., Sweet & Maxwell 2008) 337.
[488] Ibid.

the sense that it is the result of the author's own intellectual effort and is not slavishly copied from others' work.[489] Therefore, in theory, one author's work may be identical to another's and both works may still be considered original as long as the works have been created independently of each other, such that the similarity does not result from one author having copied from the other.[490] So, the originality requirement is different from that of novelty discussed in respect of patent protection previously. Multiple parties may create similar works independently, and each secures separate copyright protection. In this way, originality is not an assessment of the quality or aesthetics of a work. While the level of intellectual input that an author must invest in the creation of the work must be more than trivial,[491] there is no international consensus as to the amount or quality of the input which yields an original work. This, in fact, depends upon the facts of particular cases.[492]

In the UK, the House of Lords ruled in *University of London Press, Limited v. University Tutorial Press, Limited*[493] that a set of exam papers were original, since its questions originated from the examiner, even though they were produced quickly and were similar to the questions asked previously by other examiners. This sets the traditional threshold for originality at a low level in the UK and equates to 'not copied' from others.[494] Hence, a photograph depicting an existing object is likely to qualify as an original copyright work, provided its production involves a level of skill and effort by its photographer in selecting an appropriate composition, since the result represents the photographer's own intellectual creation.[495] The CJEU's ruling in *Infopaq International A/S v. Danske Dagblades Forening* is one which national courts within the European Union must take into consideration when examining the originality threshold. In that case, it was held that extracting text of no more than 11 words from various newspaper articles might constitute

---

[489] Garnett et al. (n 475) 141.
[490] Ibid 143–144.
[491] Ibid 141.
[492] Ibid.
[493] [1916] 2 Ch. 601, 608–609. See also *Walter v. Lane* [1900] AC 539. In this case, copyright protection was conferred to a newspaper report which the reporter took down the oral speech in his own notes. It was ruled that the reporter did take considerable skill and labors in producing a transcript of the speech.
[494] *University of London Press* (n 493) 608.
[495] *Temple Island Collections Limited v. New English Teas Limited* [2012] EWPCC 1 and Case C–145/10 *Eva-Maria Painer v. Standard VerlagsGmbH and Others* (CJEU, 7 March 2013). These two cases will be discussed below in Section 2.1.1.

copyright infringement if done without the author's consent, since it was possible that an extract of this length was original, since it could be the result of the author's own intellectual creation.[496] It was not for the CJEU to decide whether any particular short extract of text was in fact original, and therefore eligible for copyright, since this was a question of fact for the national court to determine.[497]

Prior to *Infopaq*, the traditional test of originality for a work was based upon *University Press* principles, as described above,[498] and required input of a sufficient amount of skill, labor or effort[499] and assumed that the work was not copied. Thus, the *Infopaq* decision which explicitly links 'originality' to 'creativity' seems to affect the scope of the UK copyright protection in some aspects.[500] Firstly, it seems to raise the threshold for originality, since a work that results from an input of skill and labor which might have been sufficient to meet the requirements of the UK traditional test might now fail to be original, if the author's intellectual input is not also deemed 'creative'. Thus, authors of sub-creative literary works, previously protected by copyright in the UK, might now find that their work is considered to be unoriginal and therefore unprotected by copyright. This will leave their efforts unprotected, since the UK does not have an unfair competition law as some other countries.[501]

---

[496] Case C–5/08 *Infopaq International A/S v. Danske Dagblades Forening* [2012] Bus. L.R. 102; [2009] E.C.R. I–6569; [2009] E.C.D.R. 16; [2010] F.S.R. 20.

[497] *Infopaq* (n 496) para 51.

[498] *University of London Press, Limited* (n 493) 608.

[499] Lord Reid in *Ladbroke v. William Hill* [1964] 1 W.L.R. 273, 278, [1964] 1All ER 465, 469.

[500] The discussion of the impact of the *Infopaq* holding on UK copyright law can be found, for example, at Eleonora Rosati, *Originality in EU Copyright Full Harmonization through Case Law* (Edward Elgar 2013); Estelle Derclaye, 'Infopaq International A/S Danske Dagblades Forening (C–5/08): Wonderful or Worrisome? The Impact of the ECJ Ruling in Infopaq on UK Copyright Law' (2010) *European Intellectual Property Review* 247; Andreas Rahmatian, 'Originality in UK Copyright Law: The Old "Skill and Labour" Doctrine under Pressure' (2013) *International Review of Intellectual Property and Competition Law* 4; Thomas Hopper, 'Reproduction in Part of Online Articles in the Aftermath of Infopaq (C–5/08): Newspaper Licensing Agency Ltd v Meltwater Holding BV' (2011) *European Intellectual Property Review* 331; Tanya Aplin, 'United Kingdom' in Brigitte Lindner and Ted Shapiro (eds), *Copyright in the Information Society: A Guide to National Implementation of the European Directive* (Edward Elgar 2011) 558.

[501] Derclaye (n 500) 249.

Infopaq will also affect the UK test for copyright infringement[502] since previous practice, based upon substantiality of the amount copied, appears out of line with the CJEU ruling, which bases infringement upon the originality of the part copied.[503] Thirdly, *Infopaq* calls into question whether the UK's system of exhaustive subject matter categories complies with EU law, since UK copyright law denies copyright protection to any authored intellectual creations which fall outside the subject-matter categories.

The decision of the UK courts in *The Newspaper Licensing Agency Ltd and Others v. Meltwater Holding BV and Others*,[504] which was heard after the *Infopaq* ruling, shows some changes in how UK copyright law is interpreted. The facts in *Meltwater* were similar to those in *Infopaq*. The defendant, Meltwater, provided an online media monitoring service. Customers selected particular search keywords of interest to them and received summaries from Meltwater of news items containing these particular search terms. The summaries included the article's headline along with a short extract of the text containing the keyword of interest. The High Court ruled that Meltwater's news service did require a license from the publishers of the news items, since it was possible that at least some of the headlines and extracts reproduced in Meltwater's reports were independent copyright works in their own right.[505] In this case, the Court's test for infringement was assessed on originality, rather than substantiality, since the Court indicated that the reproduced parts could express the author's own intellectual creation. This reasoning was upheld on appeal, which illustrates the impact of *Infopaq* in the UK.

In the United States, originality was considered at length in the well-known case of *Feist Publications, Inc. v. Rural Telephone Service Co.*[506] Here, the US Supreme Court refused to recognize copyright protection in an alphabetized telephone directory, holding that although the work originated from its author, it resulted purely from effort and so

---

502 Section 16(3) of CDPA 1988, see Derclaye (n 500) 250.

503 *Infopaq International A/S* (n 496) para 47–48 states, 'the reproduction of an extract of a protected work … is such as to constitute reproduction in part within the meaning of Article 2 of Directive 2001/29, if that extract contains an element of the work which, as such, expresses the author's own intellectual creation'.

504 [2010] EWHC 3099 (Ch).

505 This part of the decision was upheld by the Court of Appeal on 27 July 2011 [2011] EWCA Civ 890, [2011], [2012] Bus LR 53, [2012] RPC 1. More discussion of this case can be found, for example, in Rosati (n 500) 111–119.

506 *Feist Publications, Inc. v. Rural Telephone Service Co.* 499 U.S. 340, 348, 111 S.Ct. 1282, 1289 (1991).

lacked a minimum level of creativity required to be 'original' in an appropriate copyright sense.[507]

Therefore, copyright's originality requirement should be interpreted as not only requiring that a work originates from the author, but that such work must also possess a minimum degree of creativity.[508] As with works created on earth, space-related works need to satisfy this same originality test in order to enjoy copyright protection. As before, possible issues arising with respect to the originality of remote sensing satellite data and Hubble Space Telescope data will be considered separately from satellite broadcasting.

2.1.1   Remote sensing and the Hubble Space Telescope

Remote sensing data and Hubble Space Telescope data share similar characteristics in terms of categorization. The difference between these two activities is that while remote sensing is an activity that captures images of the earth, the Hubble Space Telescope captures images of outer space. Since the data produced from both remote sensing and via the Hubble Space Telescope are arguably the results of human intellectual creativity, which fall within the recognized subject matter categories, these both have the potential to be protected by copyright.

As previously mentioned, remote sensing and the Hubble Space Telescope both produce what are best categorized as satellite images.[509] Since any photographic image is always a reproduction of the scene which it captures, copyright protection for any photograph is always open to challenge on the basis that the work lacks originality. However, this line of argument is unconvincing. A work does not lack originality simply because it is a reproduction of something which pre-exists.[510] Rather, it is necessary to assess whether the reproduction involves sufficient talent and technical skill, to be original in its own right and therefore qualify for copyright protection.[511]

Generally, there are three steps in the production of a photograph: pre-fixation, fixation and post-fixation.[512] At the pre-fixation stage, the photographer selects the subject to be shot, arranges the angle of the camera, and adjusts levels of shadow or light, as well as the position of

---

[507]   Goldstein et al. (n 141) 192.
[508]   Goldstein et al. (n 141) 192.
[509]   See subject matter section.
[510]   Garnett, et al. (n 475) 145.
[511]   Ibid.
[512]   Sterling (n 487) 312.

the subject.[513] During the fixation stage, the photographer selects the equipment to be used (for example, which camera, what lens strength, film type, camera aperture size and shutter speed) when taking the photos.[514] At the post-fixation stage, a number of procedures might take place in terms of developing, printing the final product. At each stage, a photographer has input in terms of making decisions and selecting technique, which arguably constitute creativity in varying degrees.[515] It is therefore considered that these creative contributions are sufficient to render the results as an original work that should qualify for copyright protection.

Since there are three types of data from remote sensing satellites – 'primary data', 'processed data' and 'analyzed information'[516] – each will be assessed separately in terms of their originality.

2.1.1.1 Primary data The primary data is the most problematic type under consideration in terms of originality. To recap, primary data is 'the raw material that are acquired by remote sensors borne by a space object and that are transmitted or delivered to the ground from space by telemetry in the form of electromagnetic signals, by photographic film, magnetic tape or any other means'. In this raw state, the data is unusable without further processing. Owing to its unusable and unenhanced characteristics, which result from a purely automated process, many scholars conclude that 'primary data' lacks sufficient human intellectual input to qualify as an original creation which should enjoy copyright protection.[517]

Copyright does not subsist either in the ideas or facts *per se*, but rather its scope of protection extends only to particular expressions of those ideas or facts. The question to be answered is whether digital images from remote sensing are expressions of facts or merely facts, since the digital images represent the landscape of the earth. Some scholars argue that such satellite images should not attract copyright, since they are merely copies of the earth and lack human creativity.[518] Others believe that primary data falls outside the scope of copyright protection by

---

513 Ibid.
514 Ibid.
515 Ibid.
516 Principle I (b)(c) and (d) of the UN Remote Sensing Principles (n 112).
517 Yun Zhao, 'Regulation of Remote Sensing Activities in Hong Kong: Privacy, Access, Security, Copyright and the Case of Google' (2010) 36 *Journal of Space Law* 547, 553–554.
518 Cromer (n 447) 274.

analogy to the Berne Convention's exclusion of 'news of the day or to miscellaneous facts having the character of mere items of press information'.[519] In this regard, it is arguable that unenhanced data from a remote sensing satellite is a representation of the earth that is accessible to anyone with appropriate technology.[520] Due to the uncertain status of copyright protection, the satellite operators who collect primary data rely upon contractual license terms to protect their raw data.[521]

Since raw data are generated by the sensor technology in the remote sensing satellite, which first records information about the earth and then sends it back to a ground station by telemetry,[522] it appears that an appropriate test of its originality can be derived from an analogous examination to the originality test applied for a conventional photograph.

In *Temple Island Collections Limited v. New English Teas*,[523] the UK Patents County Court (as it then was) ruled that the plaintiff's photograph of a red bus depicted against an otherwise black and white background of Westminster Bridge was original and so qualified for copyright protection. The Court reasoned that the photograph in question was 'the result of the plaintiff's own intellectual creation' in terms not only of his choices relating to the basic photograph itself (the precise motif, angle of shot, light and shade, illumination, and exposure) but having regard to the post-fixation work in 'manipulating the image to satisfy his own visual aesthetic sense. The fact that it is a picture combining some iconic symbols of London does not mean that the work is not an original work in which copyright subsist'.[524]

In *Eva-Maria Painer v. Standard Verlags GmbH*, the CJEU held that a portrait photograph under consideration was original and therefore qualified for copyright protection. In this case, Ms Painer was a freelance photographer who had taken photographs of a girl who was later kidnapped. After the girl's escape, newspapers reporting the story reproduced the portrait photographs without first obtaining Painer's permission or attributing her as author. The Court reasoned that Painer had expended

---

[519]   Article 2(8) of the Berne Convention – see, e.g., J. Richard West, 'Copyright Protection for Data Obtained By Remote Sensing: How the Data Enhancement Industry Will Ensure Access for Developing Countries' (1990–1991) 11 *Northwestern Journal of International Law and Business* 403, 409–410.

[520]   Ibid.

[521]   Salin (n 451) 364–368.

[522]   Doldirina (n 168) 305.

[523]   *Temple Island Collections Limited* (n 495).

[524]   Ibid, paragraph 51 of [2012] EWPCC 1, at 8 <http://www.bailii.org/ew/cases/EWPCC/2012/1.html> (accessed 22 February 2016).

sufficient creative effort in choosing the background, deciding the pose, setting up the frame and arranging for the angle and lighting. Hence, the photo originated from the result of her effort and qualified for copyright protection.[525] This decision reflects Recital 17 of the Preamble of EU directive 93/98, which states that 'a photographic work is to be considered original if it is the author's own intellectual creation reflecting his personality'. Thus current European case law supports a position that a photograph can be original as long as its production involves creative human intervention.[526]

The US Supreme Court adopted similar logic in *Burrow-Giles Lithographic Co. v. Sarony*. Here, the Court overturned a lower court's decision which rejected a claim that a photograph was entitled to copyright protection and ruled that the photo was created by the plaintiff's own intellectual effort since he had arranged for the pose, the lighting as well as selecting the costume and other accessories.[527] These efforts reflected sufficient originality for the plaintiff's photograph to attract copyright protection.[528]

Nevertheless, it appears that *Sarony* can be distinguished from the automatic capture of satellite images on remote satellites, which result in factual representation of the earth.[529] Therefore, it is believed that only a thin copyright protection is applicable in this case, if any.[530] This position finds support in US case law. In *Meshwerks, Inc. v. Toyota Motor Sales U.S.A., Inc.*,[531] the Tenth Circuit, US Court of Appeals denied copyright protection for digital images modelling Toyota's vehicles that the plaintiffs had produced, ruling that these images lacked originality. The Court explained that such digitalized images did not reflect human decisions regarding 'lighting, shading, angle, background' and thus did not qualify as original works. Although the Court acknowledged that the transposition of the physical appearance of Toyota vehicles from 3-D to 2-D involved a degree of labor and skill, and that the resulting unadorned

---

[525]   *Painer* (n 495).
[526]   Yin Harn Lee, Case Comment, 'Photographs and the standard of originality in Europe: Eva-Maria Painer v Standard Verlgas GmbH, Axel Springer AG, Suddeutsche Zeitunung GmbH, Spiegel-Verlag Rudolf Augstein GmbH & Co KG, Verlag M. DuMont Schauberg Expedition der Kolnischen Zeitung GmbH & Co KG (C–145/10)' (2012) 34 *European Intellectual Property Review* 290, 291.
[527]   *Burrow-Giles Lithographic Co. v. Sarony*, 111 U.S. 53.
[528]   Ibid.
[529]   Cromer (n 447) 274.
[530]   Ibid.
[531]   528 F.3d 1258 (2008).

images accurately depicted Toyota's product, the end product did not owe any originality to the plaintiff.[532] For this reason, the digital images were denied copyright protection as lacking originality.

To conclude, taking case-law into account as a guide,[533] it is likely that raw data satellite images will only be original if the procedures used to acquire this data involve more human input (in terms of selecting locations, angles, setting etc.), than merely programming an essentially automated and automatic technological process. Otherwise the result, as in the *Meshwerks* decision, is merely an unoriginal copy of the earth's surface.

In my view, it must be acknowledged that raw data are generated automatically using computer programs which control when the sensors on any particular remote sensing satellite commences its sensing and data-capture activities for relay back to the ground station.[534] However, this process is not random, since a human operator programs the selection of location, latitudes, time and angles for data capture. Thus to me, the raw data is not merely the equivalent of a 'snapshot', but rather a result of human intellectual creativity which sufficiently qualifies it as an original work which merits copyright protection. Since case law in analogous photographic works sets the threshold of originality at a low level, it seems justified that the raw data meets the originality test.

2.1.1.2   Processed data and analyzed information   Both processed data and analyzed information are required to make raw data usable. Processing involves data correction and classification, steps in which data is manually input into computer algorithms.[535] The final step is to analyze and interpret the processed data, to transform them into analyzed information.[536] This stage requires the use of knowledge from a specialist with expertise from fields other than that of the processing itself.[537]

---

[532]   Ibid.

[533]   At present, there is no Thai Supreme Decision on the originality of photograph available. Thai Supreme Court Database (in Thai) at <http://www.deka2007.supremecourt.or.th/deka/web/searchlist.jsp> (accessed 22 February 2016).

[534]   Doldirina, 'The Common Good and Access to Remote Sensing Data' (D.C.L. thesis, McGill University, 2010) 24–25. This author views that raw data are a description of what the satellite 'see' on the surface of the earth even though what it senses is a certain part of the ground. Thus, raw data are factual information and cannot be copyrightable.

[535]   Ibid 26.

[536]   Ibid 26–27.

[537]   Ibid 27.

Creation of both processed data and analyzed information involves human intervention, in terms of translating the data into something usable. Although it might be argued that the method of retrieving processed and analyzed data is a kind of technological standard program, this does not detract from the fact that some human intervention is still needed in programming the process. More than merely a trivial amount of labor, judgment and creativity is employed. Thus, based upon the guidance provided by case-law, both processed data and analyzed information have the attributes required to be original works, and therefore should be eligible for copyright protection.

In summary, to qualify as original works, creation of the three different types of remote sensing data must each involve a certain degree of human intellectual creativity. However, irrespective of its originality, doubt has been raised whether raw data from remote sensing would merit copyright protection in the United States. This is because it is argued that raw data from remote sensing satellites are excluded from copyright protection by virtue of a provision in the US Commercialization Act which states that 'the private operator must make unenhanced data available to all users on a non-discriminatory basis'.[538] In my view, the obligation to allow access to raw data without discrimination has no impact upon the eligibility of the data for copyright protection, although it may limit the extent to which copyright owners may enforce their rights.[539] Nonetheless, considering the US case law precedent relating to originality, and by analogy with the *Sarony* case cited above,[540] it is considered that raw data from remote sensing, like processed data and analyzed information should merit copyright. However whether raw data will ultimately be considered original under the US law remains open for further discussion. At present, there is no equivalent UK law on space commercialization.

2.1.2 Satellite broadcasting

Under the UK legislation, there is no originality requirement for a broadcast. However, pursuant to US copyright law, only original broadcasts gain copyright protection.

---

[538] West (n 519) 406–407.

[539] West argues that since the private operators are obliged to make their unenhanced data available to all users without discrimination, this would prevent them from receiving royalties or fees from users of raw data, and as a result, those private operators do not attempt to copyright raw data.

[540] West (n 519).

In *Baltimore Orioles v. Major League Baseball Players*,[541] a television broadcast of a baseball game was held to fulfill the originality criteria required by US law. The Court reasoned that the selection of camera shots and angles used during the game, the use of instant replays and split screens and shading provided sufficient originality to qualify the work for copyright protection.[542] Hence, we can infer that in terms of originality, a satellite broadcast would attract copyright protection, provided that it is independently created, rather than simply reproducing another work and it must involve a minimum degree of creativity.

2.2 Fixation

Article 2(2) of the Berne Convention states, 'It shall be a matter for legislation in the countries of the Union to prescribe that works in general or any specified categories of works shall not be protected unless they have been fixed in some material form.'

Not all countries require works to be fixed for subsistence of copyright. For example, there is no fixation requirement under French Copyright legislation.[543] Similarly, the Thai Copyright Act B.E. 2537 does not explicitly require that a work to be fixed in order to obtain copyright protection. However, some members of the Union have elected to include fixation requirements in their national copyright legislation, although the exact requirements vary. For instance, Section 3(2) of the UK CDPA 88 provides that 'copyright does not subsist in a literary, dramatic or musical work unless and until it is recorded, in writing or otherwise'. While fixation is required for literary, dramatic and musical works, this provision does not extend to artistic works.

Section 101 of the US Copyright Act defines that 'a work is fixed in a tangible medium of expression when its embodiment in a copy or phonorecord, by or under the authority of the author, is sufficiently permanent or stable to permit to be perceived, reproduced, or otherwise communicated for a period of more than transitory duration'. Section 102(a) states that copyright subsists 'in original works of authorship fixed in any tangible medium of expression, now known or later developed, from which they can be perceived, reproduced, or otherwise communicated, either directly or with the aid of a machine or device'. Unlike in the United Kingdom, US copyright law requires all types of work to be fixed in order to receive copyright protection. In addition, while the

---

[541]   805 F.2d. 663 (7th Cir. 1986).
[542]   Ibid 668.
[543]   Sterling (n 487) 330.

fixation criteria is met in the UK whenever a work is reduced to a material form, regardless of whether this is done by the author, by a third party, or with the author's authorization, US law explicitly requires a work to be fixed by, or under, the authority of the author.[544]

These differences in fixation requirements impact upon whether space-related works created in outer space are eligible for copyright protection in the two jurisdictions under consideration.

2.2.1   Remote sensing data and the Hubble Space Telescope images

Although the UK CDPA 88 does not explicitly require fixation of artistic works, all the particular categories of artistic works eligible for protection require fixing in some kind of material form in order to exist.[545] In case of a photograph, for example, in reality, it is impossible for a photograph to be created without some kind of fixation being simultaneously created.

As previously mentioned, remote sensing satellites take pictures from outer space and send them back to a ground station in a digital format. It is reasonable to question whether, in such circumstances, this work is actually fixed in outer space or at the ground station. In other words, at which of the various stages are those geospatial data fixed (the collection stage, the transmission stage or the processing stage). This is significant because the point of fixation is one factor that determines the term of copyright protection.

Once a satellite takes a 'picture', the data collected may be stored in some kind of electronic memory device, such as in RAM or on the hard disk of a computer on board a spacecraft. If this is the case, the data are fixed in a material form and therefore qualify for copyright protection. The retention of those data for a period sufficient to enable the signals representing those works to be transmitted to the ground station will adequately satisfy the fixation requirement.[546] In practice, after the remote sensing satellites take pictures, those data will always be stored in the memory of the computer on board the spacecraft, either temporarily or permanently, before being transmitted to the ground station.[547] In such circumstances, because the primary data stored can be retrieved or perceived later, the data storage will constitute fixation.

---

[544]   Section 101 of the US Copyright Act.
[545]   Sterling (n 487) 330.
[546]   Ibid.
[547]   Interview with Dr. Sompong Liangrocapart (n 456) and Professor Christopher Conselice, Professor of Astrophysics, School of Physics and Astronomy, the University of Nottingham (Nottingham, 29 March 2012).

This position can be supported by guidelines set out in the UK CDPA 88. Section 17(2) provides that copying in relation to a literary, dramatic, musical or artistic work means reproducing the work in any material form and this includes storing the work in any medium by electronic means. In addition, Section 17(6) provides that copying in relation to any work includes making copies which are transient or incidental to some other use of the work. So, it is possible under the UK Act that even temporary storage of a work in an electronic medium would satisfy the fixation requirement.[548]

Under the US copyright law, Section 102 of the Act states that copyright subsists in 'original works of authorship fixed in any tangible medium of expression'. The question arises whether the storage of data from remote sensing in a digital form in an electronic medium would be sufficient. Section 101 of the Act defines that a work is 'fixed' in 'a tangible medium of expression and is sufficiently permanent or stable to permit it to be perceived, reproduced, or otherwise communicated for a period of more than transitory duration'. After satellite images are taken, they are electronically stored in a computer device on board the spacecraft and retrieved at the earth station for further use. Thus, those satellite images would appear to be fixed according to US law because they are fixed in a tangible form which is reproducible later, for more than temporary period.

In *Williams Electronics, Inc. v. Artic International, Inc.,*[549] the Federal Court ruled that the storage of the plaintiff's electronic video game in the memory device of the computer was sufficiently fixed as it was 'sufficiently permanent or stable to permit it to be ... reproduced, or otherwise communicated for more than a transitory period'.

Thus, I have no doubt that the fixation requirement is met in case of satellite images under both US and UK law.

2.2.2 Satellite broadcasting

As stated above, the UK CDPA only requires fixation in the case of literary, dramatic and musical works, and so there is no fixation requirement in the UK in the case of a broadcast. Therefore, a broadcast is protected irrespective of whether the Broadcasting Authorities retains a permanent version or not.[550] However, it has been pointed out that such a

---

[548]   Sterling (n 487) 331.
[549]   685 F.2d 870 (3d Cir. 1982). See also *MAI System Corp. v. Peak Computer, Inc.* 991 F.2d 511 (9th Cir 1993).
[550]   Bently et al. (n 207) 92.

transient broadcast would constitute one of the most intangible forms of intellectual property.[551]

However, the situation seems to be different in the United States. Under Section 102 of the US Copyright, copyright subsists in works that are fixed in 'any tangible medium of expression'. First we need to consider whether satellite broadcasting is fixed in order to fulfill the requirement stated in the US law.

National Football League v. McBee & Bruno's Inc.[552] is one case which considered the fixation criteria. In this case, the plaintiff telecast signals of a football match which were relayed via a satellite from a ground station to a receiving station. At the receiving station, commercial advertising was added before the transmission was sent out to its cable service subscribers. The defendant intercepted signal in transit between the ground station and satellite and then transmitted it to the public. The plaintiff claimed infringement of copyright in the telecasts, whereas the defendant denied copyright protection subsisted, since the signal which had been intercepted was not fixed. The court analyzed the definition of fixation pursuant to Section 101 of the Act. This states that 'a work ... being transmitted, is fixed for the purpose of the Act if a fixation of the work is simultaneously made with its transmission'. Since the telecast signals were fixed at some point during the course of their transmission, this fell within the definition of fixation, such that the work was protected by copyright.[553] A similar explanation of the application of the fixation rule was also provided in *Baltimore Orioles v. Major League Baseball Players*. Here the Court ruled that the telecast of a sports event which was videotaped simultaneously with public transmission fixed the telecast in tangible form, as defined by the Act.[554]

Thus, having regard to these US Court decisions, satellite broadcasts meet the fixation requirement, provided that as it is transmitted from space back to earth, a recording (fixation) of that work is made simultaneously, and that recording is 'sufficiently permanent or stable to permit it to be perceived, reproduced, or otherwise communicated for a period of more than a transitory duration'.[555] A satellite broadcast work is initiated with a signal from an 'uplink' ground station which is received

---

[551] Ibid.
[552] 792 F.2d 726 (8th Cir., 1986).
[553] Sterling (n 487) 333.
[554] *Baltimore Orioles* (n 541).
[555] Section 101 of the US Copyright Act.

by a transponder located on board an orbiting satellite.[556] This transponder retransmits a 'downlink' signal back to the earth, which is collected using a receiving dish at a receiving station, before transmitting it on to the public.[557] Since satellite broadcasting signals are collected in a receiving dish during transmission to the earth, and are able to be viewed by the public later, a satellite broadcast work therefore fulfills the definition of fixation under the US law. As a result, satellite broadcast works warrant copyright protection in the US, providing the other conditions required by copyright law are met.

The difference between fixation requirements in national copyright laws adds to complexity where infringement is alleged in an unfixed work. For example, during transmission of a satellite broadcast, third-party interception may occur before the signal has been fixed. Such an act is likely to be an infringement in a country without fixation requirements, whereas no infringement exists in a country where fixation is a condition of copyright protection since the signal is not fixed yet. A hypothetical case will better illustrate this problem. During a transmission from a US satellite, Viewer A intercepts the signals before the broadcast work is fixed and rebroadcasts it to a number of countries, including the United States and Thailand. If Viewer A is sued for copyright infringement in the US, the act will not amount to infringement, because an unfixed work falls beyond the scope of copyright protection under US law. In contrast, if an infringement case is brought before a Thai court, the signal itself is protected under the Thai copyright law, as there is no fixation requirement under the Thai law. Since Thailand is a member of the Rome Convention, a foreign work (in this case, the US signal) will be treated in the same way as a national work. Notwithstanding the fact that the US is not a party to the Rome Convention, but rather has agreed to equivalent provisions as a party to the TRIPs Agreement, Thailand has an obligation under the national treatment principle to protect the US broadcasts in this case.[558] The

---

[556]   Makeen Fouad Makeen, *Copyright in a Global Information Society: The Scope of Copyright Protection Under International, US, UK and French Law* (Kluwer Law International, 2000) 180. See also <http://en.wikipedia.org/wiki/Satellite_television> (accessed 26 April 2012).

[557]   Ibid.

[558]   Article 3.1 and Article 14.3 of the TRIPs Agreement. See also Section 8.1 of the Thai Copyright Act available online in English at <http://www.stop.in.th/webdatas/download/copyright_act_2537.pdf> (accessed 22 February 2016).

issue of applicable law and jurisdiction on this matter will be dealt in Chapter 5.[559]

2.3   Authorship of Work

There is no explicit reference on the term of the 'author' under the Berne Convention. So it is up to the member states to define what the author is under their domestic legislation. However, some scholars consider that 'author' and 'authorship' are to be interpreted to natural persons only.[560] The question arises regarding space-related activities whether those works are created by a natural person or purely by an automatic machine.

2.3.1   Remote sensing and the Hubble Space Telescope

As all geospatial data from remote sensing satellites and the Hubble Space Telescope may be categorized as satellite imagery, the term 'satellite images' will be used as a collective reference for the purpose of this sub-section when analyzing issues of authorship. Analysis of authorship is a crucial in the case of such satellite images, because aspects of a work's creation often involve automated processes, and so the topic needs careful consideration. In the UK, Section 9(1) of UK CDPA 88 defines an 'author' of a work as 'the person who creates it', and by virtue of Section 3(3) UK CDPA 88, the author is not necessarily the one who fixes the work. CDPA specifically covers 'computer-generated' works. Pursuant to Section 178 CDPA 88, the creator of such works is 'the person by whom the arrangements necessary for the creation of the work are undertaken. The US copyright statute, in contrast, includes no definition of 'author', but the term has been defined by the US Supreme Court as 'one to whom anything owes its origin'.[561] In the United States therefore, it appears implicit that authorship only applies to a human intellectual creation, not a machine-generated work.[562] Nevertheless, non-human generated works, including computer-generated works, can

---

[559] See Chapter 5, the hypothetical case no. 2 under the choice-of-law section.

[560] Goldstein et al. (n 141) 245. See also Martha Mejia-Kaiser, 'Copyright Claims for METEOSAT and LANDSAT Images under Court Challenge' (2006) *Journal of Space Law* 293, 300.

[561] *Burrow-Giles Lithographic Company* (n 527).

[562] See more in Pamela Samuelson, 'Allocating Ownership Rights in Computer-Generated Works' (1985) 47 *University of Pittsburgh Law Review* 1185.

be attributed with authorship, and so be eligible for copyright protection, providing the production of such a work involved human intervention and effort.[563]

Having regard to the definitions of 'author' outlined above, the question arises whether only natural persons can be authors, or whether authors may also be legal persons, such as companies and corporations, according to copyright legislation. In the United Kingdom, Section 9 of CDPA 88 does not explicitly exclude a company from authorship, and, taking the text of Section 9(2) CDPA 88 into consideration, it is likely that an author of those works covered therein could be a legal entity. For instance, the producer of a sound recording is likely to be a music production company, whereas the 'person' making a broadcast is likely to be a broadcasting company or organization. In the United States, if a work is 'made for hire',[564] the author is an employer, which may be a company, an organization or an individual.[565] Hence, in these two jurisdictions under consideration, both legal and natural persons can be the author of a copyright work.[566]

Where the work under consideration is a photograph, typically authorship will vest in a photographer. However, this would not be the case if the photographer merely 'presses the button' if another person has been substantially responsible for arranging or composing the image to be photographed. In that case, the latter would be considered to be the author instead.[567] This needs to be borne in mind when evaluating authorship where the 'photographic work' is a satellite image. Where the work is a satellite image, it may be questioned whether such an image even qualifies for copyright protection, since the image is created by apparatus located on board a satellite, not by a natural person. Alternatively, it might be argued that the work's authorship may be attributed to the person who has arranged all the processes necessary to create the

---

[563]   Halpern (n 234) 51.

[564]   Section 101 of the US Copyright Act.

[565]   See below section 201(c) of the US Copyright Act which will be discussed below in Section 4 of this chapter. More information can also be found from the United States Copyright Office <http://www.copyright.gov/circs/circ09.pdf> (accessed 22 February 2016).

[566]   Though in some cases in which a corporation is not an author, this does not prevent it from copyright protection since copyright may be transferred to such corporation by assignment or by virtue of law. It is noted that the term 'authorship' is different from that of 'ownership'.

[567]   Garnett et al. (n 475) 240.

images via the satellite,[568] since satellite images result from technology which is programmed by a human and directed to sense and capture particular images of earth.

In the UK, Section 9 of CDPA 88 stipulates that copyright will vest in the author who creates the work. Authorship of satellite images could be interpreted as analogous to computer-generated works as set out in Section 9(3) CDPA 88. In which case, the author of satellite images would be the one undertaking all necessary arrangements for their creation. In other words, the author is that person who arranges or programs the satellite equipment to capture the images, irrespective of whether those arrangements are made at a station based on earth or in a space station located in outer space.

In the United States, the author of satellite images is again analogous to the case of a computer-generated work, where the person who makes intellectual intervention in creating such work is considered as an author.[569] Thus again, the author of satellite images is the person who makes all necessary arrangements for the creation of that work.

Beyond the UK, courts in Europe have twice considered copyright in satellite images.[570] In the first case, proceedings were initiated in Germany. The European Space Agency (ESA) claimed copyright in certain satellite images taken by the Meteosat satellite, which were reproduced without consent by an advertising agency. In this case, the German Court ruled that pursuant to the German Copyright Act, only a natural person can author a copyright work. This interpretation thus excluded the ESA (clearly a legal entity) from claiming 'authorship' under German law. In these proceedings the court invited ESA to present evidence that the satellite image in dispute was in fact created by an employee of ESA in circumstances in which the right to exploit the work had been transferred from employee to employer. Unfortunately, as ESA failed to present the evidence requested,[571] the court inevitably ruled that it had not been established that the satellite image was the result of human intellectual creation. Therefore, the image did not qualify for copyright protection under German law.[572] Following the decision, Gervais, a copyright expert from the World Intellectual Property Organization commented that if ESA had properly demonstrated to the court

---

568   Mejia-Kaiser (n 560) 299–302.
569   Halpern et al. (n 234) 51.
570   There is no availability of the English version of these two cases. These cases are reported in Mejia-Kaiser (n 560) 299–302.
571   Ibid 294–302.
572   Ibid 301–302.

that a satellite 'is not taking dumb pictures, that someone has to tell it what to take the picture of, when to take the picture, that there was a human intervention', then in his view the German Court would have concluded that the photos were protected.[573]

In similar circumstances, M Sat brought copyright infringement proceedings in respect to unauthorized use of satellite images from its Landsat satellite. Unlike the German decision, the French Court was satisfied that the satellite images involved sufficient human creativity and initiative to warrant protection.[574] In reaching this decision, the Court took into account the efforts of employees of M Sat, who selected particular satellite images captured by Landsat and then utilized technology to transform and enhance the selected images. These activities provided the human intellectual intervention necessary to recognize the outputs as authorial works.[575] However, such reasoning is not uncontroversial. Pierre Sirinelli, for example, a French intellectual property expert, considers that it was inappropriate for the Court to apply criteria developed for traditional photography to the M Sat satellite images. In his view, the efforts of M Sat employees in, for example, selecting a Landsat image and then adjusting colors, contrasts, luminosity etc. are not comparable to the creative efforts of a traditional photographer (in selection of location, light, angle, subject and so on).[576] Sirinelli's views find support from commentator, Philippe Gaudrat, who considers that the act of enhancing the color in Landsat images lacked enough creativity to support copyright protection.[577]

What is also significant is that both the French and German courts were considering eligibility of the final product of satellite images for copyright protection, or in other words, the analyzed information. This still leaves unresolved the question whether French or German courts would consider raw or processed data authorial works.

---

[573] D. Gervais, 'International Aspects of Protection of Copyright Issues Related to Outer Space Activities' Workshop Proceedings on Intellectual Property Rights and Space Activities 105–106, ESA, Dec. (1994) 106.

[574] Mejia-Kaiser (n 560) 306.

[575] Ibid.

[576] Ibid 307–308. The original version of P. Sirinelli article is written in French and can be found at P. Sirinelli, 'Originalité d'images satellites ou comment distinguer la carte du territoire' 40 *Recueil Dalloz* (13 November 2003) 2754–2756.

[577] Mejia-Kaiser (n 560) 308. The original version of the Ph. Gaudrat article is written in French and can be found at Ph. Gaudrat, 'La terre vue en haut sur le puzzle des Amateurs d'en Bas: Brèves Observations à propos Riom' (Com. 14 mai 2003), 2 RTD.com, 309 (2004).

On balance, the reasoning contained in these two cases appears correct, namely that a satellite image has the potential to be an authorial work, since some level of human intellectual input is required for its creation. Here, the author is the individual who makes all necessary arrangements for the creation of satellite imagery. However, legal opinion varies as to the nature and degree of human intervention required in order to trigger copyright protection in any particular satellite image. This requires determination on a case-by-case basis, and different outcomes may result.

2.3.2 Satellite broadcasting

Satellite broadcasting appears less problematic from an authorship perspective because it more clearly involves human intervention in the creation of such a work.

In the UK, pursuant to CDPA 88, the author is defined as the person making the broadcast or, in the case of a broadcast which relays another broadcast and immediate re-transmission, the person making that other broadcast is the author of that work.[578] Thus, the author of a broadcast is the person at the ground station who arranges the broadcasting.

The interpretation of authorship for a satellite broadcast under US law would be the same as that discussed above in relation to remote sensing satellite images. Since there is no statutory definition of author given under the US law, the concept of authorship is determined by case-law precedent, which indicates that an author is the intellectual creator of a work.[579] Thus, it is reasonable to conclude that, in the case of a satellite broadcast, the author is the person who arranges and contributes to the work of broadcasting.

In considering authorship of remote sensing satellite images and satellite broadcasts, this sub-section has demonstrated that these space-related works derive from creative human intellectual effort, and are not merely the inevitable result of using automated technology. As such, these works are rightly eligible for copyright protection. Having established this preliminary point, issues of joint authorship and ownership of those works can now be considered in the following subsections.

---

[578] Section 9(2)(b) of the UK CDPA 88.
[579] *Andrien v. Southern Ocean County Chamber of Commerce*, 927 F.2d. 132 (3d Cir.1991).

3. OWNERSHIP

Normally, the author of any work is the first owner of copyright. This is provided for in Section 11(1) of the UK CDPA 88 and Section 201 of the US Copyright Act. However, in some instances, the law recognizes someone other than the author as first owner of a copyright work. The common exception is the case of a work created by an employee during the course of employment.[580] However, even if first ownership vests in a third party, rather than the author, issues of authorship of that work remains unchanged.

4. EMPLOYER/EMPLOYEE

Employment provides a common exception to the general rules of first ownership of copyright. As between an employee and employer, copyright in a work vests with the employer, when an author creates a work in the course of their employment.

In the UK, Section 11(2) of the CDPA 88 provides that the employer is the first owner of the copyright in a literary, dramatic, musical or artistic work or a film which is created in the course of employment, unless there is an agreement in place to the contrary.

In the US, the US Copyright Act also shares the rule that an employer is the first owner of an employee's work. Section 201(c) provides that 'In the case of a work made for hire, the employer or other person for whom the work was prepared is considered the author for the purposes of this title, and, unless the parties have expressly agreed otherwise in a written instrument signed by them, owns all of the rights comprised in the copyright'. Here, a 'work made for hire' is defined as 'a work prepared by an employee within the scope of his or her employment'.[581] Thus, an employer is held to be the author of any work created by an employee during the course of their employment, unless the parties have expressly agreed otherwise in writing.

Whether any particular work is made during the 'course of employment' depends upon the particular terms of the individual's contract of employment. Courts tend to equate 'course of employment' with 'scope of duties', rather than simply looking at the time and place where the work in question was created. So, the fact that an employee has created a

---

580   See Section 4 below in this chapter.
581   Section 101 of the US Copyright Act.

copyright work at home during the weekend is not decisive in determining whether the work is their own. Instead, it is proper to review whether such a work is likely to result or falls within the scope of tasks which that individual has been employed to carry out under their contract of employment. If so, then that work is likely deemed to be made in the course of their employment.[582]

Therefore, in the UK and US, there seems little doubt that first ownership of copyright works created in outer space, whether a space-related work or a general work, which arises during the course of an employee's employment will vest with their employer, provided that there is no express agreement to the contrary. For example, where an astronaut on board a spacecraft during a mission creates a copyright work, determinations of ownership depend upon their contract of employment. If the work created is a poem, then it is highly likely that he would be the author and owner of copyright in that work, but if the work is a literary copyright arising in a report regarding experimental work which has been undertaken as part of their mission, it is highly likely that this falls within the scope of the astronaut's employment, such that copyright in the report would belong to the employer.

Since space activities (remote sensing and satellite broadcasting) require high levels of investment, an employee is unlikely to create such a work successfully without significant technical and financial contributions from their employer, which would typically be either a government department or private entrepreneurial company. In addition, such works would be expected to result during the course of the employee's employment. Hence, the first ownership of these particular works seems to vest in an employer under UK and US laws. However, the situation in some jurisdictions, such as Thailand, is different.

Contrary to the provisions in the UK and US, Section 9 of the Thai Copyright Act provides that the ownership of copyright in a work created in the course of employment vests in the author, *unless* otherwise agreed to the contrary.[583] However, even in the absence of a specific agreement, an employer is entitled to communicate an employee's work to the public in accordance with the purpose of the employment.[584] Granting first

---

[582] *Missing Link Software v. Magee* [1989] FSR 361.

[583] Section 9 of the Thai Copyright Act states, 'Copyright in the work created by the author in the course of employment vests upon the author unless it has been otherwise agreed in writing provided that the employer is entitled to communicate such work to public in accordance with the purpose of the employment'.

[584] Ibid.

ownership to an employee is considered to best protect the intellectual effort of the real creator. At the same time, this situation may serve as a disincentive for any employer, having regard to their contribution in providing the circumstances necessary for the creation of that work, and given that they are likely to be better placed to exploit the works commercially, especially in the case of highly technological fields, including outer space activities.

The question of whether first ownership of a copyright work vests in an employer or employee is one of the issues examined in Chapter 5, as this may give rise to issues particularly in commercial ventures which include participants of multiple nationalities. This is not uncommon in space activities, and problems of applicable law and proper jurisdiction can result. For example, a Thai astronaut may be employed by the US government. If the astronaut writes a new computer program for use in the operation of the International Space Station, it may not be evident who the first owner of copyright in this computer program is. Under US (and UK) copyright law; the employer – i.e., the US government – would be the first owner, as the employer, whereas the astronaut might expect to be first owner of this work under Thai copyright law.[585]

Different schemes of first ownership under different national laws could be problematic, not only in terms of further assignment or licensing of the work, but also in respect of entitlement to bring proceedings in the case of alleged infringement, since these are all acts which lie with the owner of the work. Since the first ownership rule diverges between common law and civil law countries, it is useful to study further how this problem is resolved.[586]

5. JOINT AUTHORS OR CO-AUTHORS

As with other copyright works, it is quite possible that works created in outer space – both space-related works and general works – might be a work of joint authorship. A work is jointly authored when two or more authors collaborate to create a work, the nature of which is such that the contribution of each author is not distinct from that of the other author or authors.[587] In other words, the individual contributions must merge or

---

[585] However, Section 105 of the US Copyright Act disqualifies US government work from copyright protection. But the employer first ownership rule is still applicable under the US law in case the employer is a private company.

[586] See Chapter 5, the hypothetical case no. 1 in the choice-of-law section.

[587] Bently (n 207) 131.

integrate to one whole work.[588] However, not every collaborative contribution in a work will be sufficient to qualify the contributor as a joint author. Any co-author must make a substantial contribution to the work.[589]

This sub-section will focus attention upon authorship of space-related works, that is, works derived from remote-sensing satellites and satellite broadcasts. As these works are examples of computer-generated works and entrepreneurial works, determining authorship, particularly when multiple parties are involved, appears to be more problematic.

UK law makes special provision for joint authors in case of a broadcast: there will be joint authorship whenever a broadcast is made by more than one person.[590] For these purposes, the broadcast is made by the person(s) responsible for the contents of the transmitted programme and whoever makes the arrangements necessary for its transmission.[591]

Section 101 of the US Copyright Act defines a 'joint work' as one 'prepared by two or more authors with the intention that their contributions be merged into inseparable or interdependent parts of a unitary whole', In the case of *Aalumhammed v. Lee*,[592] the court ruled that to satisfy the requirement for a joint work, each author has to exercise control over the work and clearly express their intention to be a co-author; some level of creative contribution alone is not sufficient.

6. QUALIFYING CONDITIONS

Satisfaction of the protection requirements is not sufficient to qualify a work for copyright protection. Before a work receives copyright protection in a particular jurisdiction, it is also necessary that the work has a point of attachment to that country. Typically, nationality or habitual residence of the author or place of first publication of the work provides the necessary point of attachment which qualifies a work for protection. Thus, the actual place where a work is created, e.g., outer space, is irrelevant when assessing whether a work qualifies for protection. A space-related work will qualify for copyright protection, providing it satisfies at least one of the qualification requirements of the particular national legislation. Protection in a Berne Convention signatory country

---

[588]   Ibid 121–122.
[589]   Ibid 121.
[590]   Section 10(2) of the UK CDPA 88.
[591]   Section 10(2) and Section 6(3) of the UK CDPA 88.
[592]   202 F.3d 1227 (9th Cir. 2000).

provides a further mechanism for qualification, since Article 3 of the Berne Convention obliges a member state to protect foreign works which qualify for protection in another member state, based upon nationality or residence of author and country of publication. This situation is best illustrated with a specific example.

Let us take the case of a Thai national who is an astronaut. Both Thailand and the United States are Berne Convention countries. He creates a copyright work while on a US spacecraft in outer space, and the work is published on that spacecraft. His work may qualify for copyright protection in any Berne member country based upon the place of publication of the work or on his nationality or place of habitual residence, as illustrated below.[593]

As the US spacecraft is registered to the United States, it is possible that by publishing the work on the spacecraft, the place of first publication is the United States. However, even if publication on the spacecraft is not considered effective, the astronaut still has an opportunity to publish his work in any other Berne member states within 30 days of the first publication and still qualify for protection under a provision of the Berne Convention.[594] Even if he fails to do this, he still has an opportunity to qualify the work for copyright protection based upon the authorship rules instead. Because he, as author, is a national resident in Thailand, his work qualifies for copyright protection in Thailand, as well as other member countries of the Berne Convention.

Now suppose that Thailand is not a party to the Berne Convention and the spacecraft in question is the ESA spacecraft. In this case, the first publication in that spacecraft cannot be considered as if done in a Berne member state, because the ESA is not a country. However, the astronaut still has the option to arrange to have his work published in a Berne country, and if he does, his work qualifies for protection by virtue of the rule of the first publication.[595] However, even if he fails to first publish his work in a Berne Convention country, his work may still qualify for protection. Assuming now that his Thai nationality excludes his work from qualifying based upon the nationality rule, his work may still qualify for protection under the Berne Convention, based upon his place of habitual residence in a Berne Convention country. For example, as a US astronaut, he may be habitually resident in the United States. Finally, even if the habitual resident rule does not apply, his work may still be

---

[593] For examples, see Section 8 of the Thai Copyright Act, Sections 154 and 155 of the UK CDPA 88 and Section 104 of the US Copyright Act.

[594] Article 3(4) of the Berne Convention.

[595] Article 3(1)(b) of the Berne Convention.

eligible for copyright protection under national law, even if he fails to obtain protection within the Berne Convention countries.

Since any work has to satisfy only one of the three qualifying requirements in any one Berne Convention country, and bearing in mind that 167 of the 193 countries in the world[596] are Contracting Parties to the Berne Convention,[597] it is statistically unlikely that a work which is otherwise eligible for copyright will fail to be protected because it does not satisfy the qualification requirements. However, even in the worst case, that work might still be protected on a national-only basis, if copyright protection is available in that non-Berne country, as elaborated above.

7. DURATION

The Berne Convention sets the minimum term, or duration, of protection for most works to be the 'life of the author and 50 years after his death', although it sets an alternative term for special classes of works.[598] The Convention permits countries to provide for a longer period of protection in national law. For example, following an EU harmonization directive, the general term of protection within the EU is author's life plus 70 years.[599] Article 7(4) of the Berne Convention sets a shorter duration of protection for photographic works. Rather than basing the term on the life of a natural person, the term of protection is set as 'at least until the end of a period of 25 years from the making of such work.' However, as Article 7(4) sets only a minimum term, most states have chosen to implement the system of the life of a natural person plus a fixed term instead.[600]

Turning to neighboring rights, the Rome Convention sets a 20 year minimum period of protection, setting out different starting points for computing the term for different subject matters.[601] In the case of

---

[596] Basing on the number of member states of the United Nation <http://www.un.org/en/members/> but there are 206 sovereign states reported in <http://en.wikipedia.org/wiki/List_of_sovereign_states> (accessed 5 January 2016).

[597] <http://www.wipo.int/treaties/en/ShowResults.jsp?treaty_id=15> (accessed 5 January 2016). For example, Cambodia and Myanmar are not parties to the Berne Convention.

[598] Article 7(1) of the Berne Convention.

[599] E.C. Term of Protection Directive Article 1(1).

[600] See for example, Section 12(2) of the UK CDPA 88, Section 302(a) of the US Copyright Act.

[601] Article 14 of the Rome Convention.

phonograms and for performances incorporated in phonograms, the term of protection is at least 20 years from the end of the year in which the fixation was made;[602] whereas in case of broadcasts or an unfixed performance, the minimum term of protection is 20 years from the end of the year in which the broadcast or performance took place.[603]

As we have already argued that both satellite images and satellite broadcasts are eligible for copyright protection, the issue of the duration of the resulting rights lies with differing national laws. In addition, there is no special regime for the term of protection for satellite images and satellite broadcasts, so these types of work will be governed by the same criteria as other copyright works created on earth. The only particular issue which arises would be a choice of law issue, in the event that the term of protection varies between relevant states.

In the UK, Section 12(2) CDPA 88 provides a term of protection for literary, dramatic, musical or artistic works based upon the life of the author plus 70 years. Since we have classified satellite images as photographs, these will be protected by virtue of this section for the period of the life of the author plus 70 years. In the case of joint-authors, the term is based upon the life of the longest surviving author.[604] In the case of a satellite broadcast, copyright protection expires at the end of a period of 50 years from the end of the calendar year in which the broadcast was first made.[605]

The duration of copyright protection in the United States is generally the same duration as that in the United Kingdom. Thus, under the US law, a copyright work will be protected for a term of life of the author plus 70 years.[606] In case of joint authorship, again, the period will be the life of the last surviving author plus a further 70 years.[607] However, in the case of a work made for hire, the term of copyright protection is calculated as 95 years from the date of publication or 120 years from the date of creation, whichever expires first.[608] Also, US law does not make a

---

[602]   Article 14(a) of the Rome Convention.
[603]   Article 14(b)(c) of the Rome Convention.
[604]   Section 12 (8)(a)(i) of the UK CDPA 88.
[605]   Section 14 (2) of the UK CDPA 88. See also the duration of copyright in sound recordings and films in which the term of protection are set at 50 years and 70 years, respectively, on different starting points for computing the term (Section 13A and Section 13B of the UK CDPA 88).
[606]   Section 302 (a) of the US Copyright Act.
[607]   Section 302 (b) of the US Copyright Act.
[608]   Section 302 (c) of the US Copyright Act.

special case for a broadcast,[609] so the general duration rule will apply. The problem is that normally in case of broadcast, the first ownership of such a work will vest with the employer which usually is an entrepreneurial company. So, how do we measure the term of protection in such a case? A benchmark, other than the life of a natural person, is provided for calculating the term of protection pursuant to Article 12 of the TRIPs Agreement. Article 12 of the TRIPs Agreement states that:

> The term of protection of a work, other than a photographic work or a work of applied art, is calculated on a basis other than the life of a natural person, such term shall be no less than 50 years from the end of the calendar year of authorized publication, or failing such authorized publication within 50 years from the making of the work, 50 years from the end of the calendar year of making.

If we take the provision of Article 12 of the TRIPs Agreement as guidance, the duration of copyright in case of broadcast will be measured from the date of making such work plus another 50 years.

Nevertheless, in some countries, such as Thailand, the general duration of protection for all works is a life-plus-50 system, as set out in Section 19 of the Thai Copyright Act. However, in case of satellite images (which we have explained, falls within the category of photographic work) and satellite broadcasts, duration will be 50 years from authorship, provided that the work is published during this period; otherwise, copyright subsists for 50 years as from the date of first publication.[610] The 'last surviving author' rule applies in case of joint authorship, where copyright protection lasts for 50 years from the death of the last surviving author.[611]

In conclusion, the duration of copyright is normally measured by the life of the author plus a fixed term, based upon the minimum standard set out in the Berne Convention, although additional protection is provided in some countries, including those in the European Union. In addition, the term of protection in the case of joint authors follows the criterion set forth in Article 7 bis of the Berne Convention and is determined by applying a last surviving author rule.

---

[609] The protection of broadcasts under the US copyright law covers only for fixed broadcasts. Such protection is different from other jurisdictions such as the UK and Thailand, where there is no fixation requirement for broadcasts in case of the former and for all works in case of the latter. Thus, a word 'film' is sometimes suggested to be used instead of broadcasts.

[610] Section 21 of the Thai Copyright Act.

[611] Section 19 (2) of the Thai Copyright Act.

The difference in duration of protection under national copyright laws is anticipated to result in problems in terms of choice of applicable law, when the same work is protected in more than one country, but with different terms of protection. This might result in the problem of forum shopping, where a right holder who has the option of commencing proceedings in a number of countries, elects to initiate proceedings in that country which affords the longest period of protection.[612]

8. INFRINGEMENT

Matters of infringement are determined on the same basis, irrespective of whether a particular work has been created on earth or in outer space. If a third party reproduces a satellite image or re-transmits a broadcast without the consent of the right owner, such an act would normally constitute an infringement, unless the activity falls within one of the specific acts exempted by law. The question of whether a particular reproduction of a copyright work is an infringement is one determined according to national copyright law. Article 5(2) of the Berne Convention states: 'the extent of protection, as well as the means of redress afforded to the author to protect his rights, shall be governed exclusively by the law of the country where protection is claimed.' The 'country where protection is claimed' refers to the country where the alleged infringement occurs.[613] As the scope of protected rights varies according to each national law, this may result in uncertainty as to which national law is the applicable law. Apart from the choice of law, there is no specific point to be discussed here in term of infringement in space activities. Copyright infringement considered in this sub-topic applies equally to works created in outer space which are infringed on earth and works created on earth which are infringed in outer space. Additionally, since copyright protection is territorial, any particular national law is generally only applicable within that particular state's territory. Problems may therefore arise in case that an alleged infringement has occurred in outer space,

---

[612]   See Chapter 5, hypothetical case no. 3 in the choice of law section which discusses the same issue.

[613]   See, for example, Jane C. Ginsburg, 'Private International Law Aspects of the Protection of Works and Objects of Related Rights Transmitted Through Digital Networks' Group of Consultants on the Private International Law Aspects of the Protection of Works and Objects of Related Rights Transmitted Through Global Digital Networks, (Geneva, December 16 to 18, 1998), WIPO Doc GCPIC/2, 35.

which is beyond the reach of the national law of any state. The hypothetical cases below will form the basis of further elaboration of this sub-topic.

8.1   Case 1: Satellite Images from Remote Sensing or the Hubble Space Telescope

As outlined previously, satellite images are works which are eligible for copyright protection, and represent an example of a work which is created in outer space. In the event that a third party makes unauthorized copies of a protected image on earth, this is an act which would normally constitute an infringement, to be determined according to national law. Also as discussed, not all unauthorized use of satellite images will infringe copyright. For example, images – especially those of unenhanced data – may fall below the originality threshold applied in some countries, or may not be considered to be protected authorial works. In addition, satellite images which are works of the US government are excluded from copyright protection according to US law.[614] However, even this exclusion does not prevent NASA's satellite images and those from the Hubble Space Telescope from being protected in other countries where there is no equivalent exclusion barring copyright protection on government work.[615]

But even in a situation where infringement has occurred, specific exceptions arise where a finding of infringement does not incur any liability. For example, User A in Thailand makes an unauthorized and infringing copy of a photograph taken by SPOT (a French remote sensing satellite). If the copyright owner sues User A in the UK, the UK Court will apply Thai law as the applicable law in this case.[616] Imagine that the situation is complicated by the fact that the images do not qualify for copyright protection in Thailand because they are considered to lack originality, but would satisfy the UK originality criterion. Will the UK Court hold that User A's action is an infringement?

The fact that User A exploited a copyrighted work without authorization will not always amount to infringement if the use falls under any

---

[614]   Section 105 of the US Copyright Act.

[615]   Works of government are not listed as an excluded work under Section 7 of the Thai Copyright Act, and Section 163 of the UK CDPA 88 provides for the Crown copyright subsistence.

[616]   The general choice of law rule for determining whether a copyright has been infringed is the law of the country where the unauthorized use occurred. See Goldstein et al. (n 141) 93.

exceptions from infringement. For instance, under the US Copyright law, User A might escape from liability if he can demonstrate that his use is 'fair use'.[617] A similar exception is also available under UK copyright laws (where the equivalent exception is one of 'fair dealing') and Thai copyright laws.[618] However, the extent to which any unauthorized act falls within an exception is a factual issue, and one in which User A carries the burden of proof to establish to the satisfaction of the relevant courts. Generally, making use copyrighted work for the purpose of research or private study is permitted.[619]

8.2   Case 2: Transmission of Sounds and Images of Mars to Earth by Astronauts[620]

A NASA spacecraft lands on Mars and a team of astronauts (employed by the US government) step on the planet's surface and then head off to explore the vicinity. The astronauts' activities on Mars are transmitted back to the mission control on earth and immediately broadcast on to the public throughout the world. During the transmission of signals between Mars and earth, User B intercepts the signals and retransmits them to the public without NASA's permission. Has User B infringed copyright in the broadcast or may User B avoid liability? The answer may differ by virtue of applicable national laws. One fundamental problem is, at present, there is no international agreement on the place where 'communication to the public' for a broadcast is considered to take place:[621] Is it the place where the signal is emitted (and, in this case would this be the state of registration of the satellite), or is it the place where the signal is received (the satellite's foot-print country)? For example, Article 1(2)(b) of the EU Satellite Directive provides that the communication to the public occurs in the country where the signals are introduced,[622] whereas the US Court in *Allarcom Pay TV Ltd. v. Gen Instrument Corp.*, and *National Football League v. Primetime 24 Joint Venture* held that the 'performance' in dispute occurs at the place of reception where the public

---

[617]   Section 107 of the US Copyright Act.
[618]   Section 32 of the Thai Copyright Act and Sections 29 and 30 of the UK CDPA 88.
[619]   See, for example, section 32 paragraph 2 (1)(2) of the Thai Copyright Act; Section 29 of the UK CDPA 88; and Section 107 of the US Copyright Act.
[620]   This hypothetical case has been taken from Sterling (n 483) and has been modified for the purpose of this study.
[621]   Ibid 24.
[622]   Article 1(2)(b) of the EU Satellite Directive (n 150).

received satellite signals.[623] In the first case, the Court ruled that 'the unauthorized transmission from the United States to Canada implicated rights only under Canadian law' whereas in the latter case, the Court held that the performance occurs 'at every step in the process by which a protected work wends its way to its audience'.[624] These different interpretations lead to a number of possible national laws where the infringement takes place. Thus, the solution of where any infringement takes place depends upon the national law which is applicable to the case.

Another crucial problem is that while the unauthorized broadcasting will be considered an infringement in some countries, in others, only broadcasts which are fixed will be protected. For example, to be protected under the US copyright law, broadcast must be fixed simul- taneously during the transmission. In this case, broadcast of the unfixed live performance of the astronauts on Mars would not be protected by US copyright law. However, the same broadcast would be protected under UK law, since UK copyright law does not have a fixation requirement. User B's action would therefore appear to infringe UK copyright law by virtue of Section 20(1)(c) CDPA 88, but only if the broadcaster (in this case, NASA) qualifies for protection in UK. In the case of a broadcast, Section 156 CDPA 88 sets the qualification for protection based upon the place where the broadcast is made. In this case, the transmission originates on Mars. Is the broadcast an extraterritorial work? If the answer is affirmative, will the broadcast in this case be protected on the earth?[625] Though copyright is protected regardless of the location of its creation, this work might not be protected in the UK. This is because such work does not meet the qualification of protection since it was made on Mars, not in another country.

Now, suppose that the broadcast of the astronauts is fixed in a material form (on film or as a motion picture). The fixed broadcast is eligible for protection under US copyright law. In this case if the broadcast is transmitted by NASA, it would still fall foul of the bar set out in Section

---

[623] *Allarcom Pay TV Ltd. v. Gen Instrument Corp.*, 69 F.3d 381, 387 (9th Cir. 1995) and *National Football League v. Primetime 24 Joint Venture*, 211 F.3d 10, 12 (2nd Cir. 2000).

[624] These two cases are also reported in Graeme B. Dinwoodie, 'Developing a Private International Intellectual Property Law: The Demise of Territoriality' (2009) 51 *William and Mary Law Review* 713, 726–727.

[625] See more discussion of this matter in Chapter 5, the hypothetical case no. 2 in the choice-of-law section.

105 of the US Copyright Act, which excludes works of the US Government from protection. However, this exclusion relates to the USA only, such that NASA may qualify for copyright protection in Thailand, since Thai law does not include an equivalent restriction for government work to be protected. However, to gain protection, the first broadcast of the work must be made in Thailand, or in another Berne country, including the United States.[626]

8.3   Case 3: Copying Software Games While On Board a Spacecraft in Outer Space[627]

In this example, Astronaut C brings a software game on board a spacecraft. While in outer space, he makes copies of the game which he distributes to fellow astronauts, so that they too can entertain themselves. At the end of the mission, the software copies are left on board the craft for the benefit of future astronauts. Essentially, this is an example where a work created on earth is potentially infringed in outer space, where no state can claim its sovereignty.

Case 3 raises the question of whether Astronaut C is liable for infringement, since there is no copyright law applicable in outer space. The most likely possibility is that any acts on board the spacecraft, including the copying of the software, is deemed to occur in the state of registration. In this case, the national copyright law of that state would be the applicable copyright law to determine whether Astronaut C's actions are infringing. For example, if the infringing act takes place on board the ESA module in the ISS, both the EU Software Directive and national copyright law of all ESA member countries will be applicable. Can the right holder sue for any damages he suffered? Since the astronaut did not bring the copies back to earth, it is unlikely whether the action has resulted in any harm to the right holder.[628]

---

[626]   Section 8(2) of the Thai Copyright Act.

[627]   This hypothetical case has been modified from the case stated in Sterling (n 483) 29.

[628]   The number of copies and the volume of audience are some criteria which will be taken into account for determining whether such unauthorized copies are harmful to the right holder basing on the case-by-case analysis. The fact that such unauthorized use occurred within a group of people may not trigger infringement. Taking into account that there is no copyright in outer space, thus making such copies was not an infringement and basing on the fact that they did not bring those copies back to the earth, thus there was no importation to constitute an infringement.

The scenario would be more complicated if an astronaut duplicated the software during a mission on Mars. Here, any potentially infringing act would appear to have taken place in an extraterritorial area, where no national law can reach. But, is there any possibility that some national law is applicable to this case? This would depend upon whether there is a sufficiently harmful effect arising from that unauthorized act committed in the extraterritorial area, which gives cause for a national court to apply national copyright law extraterritorially.[629]

8.4   Case 4: The Astronauts' Works Created in Outer Space and Infringed in Outer Space

During a mission to the Moon, Richard (an astronaut from the US) was so inspired by the beauty of the celestial bodies around him that he penned some lyrics expressing how awesome the galaxy is. Mike (an astronaut from the UK) started playing his guitar and soon put Richard's lyrics to music. Pleased with their efforts, the two revised the words and the music together, until they were both happy with the result, and later performed that song for the other astronauts on the Moon mission. Unknown to Richard and Mike, John (an astronaut from Thailand) recorded the performance and distributed copies of the recording to the other astronauts.

Despite the fact that these works were created in outer space, they are clearly still eligible for copyright protection.[630] Assuming that both the lyrics and the music are protected by copyright (as a literary and musical work, respectively), it would be reasonable to assume that John's unauthorized copying of those works constitutes copyright infringement. However, this infringement has occurred in an extraterritorial area, where no copyright law is applicable. Given this, do Richard and Mike have any legal remedy? Would the result be different if the performance and recording occurred in the International Space Station (ISS)? In which case, would the national laws of the Partner States of the ISS apply, such that Richard and Mike could bring proceedings before the national courts of these countries? And in case of the European Space Agency, one of the

---

[629]   See Chapter 5, the hypothetical case no. 3 in the choice-of-law section.

[630]   This is because the point of attachment for copyright protection is either the author's nationality or habitual residence. However, there may be an issue if the author has no nationality of any state and the criterion of habitual residence has to be taken into account instead. And if his habitual residence becomes space, in such a case, there is no copyright protection available due to lack of point of attachment under present copyright conventions.

Partners in the ISS, should the courts and national laws of each ESA be operational in this case?

These questions all relate to choice of law and jurisdiction, which will be examined in the following chapter.[631]

9. EXCEPTIONS

National copyright law includes certain exceptions, which allow third parties to use copyright works without requiring consent from the right holders, and which do not amount to copyright infringement. Nations provide similar exceptions to copyright infringement, and since none of these specifically relates to outer space activities, these defenses will only be briefly summarized in this section. At the international level, it is recognized that reproduction of a work should only be permitted in certain cases where the third-party use does not conflict with a normal exploitation of the work and does not unreasonably prejudice the legitimate interests of the author.[632,633] This leaves room for the implementation of specific copyright exceptions at the national level.

The common exceptions are: private uses, public uses and incidental uses. In each case, a notion of fair practice is applied when determining whether the unauthorized use is justified.

9.1 Private Uses

In the UK, pursuant to Section 29(1) (2) of CDPA 88, 'fair dealing with a literary, dramatic, musical or artistic work for the purposes of research for a non-commercial purpose and also for the purpose of private study' are permitted. Similarly, US copyright law provides that 'fair use of a copyrighted work for ... purposes such as scholarship or research' is not an infringement.[634]

---

[631]   See Chapter 5, the hypothetical case no. 3 and no. 4 in jurisdiction and choice of law sections, respectively.

[632]   The Three-Step Test is incorporated in Article 9(2) and Article 13 of the Berne Convention and TRIPs Agreement, respectively. See also Article 10 of the WIPO and Article 5(5) of the E.C. Copyright in the Information Society Directive of 2001.

[633]   Article 10 and Article 10bis of the Berne Convention provide certain free uses of works (quotations, illustrations for teaching and indication of source and author) and further possible free uses of works (of certain articles and broadcast works, of works seen and heard in connection with current events), respectively.

[634]   Section 107 of the U.S. Copyright Act.

9.2 Public Uses

Several uses of a protected work in public are excluded from copyright infringement. While the particular public uses excluded differ among nations, the most common exceptions include quotation,[635, 636] educational uses,[637] library uses and archival uses.[638]

9.3 Incidental Uses

National copyright law typically exempts from infringement certain unauthorized, but incidental, uses of a copyright work when this incidental use is closely allied to the primary use.[639] Such exceptions include the right to make an ephemeral recording for broadcasting purposes[640] and any necessary reproduction, being only a transient digital copy, of a computer programme during the course of its operation, or for archival purposes.[641] Since reliance upon the notion of 'fair practice' is the most common defense raised for unauthorized use of a copyrighted work, it is

---

[635] The common law countries characterize this use as the requirements of fair dealing or fair use. See Goldstein et al. (n 141) 393. See also Article 10(1) of the Berne Convention and Article 5(3)(d) of the E.C. Copyright in the Information Society Directive.

[636] There is no parody exception explicitly allowed in UK and the US copyright law. However, parody may be assimilated to the fair dealing exemption for the purpose of criticism under the UK CDPA Act. See Goldstein et al. (n 141) 394. The U.S. Courts held that parody is regarded as fair use. See Halpern et al. (n 234) 101–103. See also Article 5(3)(k) of the E.C. Copyright in the Information Society Directive.

[637] Section 32–36 A of the UK CDPA 88, the US Copyright Act's fair use doctrine also allows the use of teaching (including multiple copies for classroom use). This exception is embodied in the Section 107 of the US Copyright Act. The exceptions of education uses are also stated in Section 110(1)(2) of the US Copyright Act. See also Article 10(2) of the Berne Convention and Article 5(3)(a) of the E.C. Copyright in the Information Society Directive.

[638] Sections 37–44A of the UK CDPA 88 and Section 108 of the US Copyright Act.

[639] Goldstein et al. (n 141) 387. ·

[640] Section 112(a) of the US Copyright Act, Section 31(1) of the UK CDPA 88. The incidental inclusion under the UK CDPA 88 applies to an artistic work, sound recording, film or broadcast. See also Article 11bis (3) and Article 5(2)(d) of the E.C. Copyright in the Information Society Directive.

[641] Section 117(a)(1)(2) of the US Copyright Act. See also Article 5(1)(2) of the E.C. Software Directive.

left to case law to explain the nature and extent of activities which unauthorized activities is likely to be 'fair'.[642]

10. CONCLUSION

The analysis undertaken in this chapter has identified the potential for certain space activities to fall outside the scope of copyright protection. Owing to their special nature, it is unclear whether particular space-related activities meet certain copyright thresholds, and this lack of clarity gives rise to uncertainty of outcome. For example, in the case of remote sensing data, it remains arguable whether raw, or primary, data would meet the requirement for originality. For similar reasons, scholarly opinion is divided as to whether remote sensing data is an authorial work which results from creative human intellectual activity, or whether it is merely a computer-generated work, which may be ineligible for protection. Clarity as to the extent to which national copyright law is applicable extraterritorially, in the absence of rules regarding jurisdiction and choice of law, is critical. This represents the most important issue which nations need to resolve, and a proposal for an international agreement which provides a specific legal regime for copyright and space activities has been suggested.[643] The next chapter will analyze whether and to what extent private international law can address the problems identified in this chapter.

---

[642] See, for instance, *Sony Corp. of America v. Universal City Studios, Inc.* 464 U.S. 417, 104 S.Ct. 774 (1984); *Harper & Row Publishers, Inc. v. Nation Enterprises* 471 U.S. 539, 105 S.Ct. 2218 (1985); Hubbard v. Vosper [1972] 2 QB 84, *Newspaper Licensing Agency v. Marks & Spencer plc* [1999] EMLR 369.

[643] Sterling (n 483) 32 and K. de la Durantaye et al., 'Space Oddities: Copyright Law and Conflict of Laws in Outer Space' (2014) 9 *Journal of Intellectual Property Law and Practice* 521, 529.

5. Intellectual property rights and private international law

As discussed in the foregoing chapters, certain works created in outer space qualify for patent and copyright protection. While intellectual property law is territorial, use of space-created works normally involves an international element. This leads to questions of jurisdiction and choice of law, both in terms of validity and infringement.

Issues of jurisdiction and choice of law fall under the area of the private international law, which is also known as the conflict of laws.[644] When a legal dispute involves a foreign element, private international law comes into play. Normally, foreign elements in a dispute may arise from foreign domicile, multi-nationalities of parties and a foreign location in terms of the place where a harmful event occurs or where any resulting damage is experienced. There is no doubt that when cases involving foreign elements take place on earth, private international law rules will be applicable. However, in the case of a dispute arising in outer space – where no state can claim its territory – it is questionable whether private international law rules will have a role.

Part 1 of this chapter concerns issues of proper jurisdiction. The analysis will examine which court can assert its jurisdiction over particular disputes. Having determined which courts are competent to assume jurisdiction, Part 2 addresses issues regarding choice of law. Finally, Part 3 deals with recognition of judgments issued by foreign courts. The hypothetical cases established in the previous chapters will also be used for discussion in this chapter. This particular study will only focus on civil jurisdiction; criminal jurisdiction is beyond the scope of this research.

---

[644] James Fawcett and Janeen M. Carruthers, *Cheshire, North and Fawcett: Private International Law* (14th ed., OUP 2008) 16–18.

1. JURISDICTION

A choice of forum arises whenever a dispute involves 'international' elements. For example, a team of research scientists of different nationalities (UK, US and Thailand) invents a new piece of apparatus in outer space. On their return to earth, each of them files a patent application at their own national patent office, and each names themselves as the sole patent applicant. Given these circumstances, any ensuing entitlement dispute among the co-inventors will involve which courts have jurisdiction to hear the case. Alternatively, if third parties in France, Germany and Singapore each use the invention without consent, which forums have jurisdiction to adjudicate a patent infringement claim – the courts where the infringements occurred (France, Germany and Singapore) or the courts where the patents were registered (UK, USA and Thailand)? Questions such as these are resolved by applying of private international law rules. However, in a scenario in which an invention is devised or infringed in outer space, can any court claim its jurisdiction over the case? Patent cases present two jurisdictional issues: relating to the validity of a patent and infringement proceedings.

Similar issues arise in copyright-based disputes. For example, if a copyright-protected broadcast is intercepted by an unauthorized third party as the satellite signal is being transmitted from Thailand, and if that third party re-broadcasts the protected work on to a number of countries worldwide, which court can assert jurisdiction to determine the right holder's claim of infringement?

In these examples, it seems very likely that more than one court could assert their jurisdiction, but this could then lead to irreconcilable judgments and forum shopping. These issues will be examined using the hypothetical cases introduced previously as the point of discussion. In each case, for a court to have impetus to determine whether it has proper jurisdiction, there must be some connection which links either a person or an event to that particular forum. The establishment of jurisdiction is generally based either upon a connection to the domicile of the defendant, or on the subject matter of the case. The former is known as the 'general rule' of jurisdiction, whereas the latter is termed 'special jurisdiction'. The jurisdictional rules of the United States and the United Kingdom will be examined to investigate whether courts in these countries can assert their jurisdiction in respect of cases concerning IP rights in outer space activities.

1.1 Personal Jurisdiction (General Jurisdiction)

Generally, a national court will have 'personal' jurisdiction to adjudicate a case if a defendant is domiciled or resident in that forum's state. Domicile or residence is the most common connecting factors which establish personal jurisdiction. This requires the physical presence of the defendants in the forum. In the United States, personal jurisdiction can be asserted without the physical presence of the defendants in the forum by using the rule of minimum-contacts. The authority of courts to adjudicate on cases brought against 'home' defendants is derived from both statutory provisions and case-law. We shall now start with an examination of issues exercising personal jurisdiction in respect of disputes relating to outer space activities.

1.1.1 United States

In the United States, a court can assert its general jurisdiction over a defendant who is either domiciled in the forum or who is conducting business in the forum. Here, personal jurisdiction is established upon the Due Process Clauses in the US Constitution.[645] Actual physical presence within a state represents an important factor when establishing personal jurisdiction, following the US Supreme Court ruling in *Pennoyer v. Neff*.[646] Subsequently, the US courts have developed personal jurisdiction over non-resident defendants insofar as temporary presence in a forum state may constitute sufficient basis for personal jurisdiction. Further, in *Burnham v. Superior Court*,[647] it was held that a court can assert personal jurisdiction over a non-resident who was personally served with process while temporarily present in the state, even though the purpose of his presence was unrelated to the matter in dispute before the court.

Also, personal jurisdiction is sometimes exercised over an out-of-state defendant. At present, most of US states have 'long-arm' statutes which permit state courts to assert personal jurisdiction over a non-resident defendant,[648] provided certain requirements under the statutory provision

---

[645] Due Process Clause of the Fourteenth Amendment (US Constitution) (1865), Trevor C. Hartley, *International Commercial Litigation* (1st ed., Cambridge University Press 2009) 136–137, R.D. Rees, 'Plaintiff Due Process Rights in Assertions of Personal Jurisdiction' (2003) 78 *NYU Law Review* 405, 405–406.

[646] 95 U.S. 714, 729 (1877).

[647] 495 U.S. 604 (1990).

[648] Jay Kesan, 'Personal Jurisdiction in Cyberspace: Brief Summary of Personal Jurisdiction Law' 2, <http://www.cyberspacelaw.org/kesan/kesan1.html> and <http://mycivpro.pbworks.com/w/page/21954161/cyberspace-jurisdiction>

and Constitutional Due Process requirements are properly met.[649] Also, the 'minimum contact' rule, discussed below, establishes another way for a court to establish jurisdiction over an out-of-state defendant.

In *International Shoe Co. v. Washington*,[650] the US Supreme Court ruled that a forum state may assert its jurisdiction if it appears that a defendant has at least a minimum level of contact with that state and provided that exercise of such jurisdiction is not contrary to fairness and substantial justice. This particular case questioned whether a defendant company incorporated in Delaware and having a principal place of business in Missouri could be sued in the state of Washington, since a number of employed salesmen operated there, selling products under the supervision of a manager based in Missouri. It was ruled that this connection to Washington state satisfied a 'minimum contacts' requirement and this established valid grounds for recognizing personal jurisdiction. In *Akro Corp. v. Ken Luker*[651] the Federal Circuit court established a three-prong test for determining personal jurisdiction, requiring purposefully directed activities, a relationship between those directed activities and the cause of action, and the constitutional reasonableness of jurisdiction.[652] In *Burger King Corp. v. Rudzewicz*,[653] an out-of-state franchisee defendant sent payments to the plaintiff franchisor's office in Florida and received training from the plaintiff in Florida. The US Court was satisfied that these circumstances established sufficient contact between the defendant and Florida for the Florida court to exercise personal jurisdiction over the defendants in this case. In *World Film Services v. RAI Radiotelevisione Italiana*,[654] the Court ruled that the fact that the foreign corporation defendant held a local subsidiary operating within forum was enough to establish that the defendant was 'doing business' in the forum and thus justify personal jurisdiction. In *Asahi Metal Industry Co. v. Superior Court*, a foreign corporation's awareness that a faulty product which it supplied could end up in the

---

(accessed 3 February 2014 and 12 March 2016, respectively). Roberto Garza Barbosa, 'International Copyright Law and Litigation: A Mechanism for Improvement' (2007) 11 *Marquette Intellectual Property Law Review* 78, 106–107.

[649]   Barbosa (n 648) 107.
[650]   326 U.S. 310 (1945) 316.
[651]   45 F. 3d 1541,1545 (Fed.Cir 1995).
[652]   Fritz Blumer, 'Patent Law and International Private Law on Both Sides of the Atlantic' (WIPO Forum on Private International Law and Intellectual Property, Geneva, January 2001) (WIPO/PIL/01/3) 25.
[653]   471 U.S. 462 (1985).
[654]   50 U.S.Q.2d 1187 (S.D.N.Y. 1999).

forum state was held sufficient to satisfy the requirement for minimum contacts under the Due Process Clause.[655]

Thus, a plaintiff must demonstrate that a defendant has a minimum level of contact with any particular forum in order to establish personal jurisdiction in the case of a non-resident defendant. Courts will determine this on a case-by-case basis. Several decided cases which involved foreign defendants demonstrated insufficient contact with a US forum to establish personal jurisdiction. For instance, in *World-Wide Volkswagen Corp. v. Woodson*,[656] the out-of-state defendant was a distributor and car dealer who neither sold cars nor conducted any business in the forum state. Here, the likelihood that the defendant's products might find its way into the forum state was held insufficient to establish personal jurisdiction.[657] In another case, the fact that a website illustrating the product was accessible within the forum state, was insufficient ground for establishing jurisdiction, because the website did not allow an online transaction with the forum to take place.[658]

The ability of US courts to assert personal jurisdiction over a defendant without requiring their physical presence in the forum could prove to be advantageous if US courts are called upon to adjudicate cases relating to outer space activities, where the defendant is not domiciled in any country, but has a sufficient level of contact with the United States.

1.1.2 United Kingdom

Since the United Kingdom is a European Union (EU) member state, jurisdictional rules previously developed under English common law have been replaced by European Union law in circumstances where the defendant is domiciled in the United Kingdom, another EU member state, or in a state which is party to the Lugano Convention.[659] The traditional English common law rules still apply to defendants domiciled in non-EU or Lugano countries. This means that it is necessary to consider both the relevant European Union law on jurisdiction, as well as traditional English rules.

---

[655] 480 U.S. 102 (1987).

[656] 444 U.S. 286 (1980).

[657] Ibid.

[658] *Westcode v. RBE Electronics*, 2000 U.S. Dist. LEXIS 815 (E.D. Pa. Feb. 1, 2000).

[659] Hartley (n 645) 77.

1.1.2.1 Brussels regime   With the EU, the Brussels regime allocates jurisdiction as between European Union countries. Although the complete regime consists of the Brussels Convention,[660] the Brussels I Regulation (recast)[661] and the Lugano Convention,[662] since the basic principles of all three instruments are very similar, we shall base our study on the Brussels I Regulation (recast), as being both the most important and most recent of the legislation. However, since the Brussels I Regulation[663] still continues to apply to proceedings instituted before the recast came into force on 10 January 2015,[664] the provisions of the Brussels I Regulation, which are similar to those of the Brussels I Regulation (recast), will also be cited in footnotes for further reference.

The Brussels I Regulation (recast) applies in the case where a defendant is domiciled in the EU member state. However, where a defendant is not present in any member state, jurisdiction is determined based upon the domestic jurisdiction rule of the forum,[665] such that when the defendant is domiciled within the UK, an English court will apply the English traditional common law rules to determine whether it has power to hear the case.

Article 4 of the Brussels I Regulation (recast)[666] provides the general rule that a defendant domiciled in a member state shall be sued in the court of that Member State, regardless of their nationality.[667] However, there are exceptions to this general jurisdiction rule. Article 7(1) provides that in a dispute relating to a contract, a person domiciled in one member state may be sued in another member state which is the place that performs the contract.[668] A second exception is provided in Article 7(2) of the recast. This provides that in a dispute relating to tort, a defendant

---

[660]   The Brussels Convention of 27 September 1968 on Jurisdiction and the Enforcement of Judgments in Civil and Commercial Matters (OJ 1978 L 304).

[661]   Regulation (EU) No. 1215/2012 of the European Parliament and of the Council of 12 December 2012 on jurisdiction and the recognition and enforcement of judgments in civil and commercial matters (recast).

[662]   The Lugano Convention of 16 September 1988 on Jurisdiction and the Enforcement of Judgments in Civil and Commercial Matters (OJ 1988 L 319).

[663]   Council Regulation (EC) No 44/2001 of 22 December 2000 on Jurisdiction and the Recognition and Enforcement of Judgments in Civil and Commercial Matters (2001) OJ L12/1.

[664]   See Article 66 of the recast.

[665]   Article 6 of the Brussels I Regulation (recast).

[666]   Article 2 of the Brussels I Regulation.

[667]   See Articles 62 and 63 of the Brussels I Regulation (recast) for further elaboration on domicile (Articles 59 and 60 of the Brussels I Regulation).

[668]   Article 5(1) of the Brussels I Regulation.

may be sued in the state where the place of harmful event occurred.[669] In addition, Article 24(4) of the recast determines an exclusive jurisdiction in disputes relating to the validity of IP rights. Here jurisdiction vests in the courts of the state where the IP right is registered or deposited, notwithstanding that no party to the dispute is domiciled in any member state.[670] These rules establish 'special jurisdiction' as exceptions to the general jurisdiction rule, which will be discussed in a subsequent section devoted to this topic.

1.1.2.2 English traditional rules The jurisdiction of the forum based upon where the defendant is domiciled is also entrenched in the traditional English common law rules.[671] Under these traditional rules, the English court has jurisdiction in three circumstances: (1) the defendant is present in England when the action is served; (2) the defendant submits to the jurisdiction of the court; and (3) the claim falls under the scope of para 3.1 of the Practice Directive 6B of the Civil Procedure Rules, and the court gives the permission to serve the claim form out of the jurisdiction.[672] However, in this sub-section, we shall only address the first two options, as service out of jurisdiction will be considered later in a sub-section relating to tort disputes involving multiple parties.[673]

Service of a claim form within the jurisdiction applies either when the defendant is present in the forum, or where the defendant submits to the court's jurisdiction.

In the case of an intellectual property dispute, the English Court is competent to determine a case when the defendant, either a natural or legal person, is present within the jurisdiction, even if this is only temporarily and irrespective of the nationalities of the parties or place of infringement.[674] Consider the following example.

Astronaut B (a US resident) writes a book while in the International Space Station. Businessman A (a Thai resident) visits London on business. During his stay, he copies B's book, and uploads this unauthorized copy of the book to his website in Thailand. In this case, the High

---

[669] Article 5(3) of the Brussels I Regulation.

[670] Article 22(4) of the Brussels I Regulation.

[671] Abla Mayss, *Principles of Conflict of Laws* (3rd ed., Cavendish Publishing 1999) 58.

[672] C.M.V. Clarkson et al., *The Conflict of Laws*, (4th ed., OUP 2011) 102–103.

[673] See below Section 1.2.3.2.

[674] *Maharanee of Baroda v Wildenstein* [1972] 2QB 283. See also C.M.V. Clarkson (n 672) 102–103.

Court in London would have authority to determine allegations of copyright infringement brought by Astronaut B against Businessman A, even though this case has no subject-matter connection with the UK. Here, A's presence in the UK while committing infringement establishes a sufficient point of attachment to the forum.

The English court also has power to adjudicate any case where the defendant submits to the jurisdiction of the court. When the defendant is willing for the English court to determine a dispute, both the nationality of the parties and the place of infringement are irrelevant. This may be relevant in the case of a dispute relating to outer space activities.

1.2   Subject-Matter Jurisdiction (Specific Jurisdiction)

Special rules exist which allow courts to adjudicate cases despite an absence of personal jurisdiction. Here, there must be an appropriate connecting factor between the cause of action and the forum to justify assertion of this special jurisdiction.[675] An alternative basis for a court to assume jurisdiction is based upon a connection between the subject matter of the dispute and the forum. In this sub-section, we shall focus on when special jurisdiction arises in particular circumstances.

1.2.1   Jurisdiction in case of validity

Article 24 of the Brussels I Regulation (recast) provides for an exclusive jurisdiction, which overrides consideration of the defendant's domicile. This means that when this provision applies, a non-EU resident will be subject to the exclusive jurisdiction of an EU court.[676] We are concerned with Article 24(4) of the Regulation. In the case of a dispute which relates to a validity or registration of a registered or deposited IP rights, Article 24(4) provides exclusive jurisdiction to the court where the IP right in dispute was registered or deposited.[677] As this exclusive jurisdiction clause applies to the registerable IP rights only, copyright and other unregistered IP rights fall outside the scope of this provision. However, for registered IP right this exclusive jurisdiction rule is mandatory, and so the parties cannot agree between themselves to derogate from it.[678]

---

[675]   Hartley (n 645) 40.

[676]   Ibid 70.

[677]   Article 22(4) of the Brussels I Regulation.

[678]   Article 25(4) of the Brussels I Regulation (recast), (Article 23(5) of the Brussels I Regulation), see more in Luigi Fumagalli, 'Litigating Intellectual

It is also significant that infringement proceedings relating to registered IP rights are not governed by Article 24(4), but by the general rules of the Regulation. However, since a defendant in an IP infringement case will typically defend infringement allegations by raising issues of validity in a counterclaim, it is necessary to consider whether the court designated under Article 22(4) would be competent to hear the case in such circumstances. In *GAT v. LuK*,[679] a patent infringement claim based upon a French patent was brought before a German Court, where the alleged infringement had occurred. In their defense, the defendant claimed that the patent in suit was invalid, and whether the German Court had proper jurisdiction according to the Regulation was contested. The CJEU confirmed that as French patent rights were relied upon in the claim, the French courts had exclusive jurisdiction to determine the case, since the patent was registered in France, notwithstanding the location where the infringement took place. The exclusive jurisdiction rule in Article 24(4) (previously Article 22(4)) empowered the relevant court to determine every case of validity of those registered IP rights, irrespective of the manner in which the validity was challenged.

The CJEU clarified in *Duijnstee v. Goderbauer*[680] that the phrase 'proceedings concerned with the registration and validity' of patents or other registered IP rights caught by Article 24(4) (previously Article 22(4)) does not cover claims related either to initial ownership or attribution of ownership in case of employee inventions.

It is therefore noted that the exclusive jurisdiction provided under Article 24(4) of the Brussels I Regulation (recast) only limits an EU national court's jurisdiction when determining validity of nationally registered IP rights which are registered within its forum.

This exclusive jurisdiction, however, does not explicitly exist under the US jurisdictional rule. But here instead, the Court of the country of registration may seize jurisdiction to hear a claim on its merit based upon subject-matter jurisdiction.[681] Therefore, there is no specific problem when applying exclusive jurisdiction to intellectual property rights in

---

Property Rights Disputes Cross-Border: Jurisdiction and Recognition of Judgments Under the Brussels I Regulation' in Stefania Bariatti (ed.), *Litigating Intellectual Property Rights Disputes Cross-Border: EU Regulations, ALI Principles, CLIP Project* (Wolters Kluwer Italia Srl, 2010) 19.

[679] Case C–4/03 (13 July 2006).

[680] Case C–288/32 (15 Nov 1983).

[681] See 28 U.S.C. 1338(a). This provision states that courts have jurisdiction over patents, trademarks and copyrights. The scope of application is wider than that of Article 24(4) of the Brussels I Regulation (recast).

outer space cases, since the point of attachment is based upon the place where the relevant IP rights are registered.

1.2.2   Jurisdiction in the *forum delicti*

While the Brussels I Regulation (recast) establishes a specific and exclusive jurisdiction in certain disputes relating to intellectual property rights, in the remaining circumstances, jurisdiction will be determined based upon *forum delicti*. *Forum delicti* establishes jurisdiction by connecting a particular forum to the place where the infringement takes place. Owing to the territorial nature of IP rights, national courts generally only assert jurisdiction over allegations of infringement concerning IP rights conferred by their domestic laws, and thus protection is only given to unauthorized acts taking place within their territories.[682] This raises the question of whether a national court can establish jurisdictions based upon *forum delicti* if the alleged infringement occurs in outer space.

1.2.2.1   United States   A connection between a cause of action and the forum does not entitle US Courts explicitly to assume jurisdiction over a case. Rather, US Courts tend to assert jurisdiction in a case where the Court appears to have *both* personal jurisdiction and subject-matter jurisdiction.[683] Even if a US Court finds it has personal jurisdiction, it will not hear a case if it does not also have subject-matter jurisdiction.

The United States is a federal country which operates both state and federal courts. As a first step, a US court has to determine whether the dispute before them falls within the jurisdiction of a state or federal court. The Federal Court circuit has subject-matter jurisdiction over any disputes arising under the US Copyright Act or the US Patent Act, whereas disputes arising from contractual arrangements concerning IP rights (for example, patent and copyright assignments or licenses) fall within the jurisdiction of state courts.[684] In any claim involving foreign intellectual property rights, a US Court will establish its supplemental jurisdiction by virtue of 28 U.S.C. 1367.[685]

---

[682]   Dinwoodie (n 624) 733.
[683]   Toshiyuki Kono ed., *Intellectual Property and Private International Law Comparative Perspectives* (Hart Publishing 2012) 22.
[684]   28 U.S.C. 1338(a) 2006. Under this section, the federal district courts have 'original jurisdiction of any civil action arising under any Act of Congress relating to patents, plant variety protection, copyrights and trade-marks'.
[685]   28 U.S.C. 1367 states that 'in any civil action of which the district courts have original jurisdiction, the district courts shall have supplemental jurisdiction

Although the specific test for jurisdiction over a tort claim, such as trademark infringement, varies from state to state, under a typical state 'long-arm' statute, jurisdiction for a trademark claim against a non-resident defendant is normally based upon the state in which the harm occurs.[686] Furthermore, if an infringing act is committed in the forum, a US Court will assert its jurisdiction, regardless of the quantum of harm which results from that infringement. For instance, a US Court exercised its jurisdiction over a defendant, even though only a single unauthorized copy had been distributed with that forum.[687]

In *Itar-Tass Russian News Agency v. Russian Kurier Inc.*,[688] the defendant copied substantial parts of the plaintiff's published news reports and circulated them in New York. The US Court asserted subject-matter jurisdiction over the case, since unauthorized use took place in the United States.

In *Mars Inc. v. Nippon Conlux Kabushiki-Kaisha*,[689] a US Court declined a case based upon lack of subject-matter jurisdiction. Here, the plaintiff alleged that the defendant had infringed its US and Japanese patents which related to 'coin changing' apparatus used in vending machines to distinguish between genuine and counterfeit coins, and to distinguish among coins of different value. The defendant manufactured similar coin changers in Japan and exported them for sale in the United States. The US Court of Appeals ruled that the US District Court lacked subject-matter jurisdiction to determine allegations of infringement of the Japanese patent based upon both original jurisdiction[690] and supplemental jurisdiction,[691] despite the fact that the US and Japanese patents covered equivalent subject matter. The Court reasoned that 'a claim of infringement of a foreign patent does not constitute a claim of unfair competition within the meaning of section 1338(b)'[692] and 'the foreign patent

---

over all other claims that are so related to claims in the action within such original jurisdiction that they form part of the same case or controversy under Article III of the United States Constitution'.

[686] *Worldwide Volkswagen* (n 656), *Asahi Metal Industry* (n 655).

[687] *Blue Ribbon Pet Prods. v. Hagen Corp.*, 66 F.Supp.2d. 454 (E.D.N.Y. 1999), *Cordon Holding B.V. v. Northwest Publishing Corp.*, 49 U.S.P.Q. 2d 1697 (S.D.N.Y. 1998).

[688] 153 F 3d 82, 47 U.S.P.Q. 2D 1810 (2d Cir 1998).

[689] 24 F.3d 1368, 62 USLW 2720, 30 U.S.P.Q. 2d 1621.

[690] 28 U.S.C. 1338(b).

[691] 28 U.S.C. 1367.

[692] 24 F.3d 1368, at paragraph 16.

infringement claim at issue is not so related to the US patent infringement claim that the claim form part of the same cause or controversy and
would thus ordinarily be expected to be tried in one proceeding'.[693]

In *SubaFilms, Ltd v. MGM-Pathe Communications Co.*,[694] the defendant mistakenly believed that it owned worldwide distribution rights for a
particular videocassette and so authorized its distribution on a worldwide
basis. However, the Court of Appeals held that since US copyright law
has no extra-territorial force, authorization given abroad for distribution
within the United States was insufficient for US courts to assert jurisdiction in respect of any allegations of infringement which occurred
beyond the US border.

1.2.2.2   UK   As mentioned above, when considering the position in the
United Kingdom, it is necessary to consider both the Brussels Regime
and the English jurisdictional rules.

BRUSSELS REGIME   As discussed in Section 1.1.2.1, Article 7 of the
Brussels I Regulation (recast) determines special provisions where a
person domiciled in one EU member state may be sued in another.[695]
Article 7(2) of the Brussels I Regulation (recast) is the provision which is
applicable in cases of claims for infringement of intellectual property
rights. This states that a person domiciled in one member state may be
sued 'in matters relating to tort, delict or quasi-delict, in the Courts for
the place where the harmful event occurred or may occur'.[696]

This provision raises questions as to how 'the place where the harmful
event occurred' is identified; for example in a case where an act is
initiated in one country, but the actual damage takes place in another
country.[697] The relevant place, where the harmful event occurred, has
been widely interpreted to cover both the place where the initiating event
took place and the place where the damages were suffered. In *Handelskwekerij Bier BV v. Mines de Potasse d'Alsace SA*,[698] the CJEU confirmed
that Article 7(2) of the recast (previously Article 5(3)) covered *both*
places, thus giving courts in more than one member state jurisdiction,

---

[693]   24 F.3d 1368, at paragraph 25.
[694]   24 F.3d. 1008 (9th Cir. 1994).
[695]   Article 5 of the Brussels I Regulation.
[696]   Article 5(3) of the Brussels I Regulation. See more details in James J.
Fawcett and Paul Torremans, *Intellectual Property and Private International Law*
(2nd ed., OUP 2011) 150–152.
[697]   Ibid 154–156.
[698]   Case 21/76 [1978] QB 708, [1976] ECR 1735.

and the rights holder a choice of member states in which to commence infringement proceedings.

In *Shevill and Others v. Press Alliances SA*,[699] the CJEU provided further guidance in identifying 'the place where the harmful event occurred'. In this defamation case, newspapers containing an allegedly libelous statement were distributed in a number of contracting states to the Brussels Convention. The Court confirmed that the plaintiffs could either bring their case in the member state where the damage occurred, or in the member state where the event giving rise to that damage – in this case, the place where the newspapers were printed.[700] However, while the Court in the place where the damage occurred would only have jurisdiction to determine damage which occurred in their own jurisdiction, the Court in the member state where the event giving rise to the damage has jurisdiction to adjudicate on the totality of the damage caused by that event, which in this particular case was damage to the victim's reputation.[701] The CJEU ruling identified that the place of the event giving rise to the damage could only be 'the place where the publisher of the newspaper in question is established since that is the place where the harmful event originated and from which the libel was issued and put into circulation'.[702] The Court of the defendant's domicile therefore had jurisdiction to determine the full extent of the damage caused from events originating within its jurisdiction.

However, interpretation of the term 'place where the harmful event occurred' in Article 7(2) (previously Article 5(3)) cannot be stretched to include any place where adverse consequences of that event can be felt, if initial damage was suffered in other member states.[703]

In the two cases: *Edate Advertising v. X*[704] and *Martinez v. MGN Ltd*,[705] the CJEU considered infringement of personal rights arising from publications on the internet. The Court ruled that individuals that were the subject of actionable stories published online not only had the choice to sue the publisher in the state of domicile of the publisher, or in the member state where they, as claimant, had their 'centre of interests', but

---

[699] Case C–68/93 [1995] 2 WLR 499.
[700] Ibid.
[701] Ibid 540.
[702] Ibid.
[703] Case C–364/93 *Antonio Marinari v Lloyds Bank plc and Zubaidi Trading Company* [1995] ECR I–2709, para 14–15. See also Kono (n 683) 55–56.
[704] Case C–509/09.
[705] Case C–161/10.

also in any member state where damage had been suffered as a result of the accessibility of the online content in that member state. Thus, the special jurisdiction under Article 7(2) (previously Article 5(3)) in case of internet infringement of personal rights has a broad reach, covering the place where the publisher is based, the place where the claimant has their 'centre of interests', and the place where the actionable content is accessible.

However, the CJEU has interpreted the 'place where the harmful event occurred' differently in an IP infringement case. In *Wintersteiger*,[706] an Austrian company, owner of an Austrian registered trademark, commenced infringement proceedings in an Austrian Court against a German company. The infringement claim arose from use of the registered mark on a German website, google.de, which was accessible in Austria. The CJEU was asked to determine whether the Austrian Court had proper jurisdiction under Article 7(2) (previously Article 5(3)). Here the alleged infringement took place when the Austrian trademark was used as a keyword by unauthorized advertisers to trigger their adverts on the German website when users entered the Austrian trademark into the search engine. Here, the CJEU ruled that 'the place where the damage occurred' in case of infringement of a registered trademark could only be the place where the particular mark had been registered, whereas the 'place of the event giving rise to the damage' would be the place where the advertiser was established. In this regard, the CJEU opined that the place where an offending advertisement was *displayed* (in this case was Austria) was not relevant to Article 7(2) (previously Article 5(3)) analysis.[707] Thus, the mere fact that a website is accessible in a particular member state is not sufficient in itself to establish jurisdiction under Article 7(2) (previously Article 5(3)). Hence, in the case of litigation relating to trademark infringement occurring in online content, both the Courts of the member states where the trademark is registered, and the member state where the defendant is established, have jurisdiction to determine the case.

More recently, the CJEU has considered interpretation of Article 7(2) (previously Article 5(3)) in the case of online copyright infringement. The case of *Pinckney v. KDG Mediatech AG*[708] concerned the plaintiff's claim for damages arising from the infringement of its copyright in 12 songs which were copied without consent by the defendant, established

---

[706] Case C–523/10 (19 April 2012).
[707] Ibid, paragraph 34.
[708] Case C–170/12, (3 Oct 2013).

in Austria, and then marketed by two British companies through various internet websites which were accessible in France, where the plaintiff was resident. The defendant challenged the French court's jurisdiction.

The CJEU determined that in the case of copyright infringement in these circumstance, (copyright is protected in the member state of the Court seized and online infringement occurs on a website accessible in that member state, but copyright infringement proceedings are brought against a defendant domiciled in another member state), Article 7(2) (previously Article 5(3)) limits the damages recoverable to damage caused in that particular member state only. Thus, in the particular case, the French court has jurisdiction to hear the claim and award compensation for damages caused by the infringement only in France. Thus, the CJEU has established a different precedent with copyright than for registered trademarks. However, since copyright protection arises automatically without registration, this different interpretation is justifiable. Given that within the EU copyright protection is already established in the court seized, in my view, the CJEU ruling in *Pinckey* does not conflict with its stance in *Wintersteiger*.

The allocation of jurisdiction to any court where damage has occurred may lead to forum shopping in situations where damage has occurred in multiple EU states. For instance, in the case of an infringement of a satellite broadcast, all countries falling under the satellite's footprint would be interpreted as places of infringement, and thus the Courts of all these countries are competent to hear an infringement case. Nevertheless, any national court's jurisdiction to award damages is limited only to the damage suffered in that forum, whereas the Court of the member state where the harmful event originates has power to award full compensation for all damage which results from the unauthorized broadcast.[709]

ENGLISH RULES   Pursuant to PD 6B paragraph 3.1, an English Court has the power to assert its jurisdiction in a case where the defendant is neither present in the forum nor submits to the jurisdiction, provided that the such claim meets three requirements set forth in this provision. Firstly, the claimant must show that their claim falls within one of the heads of jurisdiction contained within PD 6B paragraph 3.1. Secondly, the claimant must have a reasonable prospect of success; and finally the court needs to exercise its discretion to allow service of a claim form out of the jurisdiction. The relevant rules in case of IP infringement are PD 6B paragraph 3.1 (9), (3) and (2).

---

[709]   *Shevill* (n 699).

The provision which empowers an English court to assert its jurisdiction for service out in case of tort is stated in CPR PD 6B para 3.1(9). A claim in tort is permitted to be served out if: (a) damage was sustained within the jurisdiction or (b) the damage sustained resulted from an act committed within the jurisdiction. It is noted that the special jurisdiction under CPR PD 6B para 3.1(9) is identical to that of Article 7(2) of the Brussels I Regulation (recast).

1.2.3   Jurisdiction in case of multiple defendants

It is highly likely that an outer space IP dispute would involve multi-state claims, like that of a cross-border IP dispute. Thus, a consolidation of proceedings would appear to be an efficient measure for any such litigation. This section will examine whether a consolidation of proceedings is likely to be possible in the case of multiple-party outer space IP claims under the present rules of the two jurisdictions under consideration.

1.2.3.1   United States   Any assertion of jurisdiction over multiple defendants such that a co-defendant could be sued in a court where any other co-defendant is domiciled would be unconstitutional in the United States.[710] This is because the US requirement of minimum contact has to be met separately by each defendant.[711] Application of this rule is illustrated by the case: *Helicopteros Nacionales de Colombia v. Hall.*[712] Here a number of out-of-state defendants were sued in the same proceedings for injuries caused in a helicopter crash. In this case, WSH, an American company with its headquarters in Texas, established a Peruvian consortium, Consorcio, based in Peru to build an oil pipeline. WSH and Consorcio contracted with Helicol, a Colombian company, to provide helicopter transport services, and one of Helicol's helicopters crashed in Peru. The families of American victims killed in that accident brought proceedings against WSH, Consorcio and Helicol before a court in Texas. That court ruled that it had no jurisdiction over Helicol, since its contact with the Texan forum was insufficient to satisfy the minimum contact requirement. This case demonstrates how a foreign defendant, having neither domicile nor residence in the US, benefits from the protection of 'minimum contacts'.

---

[710]   Hartley (n 645) 63.

[711]   Ibid.

[712]   466 U.S. 408 (1984), see the analysis of this case in ibid 142–144.

The result of the case would have been different if the Texas connection was replaced with an English one, such that jurisdiction would be allocated under the Brussels I Regulation (recast) and English Traditional Rules. Here, a foreign defendant could be sued in forum provided that an 'anchor' defendant is domiciled in England.[713]

1.2.3.2   UK

BRUSSELS REGIME   Article 8(1) of the Regulation also allows a claimant to sue two or more joint defendants in a single court.[714] This article enables a court of one member state where one defendant is domiciled to assume jurisdiction over another defendant who is domiciled in another member state, provided 'the claims' against the two defendants 'are closely connected that it is expedient to hear and determine them together to avoid the risk of irreconcilable judgments resulting from separate proceedings'.[715]

In *Kalfelis v. Bankhaus Schroder*, the CJEU ruled that the jurisdiction pursuant to Article 8(1) was an exception to the general jurisdiction of the court in which a defendant is domiciled, as set out in Article 4 (previously Article 2) of the Brussels I Regulation (recast).[716] However, the special jurisdiction of Article 8(1) is not applicable in the case of infringement of a bundle of national rights under a European patent. In *Roche Nederland v. Primus*,[717] proceedings were launched against a Dutch company and its eight subsidiaries for infringement of parallel national patents in the Netherlands and in other European countries. The CJEU denied a consolidation of proceedings since there was no risk of irreconcilable judgments within the meaning of Article 8(1) of the Brussels I Regulation (recast). Although the alleged infringing products were identical in each case, the unauthorized acts were conducted by different parties in different member states, and issues concerning whether such use amounted to infringement of each national patent was to be determined according to different national law. Thus, neither the factual nor legal situations were the same, as is necessary to give rise to a consolidation of the separate claims.

---

[713]   See below on the Brussels Regime and English rules.
[714]   Article 6(1) of the Brussels I Regulation.
[715]   Article 8(1) of the Brussels I Regulation (recast).
[716]   C–189/87 [1988] ECR 5565 para 8.
[717]   C–539/03.

However, a different decision was reached in the case of *Solvay v. Honeywell*.[718] Here, Solvay, the proprietor of a European patent registered in a number of member states, sued the defendants for infringement of the national parts of the patent in force in several European Union countries. The facts in this case were different from the *Roche* case, because in this case, the co-defendants infringed the same national part of the European patents in at least one EU member state. The CJEU ruled that separate proceedings for infringement of the same national part of the European patent in different national courts may result in different judgments. Thus, it was reasonable to join claims before a single court, so as to avoid the risk of irreconcilable judgments.

ENGLISH RULES   The CPR 6.36 and PD 6B[719] para 3.1(3) grants permission for service out of the jurisdiction if (a) there is, as between the claimant and a first defendant, a real issue to be tried; and (b) the claimant wishes to serve the claim form on another defendant who is a necessary or proper party to that claim.[720]

Under this provision, two requirements have to be met in order to institute a claim against multiple defendants. The first requirement is that there must be a real issue between the claimant and the first defendant ('the anchor'). Secondly, each defendant is a necessary and proper party to the claim. While this provision is similar to Article 8(1) of the Brussels I Regulation (recast), its scope is wider because the 'anchor' defendant can be sued in the forum without requiring them to be domiciled there, and the claims do not have to be closely connected in order to be heard together as required in Article 8(1) of the Brussels I Regulation (recast).[721]

Moreover, CPR PD 6B para 3.1(4) provides that the permission of the court is granted for service out of the jurisdiction for an additional claim under Part 20 (third-party proceedings), where the third party to be served is a necessary or proper party to the claim.

It can be concluded that suing multiple defendants in the same proceedings, even in respect of claims relating to outer space activities, is allowed under the two jurisdictions. This is because the criteria for enjoining cases are the domicile of defendants and the close connection of disputes, which bear no connection to outer space.

---

[718] C–616/10.
[719] Civil Procedure Rules 6.36 and CPR Practice Direction 6B.
[720] Clarkson et al. (n 672) 112–113.
[721] Hartley (n 645) 101.

1.2.4 Jurisdiction in outer space (quasi-territorial jurisdiction)

Since outer space is *res communis*, a place where no state can claim sovereignty,[722] states have already developed certain principles which enable them to seize jurisdiction in outer space.

The general principle is that a state has jurisdiction over people and property within its territory.[723] However, in certain circumstances, an incident may occur beyond a state's border and yet that place is deemed part of its territory. This is the case on board national aircraft flying over a foreign airspace or on a spacecraft in outer space.[724] A vessel (typically understood to mean a ship or aircraft) takes on the nationality of the state in which it is registered, and is subjected to the jurisdiction of that 'flag state'.[725] While international treaties confer nationality in case of ships and aircraft, there is no equivalent space treaty which confers nationality on spacecraft.[726] Thus, in the case of a space object, the connecting factor which links it to a particular state's jurisdiction is its registration. Article VIII of the Outer Space Treaty provides that the State of Registry of a space object 'shall retain jurisdiction and control over such object and over any personnel thereof, while in outer space or on a celestial body'.[727] The jurisdiction of the State of Registry, in the case of a space object, is not the quasi-territorial jurisdiction rule as in the case of ships and aircraft, but is only similar to that of quasi-territorial jurisdiction.[728] Jurisdiction of the State of Registry established under Article VIII only extends to personnel, whereas the nationality jurisdiction established in the case of ships and aircraft extend to everyone on board. Thus, the State of Registry of a space object does not have jurisdiction over other people on board, such as passengers.

The International Government Agreement (IGA) of 1998 provides another legal basis for establishing a state's jurisdiction in outer space. Article 5(2) of the IGA establishes, as between partner states, jurisdiction

---

722 Article 1 of the Outer Space Treaty.
723 Oduntan (n 202) 36.
724 Ibid.
725 Article 91 of the United Nations Convention on the Law of the Sea, Dec. 10, 1982, 1833 U.N.T.S. 3, 397; 21 I.L.M. 1261 (1982) and Article 17 of the Convention on International Civil Aviation signed at Chicago on 7 December 1944.
726 For discussion on nationality of spacecraft, see Cheng (n 26) 482.
727 The 'state of registry' is defined as a 'launching state'. In case there is more than one launching state in respect of a space object, they shall jointly determine which one of them shall register that space object. Articles 1(c) and Article 2(2) of the Registration Convention.
728 Cheng (n 26) 488.

and control of the International Space Station to the state of registry of each individual element of the space station.[729] Regarding the European element of the ISS, the European partners have delegated this responsibility to the European Space Agency.[730] Thus, ESA is the 'state of registry' for any European Partner elements.[731] However, since ESA is an international intergovernmental organization, it is questionable whether ESA can exercise jurisdiction and control as the State of Registry, as set out in Article VIII of the Outer Space Treaty, since Article VIII specifically refers to 'states' to the treaty. Moreover, according to the provisions of the ESA Convention, it does not appear that ESA member states have entrusted ESA with the competence to exercise full jurisdiction and control over space objects which are registered by ESA.[732]

However, Article 21 of the IGA, which exclusively applies to intellectual property matters, establishes a much clearer picture. This provision stipulates that the space elements of the ISS are deemed to be national territory of the relevant partners and, in the case of ESA, the territory of each ESA member state.[733] Thus, in case of intellectual property rights,

---

[729]   Article 5.2 of the IGA states, 'Pursuant to Article VIII of the Outer Space Treaty and Article II of the Registration Convention, each Partner shall retain jurisdiction and control over the elements it registers in accordance with paragraph 1 above and over personnel in or on the space station who are its nationals. The exercise of such jurisdiction and control shall be subject to any relevant provisions of this Agreement, the MOUs, and implementing arrangements, including relevant procedural mechanisms established therein'. The partner states are the USA, the European Space Agency, Canada, Japan and the Russian Federation.

[730]   Article 5.1 of the IGA (n 416).

[731]   Though Article II of the 1978 Registration Convention provides that the launching State is the state which is responsible for the space registration, Article VII (1) of the Convention states that 'in this Convention, reference to States shall be deemed to apply to any international intergovernmental organization which conducts space activities if the organization declares its acceptance of the rights and obligations provided for in this Convention'. ESA's Declaration of Acceptance of the Registration Convention was done on 2 June 1979. See G. Lafferranderie, 'The United States Proposed Patent in Outer Space Legislation: An International Perspective' (1990) 18 *Journal of Space Law* 1, 9.

[732]   Vahrenwald (n 368) 320.

[733]   Article 21(2) of the IGA states, 'Subject to the provisions of this Article, for purposes of intellectual property law, an activity occurring in or on a space station flight element shall be deemed to have occurred only in the territory of the Partner State of that element's registry, except that for ESA registered elements any European Partner State may deem the activity to have occurred within its territory'.

by virtue of Articles 5(2) and 21(2), the State of Registry for each space element has jurisdiction and control over the space object and personnel, and in the case of ESA, each ESA member state is individually competent. Nonetheless, these provisions are only applicable to partner states. The IGA is not binding and so has no effect on non-partner states.[734]

Having established the general principles and reviewed international law, we shall now examine national legislation to determine whether any of the countries under consideration have explicitly implemented this quasi-territorial jurisdiction over its spacecraft.

The United States has exhibited a tendency for asserting quasi-territorial jurisdiction. For example, US courts have asserted quasi-territorial jurisdiction to hear disputes relating to alleged patent infringement based upon unauthorized acts which occurred on board US ships on the high sea. In *Gardiner et al. v. Howe*,[735] a US court deemed that activities which took place on board a US-flag vessel on the high sea was deemed to have taken place in the territory of the United States. Thus, the plaintiff in this case was entitled to damages for infringement of their US patent. As US patent law gives extraterritorial effect to any invention made, used or sold on any US space object,[736] it is assumed that the US Courts' stance on exercising quasi-territorial jurisdiction might extend to infringement of IP rights in a US spacecraft. In contrast, there is no provision on the quasi-territorial jurisdiction in the UK legislation.

1.3 Limitation to Jurisdiction

Although national courts may have, in principle, adjudicative authority to decide a particular case, it is possible that the claim may still be dismissed. The territoriality principle of IP rights is a common reason used by courts in many countries to decline to hear a case which concerns infringement of foreign IP rights, even though the court has jurisdiction to try that case based upon the defendant's domicile or the place of infringement.[737] The doctrine of *forum non conveniens* also

---

[734] See also Section 6 in Chapter 3.
[735] Gardner et al. (n 372).
[736] 35 U.S.C. 105 (n 379).
[737] In *Lucasfilm Ltd v. Andrew Ainsworth* [2009] EWCA Civ 1328, the UK Court declined to deal with a claim concerning the infringement of the US copyright law by arguing that the infringement of foreign copyright is not justiciable. In Thailand, the Thai Supreme Court in its decision no. 3094/

provides a basis to decline jurisdiction. Here, a court determines that despite the fact it could establish jurisdiction, an alternative forum would be a more appropriate one to hear the particular case. It is therefore necessary to examine whether it is possible that courts in the two jurisdictions of interest might refuse to hear an IP case on such grounds.

1.3.1 Foreign IP rights

United States The case of *Voda v. Cordis Corporation*[738] concerned alleged infringement of the plaintiff's US patent rights, as well as equivalent national patents elsewhere. Instead of bringing multiple suits in each country where infringement was suspected, the plaintiff sought the US Court to add the claim of foreign infringement (in the UK, Canada, France and Germany) to his claim for infringement of the US patent claim. The US court declined to consider the claim for infringement of foreign patents on the basis that it lacked subject-matter jurisdiction over any foreign patent claim.[739] The court also rejected the notion that its supplemental jurisdiction could be used to bring foreign patents before a US court.[740]

2549(2006) refused to enforce a claim relating to the infringement of the US patent against the defendants on the ground of the territoriality of the patent regardless of the facts that the defendants were domiciled in the forum and that the infringements took place in the forum.

[738]   476 F.3d 887 (Fed. Cir 2007).

[739]   Ibid.

[740]   See also *Mars Inc.* (n 689) in which the US court refused to hear foreign patent claims due to lack of subject-matter jurisdiction. It was arguable whether the US Courts have subject-matter jurisdiction over foreign patent infringement claims under the provisions of 28 U.S.C. 1338 (b) which reads, 'The district courts shall have original jurisdiction of any civil action asserting a claim of unfair competition when joined with a substantial and related claim under the copyright, patent, plant variety protection or trademark laws'. and 28 U.S.C. 1367(a) which stipulates, 'Except as provided in subsections (b) and (c) or as expressly provided otherwise by Federal statute, in any civil action of which the district courts have original jurisdiction over all other claims that are so related to claims in the action within such original that they form part of the same case or controversy under Article III of the United States Constitution'. See more in Marko Schauwecker, 'Extraterritorial Patent Jurisdiction: Can One Sue in Europe for Infringement of a U.S. Patent?' TTLF Working Paper No. 10 (2011) 5–11 <https://www.law.stanford.edu/sites/default/files/publication/205085/doc/slspublic/schauwecker_wp10.pdf> (accessed 12 March 2016).

United Kingdom In several cases, UK courts also seemed to dismiss cases concerning non-UK IP rights. In *Coin Controls v. Suzo International et al.*,[741] for example, a dispute concerning infringement of foreign patent rights, the High Court declined jurisdiction based upon public policy considerations which the court felt prevented it from adjudicating foreign IP right. Similarly, in *Tyburn v. Conan Doyle*,[742] the High Court ruled that it had no jurisdiction to hear an action which asserted US copyright and trademarks in the Sherlock Holmes and Dr. Watson characters.

In *Lucasfilm Ltd. v. Ainsworth*,[743] the Court of Appeal held that English Court had no power to adjudicate a dispute concerning a claim for infringement of US copyright, even though the alleged infringer was domiciled in England. However, this finding was later overturned by the UK Supreme Court, which held that it was justifiable for an English court to assume jurisdiction in a case concerning foreign copyright, provided that the court had personal jurisdiction over the defendant.[744]

Subsequent to the *Lucasfilm* decision, English courts are now more inclined to assert jurisdiction over claims which relate to foreign intellectual property rights. The recent case of *Actavis Group HF v. Eli Lilly and Company*[745] concerned a patented cancer treatment, Pemetrexed, owned by Eli Lilly. Actavis, wanting to launch an equivalent *pemetrexed dipotassium* product in UK and elsewhere in Europe, applied to the High Court seeking a declaration of non-infringement, not only for the UK designation of Eli Lilly's European patent, but also in respect of the equivalent French, German, Italian and Spanish designations, too. Overturning the High Court's refusal, the Court of Appeal applied the *Lucasfilm* reasoning and ruled in favor of Actavis, holding that English courts did have jurisdiction to adjudicate in respect of both the UK and non-UK patents.

1.3.2 *Forum non conveniens*

As mentioned above, even though a Court has jurisdiction over the case, it may still decline its jurisdiction based upon *forum non conveniens*.

---

[741] [1999] Ch 33.
[742] [1991] Ch. 5 (Ch D).
[743] [2011] UK SC 39. See the Court of Appeal decision of this case at [2008] EWHC 1878, [2009] FSR 2, Ch. [2009] EWCA Civ 1328, [2010] FSR 10, CA.
[744] [2011] UK SC 39.
[745] [2013] EWCA Civ 517 (21 May 2013). See also the High Court (Patent Court) decision in this case at [2012] EWHC 3316 (Pat) (High Court 2012).

Although an English court rarely rejects a case on this basis under the English Traditional Rules,[746] a US court is more likely to apply this principle.

In *Gulf Oil Corp. v. Gilbert*,[747] the US Supreme Court established private and public factors, including availability of evidence, convenience and expense of a trial, and difficulty when applying foreign law to a case, to deny jurisdiction on the basis of *forum non conveniens*. Instead of refusing to hear a case, an English court is more likely to grant a stay of proceedings, only if there is an available forum which is more appropriate than the English Court.[748]

In *Andrew Owusu v. N.B. Jackson*, a defendant challenged an English court's jurisdiction on the basis that a Jamaican court was a more suitable forum, since this was the place where the accident causing the dispute had occurred. The CJEU held that an EU court which is exercising jurisdiction under the Brussels I Regulation is precluded 'from declining to exercise jurisdiction on the ground that a court in a non-Contracting State would be a more appropriate forum for the trial of the action'.[749] Thus, *forum non conveniens* is only available to English courts in respect of cases brought under the traditional rules.

1.4 Hypothetical Case

Having identified the relevant principles of jurisdiction under private international law, the principles will be examined further using a series of hypothetical cases. The purpose of these cases is to determine which courts are competent to hear a case. Issues of how courts should proceed in the event of parallel proceedings are beyond the scope of this study.

1.4.1 Case 1 (work created in outer space but infringed on the earth)
A is a US astronaut. While on a Moon walk, Astronaut A films what he can see as he explores the Moon and then broadcasts the results back to earth via a control station located in the United States. As the signal is being transmitted, it is illicitly intercepted and rebroadcast to recipients in the UK and other European countries by Viewer B, a Thai resident.

In this case, since B is a resident of Thailand, the Thai court is competent to try this case as the court of the defendant's domicile in

---

746   Clarkson (n 672) 122–123.
747   330 U.S. 501 (1947).
748   *Spiliada Maritime Corp. v Cansulex Ltd* [1987] AC 460.
749   C–281/02, OC 2005, I–1383, 46.

accordance with Section 4(1) of the Thai Civil Procedural Code.[750] Perhaps surprisingly, UK courts, and courts in other European countries have no jurisdiction over this case even though these are the countries where the unauthorized broadcast took place, such that these are the places where the harmful event occurred. Because jurisdiction based upon Article 7(2) of the recast (previously Article 5(3) of the Brussels I Regulation) requires a defendant to be domiciled in an EU member state, jurisdiction based upon a tortious ground applies only to an EU-domiciled defendant,[751] although the recast version does allow EU courts to adjudicate cases against non-EU defendants in certain situations.[752]

Let us modify the facts. Now assume the defendant in this case is domiciled in an EU member state, and suppose that a motion picture in this case was a work protected by UK copyright law, but the rebroadcast occurred within the EU, but excluding the UK. Can an English court assert jurisdiction in this case, since the case is based upon a UK right whereas the unauthorized act took place outside the UK? In its decision *Def Lepp Music v. Stuart-Brown*,[753] the High Court refused jurisdiction in a similar case where the claimant tried to rely upon UK copyright where the defendant's use was abroad. However, in *John Walker & Sons Ltd v. Ost*,[754] the High Court did assume jurisdiction where, although an act was done in the UK, the damage sustained was abroad. In our hypothetical case, since facts more closely resemble the former case, rather than the latter, such that there might be insufficient connecting factors for an English court to establish jurisdiction in this case. Similarly, US courts have no jurisdiction either, since there is no connecting factor to establish personal jurisdiction over B.

1.4.2 Case 2 (work created on earth, infringed in outer space and on the earth)

B is a Thai national and owner of copyright in a number of songs which were first published in Japan. During a mission to Mars, A, (domiciled in the UK) uploads his favorite of B's songs to an unauthorized file-sharing

---

[750]   See Section 4(1) of the Thai Civil Procedural Code, which states that 'the plaintiff shall submit to the Court within the territorial jurisdiction in which the defendant is domiciled, or to the Court within the territorial jurisdiction of which the cause of action arose, whether the defendant shall have domicile within the Kingdom'.

[751]   See Article 7(2) of the Brussels I Recast.

[752]   See Recital 14 and Article 6 (1) of the Brussels I Recast.

[753]   [1986] R.R.C. 273.

[754]   [1970] 2 All ER 106.

website, making them freely available to download on earth. C, a French national domiciled in France, downloads B's songs to his own computer in a hotel in Denmark. B wishes to bring copyright infringement proceedings against both A and C.

Since both A and C are domiciled within the EU, jurisdiction will be determined by the Brussels I Regulation (recast). Hence, UK and French courts, where A and C are domiciled, respectively, are competent to hear separate proceedings based upon personal jurisdiction pursuant to Article 4 of the recast.

However, given the causal connection between A and C's infringement and the common subject matter, is B able to sue A and C together in a single forum pursuant to Article 8(1) of the recast? To enjoin A and C as co-defendants, the claims against them must be closely connected, and it must be expedient to try them together so as to avoid irreconcilable judgments.[755] In our case, the facts are different even though both defendants have both copied the same copyright work.[756] This is because the place of use is different: A copied the work on Mars in an extraterritorial area, whereas B's copying took place in Denmark. Normally, the general jurisdiction of Article 4 applies, irrespective of where the alleged infringement occurred. This means that the unconventional place of A's activity makes no difference when determining the competence of a court. Whether A's unauthorized copying would be considered an infringement of B's copyright then becomes a matter of substantive law which might differ according to particular national law. Taking account of the territorial nature of copyright, courts might reasonably rule that any action against A is groundless, since copyright law does not extend to Mars. Therefore, given these differences between B's claim against A and C, in my opinion, it is not justifiable to enjoin both A and C in the same proceedings.

C's unauthorized copying of B's song took place in Denmark. Unlike the case against A, this act may be an infringement on the earth where courts may legitimately claim jurisdictions. As discussed above, based upon C's domicile in France, a French court is competent to try this case. The Thai court also has jurisdiction, based upon nationality, since B is

---

[755]   Article 8(1) of the Brussels I Regulation (recast).
[756]   See *Roche Nederland* (n 717). In this case, the CJEU ruled that 'in case of parallel patent rights, factual situations are not the same because different persons are sued in different Member States for varied infringing acts'.

the Thai national.[757] A Danish court might also have jurisdiction, based upon the place where the harmful event takes place.

Although Denmark is a member state of the EU, neither the Brussels Convention nor the Brussels I Regulation (recast) applies to Denmark. Rather, it is the Lugano Convention which is relevant. In addition to Denmark, this Convention applies to the member states of the European Free Trade Association (EFTA). However, the provisions of the Lugano Convention mirror those of the Brussels Convention and Brussels I Regulation (recast), thus applying the Lugano Convention to this hypothetical case, Danish courts also have jurisdiction over C.

Now assume that A was a space tourist in a US spacecraft when he copied B's protected songs. While the United States is the state of registry, it is questionable whether a US court could assert jurisdiction over the case. While Article VIII of the Outer Space Treaty provides jurisdiction and control for the state of registry over such object and any personnel, as previously identified, here the term 'personnel' only includes those who work on board a spacecraft and does not extend to other persons including passengers. For this reason, it is unlikely that a US court could assume jurisdiction based upon its state of registry.[758]

1.4.3 Case 3 (work created in outer space, infringed in outer space)

While on a Moon walk, A, a US national and astronaut, composes a poem which he stores on his smartphone. B, a UK scientist working in the ESA space element in the ISS, joins Astronaut A on his walk, and (while A is distracted by the spectacular views of the universe) copies the

---

[757] Section 4 of the Thai Civil Procedural Code allows the Thai court to hear a case, if the plaintiff has Thai nationality or is domiciled in Thailand, even though the defendant is not domiciled in the forum and the cause of action did not arise within the forum. Notwithstanding its existence, there is no report that a Thai court has ever exercised its jurisdiction on the basis (according to the Thai Supreme Court database available online at http://www.supremecourt.or.th> accessed 12 March 2016). This basis of jurisdiction is not available in every country, and, indeed, some countries consider it to be an exorbitant jurisdiction (See, for example, Olivia Struyen, 'Exorbitant Jurisdiction in the Brussels Convention' <https://www.law.kuleuven.be/jura/art/35n4/struyven.htm> accessed 12 March 2016). This jurisdictional rule is arguably unjustified, since the court seized lacks sufficient connection to the case. Neither the US nor the UK asserts jurisdiction based upon the plaintiff's nationality. However, in a situation in which infringement of IP rights takes place in outer space, in a location where no state can claim sovereignty and jurisdiction, the nationality principle could serve as an alternative principle for establishment of jurisdiction.

[758] See sub-topic of quasi-territorial jurisdiction.

poem from A's smartphone and sends it to C in Italy. Here, although Scientist B is a national of UK, he is not domiciled in any country on earth, since he has taken up permanent residence in the ISS.

In this scenario, not only does the unauthorized copying take place in outer space, but the copier, B, is not domiciled on earth. The fact that Scientist B copied Astronaut A's work on the Moon – an area which belongs to no state – makes the action unlikely to attach jurisdiction to any forum, based on tort, since the wrongful act occurred beyond any state's territory.

Considering now whether it is possible to establish a forum based upon personal jurisdiction, Scientist B's lack of an earth-based domicile causes difficulties, but perhaps it is possible to derive domicile based upon his occupancy within the ISS. However, since B occupies an ESA space element, it is not clear that this can be considered as B's domicile. It is necessary to take into account the fact that ESA is an intergovernmental organization, and so it is questionable which ESA partner court might assert personal jurisdiction over such a case. Might courts of all ESA partner countries be competent? Considering that Article 21(2) of the IGA provides that any European partner state may deem that an activity occurring in the ESA-registered elements to have occurred within its territory, it is possible to interpret that Scientist B is domiciled in each of the European partner state of ESA.

Article 62 of the Brussels I Regulation (recast) states that a domicile of a party is to be determined by the domestic law of the court where the case is seized. This means that were B to initiate copyright infringement proceedings at the High Court in London, it would be necessary to look at the definition of domicile under English law. An individual is domiciled in the United Kingdom if they are resident in the United Kingdom and the nature and circumstances of their residence indicate that they have a substantial connection with the UK, which will be presumed to be so if they have been resident in the UK for the last three months or more.[759]

Thus, if the High Court accepts that a person domiciled in ESA space element is deemed to be domiciled in any European partner state of ESA, then under English law, Scientist B would be domiciled in the UK, since he is in the ESA space element, the UK is a partner state of the ESA, and he has stayed there for more than the last three months. Hence, the English court could assert personal jurisdiction over B. In addition, the

---

[759]   Civil Jurisdiction and Judgments Order 2001, SI 2001/3929, sch 1, para 9(2),(6). See more in Clarkson (n 672) 68–69.

courts of the other European partner states of ESA could also assume jurisdiction over Scientist B, if those courts, like the UK, were willing to accept the concept of domicile may extend not only to their territory, but to places deemed to be their territory as well.

As we can see from these hypothetical cases, there are always grounds for at least one court to assert jurisdiction over a dispute relating to outer space activities. The concept of 'specific jurisdiction' is not an issue in case of intellectual property rights in outer space. This is because the connecting factors for establishing jurisdiction are generally based upon the domicile of the defendant and the subject-matter of the case, unless outer space becomes the place of defendant's domicile and the place where the infringement takes place. However, the jurisdictional rules in some countries allow jurisdiction to be based upon a plaintiff's nationality. Hence, there is still some room to establish jurisdiction, unless there really is no connecting factor to any jurisdiction, where neither party is domiciled in any country, nor the cause of action arises in outer space. Such a scenario seems extremely implausible. However, were such an event to arise, the rules of private international law, which attaches to territorial boundaries, will be unable to fill this gap. Thus, a specific regime on jurisdictional rules might prove necessary.

Once the appropriate forum to hear a particular dispute is determined, the next question to consider is what the applicable law will be. Although a case is brought to a court in a particular jurisdiction, it does not necessarily follow that the law of that forum will be applied in such case to determine the outcome. As will be seen, determining a single choice of law seems to bring with it more concerns than in case of jurisdiction, where a single set of facts may permit an outcome where multiple courts may each assert jurisdiction. The analysis on this issue will be discussed below by using the same hypothetical cases in the jurisdiction part.

2. CHOICE OF LAW

Once a court asserts its jurisdiction over a case, its next step is to determine the applicable law. If a dispute involves no 'foreign elements', generally the domestic law of the forum will be used to determine the outcome of the case. However, where foreign elements are involved, the position becomes more complex, and a forum might be presented with various alternatives. Here a choice is needed to which national law should be applied.

While IP disputes frequently include foreign elements, none of the international conventions on intellectual property rights explicitly sets out principles for determining choice of law. Although Article 5(2) of the Berne Convention refers to the law of the country where protection is claimed, this is not considered as a choice-of-law rule.[760] The question as to which national law is applicable is therefore left to be determined by domestic private international law.

In the field of intellectual property rights, there are several choice-of-law principles used to determine the applicable law. A court will be faced with the following alternatives: the law of the protecting country (*lex loci protectionis*); the law of the country of origin (*lex originis*); the law of the contract (*lex contractus*); and the law of the forum (*lex fori*). In this section, we shall examine these alternatives to find out what they mean and how each is applied in intellectual property cases, specifically in cases relating to entitlement and infringement, before considering whether the rules may be applied fittingly in the case of space activities. Of the various intellectual property rights, this section will be limited only to the study of choice-of-law rules in copyright and patent cases, reflecting the primary focus of this research.

2.1 Choice-of-law Rules

The primary choice-of-law rule relevant to intellectual property is termed 'the law of the protecting country' or *lex loci protectionis*. However, there is no universal definition of what this term actually means. This term is sometimes used to refer to the law of the granting state.[761] In infringement cases, this leads to the law of the country where the infringement occurs.[762] This term appears in some international conventions. For example, Article 5(2) of the Berne Convention states that 'the extent of protection, as well as the means of redress afforded to the author to protect his rights, shall be governed exclusively by the laws of the country where protection is claimed'. The Rome II regulation also applies the *lex loci protectionis* rule to the intellectual property rights

---

[760] See Section 2.2.

[761] Rita Matulionyte, 'IP and Applicable Law in Recent International Proposals' (2012) 3 *Journal of Intellectual Property, Information Technology, and Electronic Commerce Law*, 263, 265.

[762] Richard Fentiman, 'Choice of Law and Intellectual Property', in Josef Drexl and Annette Kur (eds), *Intellectual Property and Private International Law: Heading For The Future* (Hart Publishing 2005) 130.

infringement case.[763] The application of the *lex loci protectionis* rule is widely accepted since it is considered consistent with the territorial character of an intellectual property right.[764]

Adopting the law of the forum (*lex fori*) applies the national law of the country where the court seized of the case is situated. Adopting the law of the country of origin (*lex originis*) rule, the forum seized applies the national law of the country where the intellectual property work was created or first published. In some cases, this leads to the law of the country based upon the right holder's nationality.[765] The law of the contract (*lex contractus*) refers to the law of the place of where a relevant contract was made or performed.[766]

2.2 Which Law Should be Applicable?

Given this selection of possible choice-of-law rules to apply, this section examines the process of determining the application of law in IP matters, first in the case of proprietary matters arising from ownership, and then in matters of infringement.

2.2.1 Proprietary matters of IP rights

Ownership of IP rights gives rise to a number of proprietary matters which may give rise to disputes, including issues of initial ownership, creation, existence, content, limitations, exceptions and transferability.[767] Different countries apply different choice-of-law rules when considering these proprietary matters. For example, it is controversial which choice-of-law rule should be applied in a case relating to initial ownership of a right, whereas other proprietary issues are far less controversial and tend to be governed more universally by the law of the protecting country.[768]

In terms of initial ownership of a copyright work, international copyright conventions provide little guidance as to the appropriate

---

[763] Article 8 of the Rome II regulation provides that the 'law applicable to a non-contractual obligation arising from an infringement of an intellectual property right shall be the law of the country for which the protection is sought'.

[764] Fentiman, (n 762) 148.

[765] Ibid 135.

[766] <http://www.duhaime.org/LegalDictionary/L/LexLociContractus.aspx> (accessed 17 January 2016). See also Beverly May Carl, 'The Need for a Private International Law Regime in Antarctica' in Chirstopher C. Joyner and Sudhir K. Chopra (eds), *The Antarctic Legal Regime* (Kluwer Academic Publishers 1988) 83.

[767] Kono (n 683) 135.

[768] Fawcett and Torremans (n 696) 705–715.

choice-of-law rule, other than in Article 14bis (2) of the Berne Convention. Here, in relation to a cinematographic work, initial ownership is determined by the law of the protecting country.[769]

Traditionally in common law countries, such as England and the United States, a party's interest in property is determined by the *situs* of that property.[770] Since 'the essence of an intellectual property right is the owner's right to take action to prevent others from engaging in certain types of activity in a given territory', it is reasonable to infer that a patent or a copyright 'is situated in the country whose law governs its existence'.

According to the US Restatement (Second) of the Conflict of Laws ('2nd Restatement'), the applicable law in the United States is determined as the law of the country with the 'most significant relationship'.

In *Itar-Tass Russian News Agency v Russian Kurier, Inc.*,[771] the defendant in this case copied articles, pictures, headlines and graphics from the plaintiff's Russian-language content, which was published in New York without authorization. Issues of initial ownership as well as infringement arose. With regard to the issue of initial ownership, the Second Circuit adopted the approach of the 2nd Restatement and looked to determine the place with 'the most significant relationship'. Since the works in dispute were created by Russian nationals and were first published (*lex origin*) in Russia, the court held that issues of ownership should be determined by Russian law because Russia had the most significant relationship with this work.[772]

In *Bridgeman Art, Inc. v. Corel, Inc.*,[773] the plaintiff in this copyright dispute was a UK-based company with an office in New York. The company acquired the right to market reproductions of public domain works of art owned by museums and other collectors. The defendant, a Canadian company, copied the reproductions but refused accusations of copyright infringement, arguing that the works copied were not eligible for copyright protection. When considering the matter, the US court

---

[769]   Ibid 718.

[770]   Graeme Austin, 'Private International Law and Intellectual Property Rights: A Common Law Overview' WIPO Forum on Private International Law and Intellectual Property Paper WIPO/PIL/01/5 (2001) 14 www.wipo.int/edocs/ .../en/wipo.../wipo_pil_01_5.doc (accessed 17 January 2016).

[771]   *Itar-Tass Russian News Agency* (n 688).

[772]   Regarding the infringement issue, the Court ruled that the applicable law should be the law of the location of harm.

[773]   25 F.Supp. 2d 191 (S.D.N.Y. 1999), aff'd on reconsideration, 36 F.Supp. 2d 191 (S.D.N.Y. 1999).

applied UK copyright law, since the United Kingdom had the most significant relationship in this matter; whereas the infringement claim was governed by US law, since the harmful event took place in New York.

This decision is consistent with Section 104A of the US Copyright Act which addresses questions of ownership of a foreign work where copyright protection has been restored. This provision provides that 'a restored work vests initially in the author or initial right holder of the work as determined by the law of the source country of the work'.

However, contrary to the *lex originis* approach in the United States, most European countries, including the UK, apply the law of the protecting country to matters pertaining to initial ownership.[774] The law of the protecting country also plays a role in patent cases. Matters relating to acquisition, scope of transferability and termination of patents, as well as initial ownership are governed by the law of the country for which the protection is sought.[775] This leads to the law of the country of registration.[776]

The European Patent Convention includes a special choice-of-law rule in the case of an invention devised during the course of employment. In these circumstances, Article 60 EPC identifies the applicable law as the law of the country in which the employee is mainly employed.[777]

In conclusion, the law of the protecting country seems to be widely accepted as an applicable law for issues relating to proprietary matters, except in case of initial ownership in copyright case in which states adopt two different approaches: the law of the protecting country and the law of the country of origin.

2.2.2 Infringement

The *lex loci protectionis* rule plays an important role in determining the applicable law in a case of intellectual property infringement. There is no

---

[774] Kono (n 683) 139; Axel Metzger, 'Applicable Law Under The CLIP Principles: A Pragmatic Revaluation of Territoriality' in J. Basedow, T. Kono and A Metzger (eds), *Intellectual Property in the Global Arena* (Tubingen 2010) 160.

[775] Fawcett and Torremans (n 696) 687, 727 and 732.

[776] Ibid 732.

[777] Article 60 (1) EPC states, 'The right to a European patent shall belong to the inventor or his successor in title. If the inventor is an employee, the right to a European patent shall be determined in accordance with the law of the State in which the employee is mainly employed. If the State in which the employee is mainly employed cannot be determined, the law to be applied shall be that of the State in which the employee has the place of business to which the employee is attached'.

explicit provision under any international intellectual property instruments on choice-of-law rule in terms of infringement. Some scholars believe that the national treatment principle of Article 2(1) of the Paris Convention implicitly identifies a choice-of-rule of the *lex loci protectionis*,[778] however, whether this is the case is arguable.[779] In terms of copyright, Article 5(2) of the Berne Convention states that copyright disputes shall be governed by the law of 'the country where protection is claimed'. However, again, there is no agreement among commentators whether this provision of the Berne Convention is explicitly a choice-of-law rule.[780] Article 3(1) of the TRIPs Agreement, containing a principle of national treatment, reflects the earlier two conventions on the choice-of-law issue.[781] Thus, this leaves the question of the applicable law and the choice-of-law rules to be decided by the forum state.

According to the practice of the US courts, the law of the country where the infringement occurs will be applied to the case. In *Itar-Tass Russian News Agency v. Russian Kurier, Inc.*,[782] the court applied the US law to determine the infringement claim, since the unauthorized conduct (copying of the plaintiff's work) took place in New York. In *Creative Technology Ltd v. Aztech Sys PTE*,[783] another copyright infringement case, the US court also applied the law of the country in which the infringement occurred, not the law of the country in which the author is a citizen or in which the work was first published. *Subafilms Ltd v. MGM-Pathe Communications Co.*[784] further supports the fact that US practice looks to apply the law of the place where the wrong occurs. In fact, this case does not directly deal with application of the law of the protecting country to infringement issues, but rather the reverse. Here, the US court refused to apply US copyright law extraterritorially to an infringing act which occurred abroad. It might be assumed that if the court had applied an applicable law for infringement, the law of the protecting country would have been applied.

Within the EU, Article 15 of the Rome II Regulation refers to the scope of the law applicable to non-contractual obligations under the regulation. However, there is no agreement whether Article 15 covers all

---

[778]   Sender (n 357) 221–222 and 229.
[779]   Ibid 231.
[780]   Rita Matulionyte, *Law Applicable to Copyright: A Comparison of the ALI and CLIP Proposals* (Edward Elgar 2011) 28–33.
[781]   Sender (n 357) 221–230; Fawcett and Torremans (n 696) 481.
[782]   *Itar-Tass Russian News Agency* (n 688).
[783]   61 F 3d 696 (9th Cir. 1995) 700.
[784]   *Subafilms Ltd* (n 694) 1097.

the intellectual property matters or only certain ones, since the opinions of commentators diverge. However, the dominant view is that only infringement issues fall within the scope of Article 15.[785] If this is the case, then the applicable law in case of intellectual property rights is the law of the country for which the protection is claimed as stated in Article 8(1) of the Regulation.[786]

In the UK, Section 11(1) of the Private International Law (Miscellaneous Provisions) Act of 1995 (hereafter the UK Private International Law Act) refers the choice-of-law rule to the law of the country where an act of infringement takes place. However, since the Rome II Regulation has come into force, choice-of-law issues in the intellectual property cases are regulated under the Rome II Regulation instead. The UK Private International Law Act will continue to apply, but only to those matters that fall outside the scope of the Rome II Regulation.

Adoption of the *lex originis* rule has found few supporters for infringement cases.[787] Application of this rule would lead back to universal application of a single national law, which is obviously contrary to the territorial nature of intellectual property rights. Though applying the *lex loci protectionis* rule gives rise to multiple applicable laws, this is a far better fit with the territorial nature of intellectual property rights. More importantly, it is the effect of the national treatment principle embodied in international intellectual property rights instruments and, most recently the TRIPs Agreement, which prevents application of other choice-of-law rules (the law of the country of origin, the law of the forum), as this would be in breach of Article 3 of the TRIPs Agreement.[788]

Since the *lex loci protectionis* rule seems to play a dominant role in determining the applicable law in intellectual property rights cases, the next section will examine application of the *lex loci protectionis* rule in outer space. Other choice-of-law rules will also be taken into account, as relevant.

---

[785] There are three different opinions on the scope of Article 15 of the Rome II Regulation. The first group is of the view that the scope of Article 15 covers all proprietary and infringement matters, whereas the second group believes that the initial ownership issue falls outside the scope of the regulation. The other position suggests that only infringement issue is governed. See Matulionyte (n 761) 45–46.

[786] Article 8(1) of the Rome II Regulation.

[787] Sender (n 357) 259.

[788] Fawcett and Torremans (n 696) 691.

2.3   Applying the *Lex Loci Protectionis* Rule in Outer Space Activities

Application of the *lex loci protectionis* rule may be seen as posing problems in the case of multiple claims of infringement. Satellite broadcasting is a good example in which multiple infringing acts may occur in a number of countries. Both uplink countries (i.e., the country where a broadcast is transmitted to the satellite) and downlink countries (i.e., countries which receive the broadcast from a satellite) may be considered the place where infringement has taken place. Under the *lex loci protectionis* rule, this would lead to the application of national law of each country where an infringement occurs. An equivalent situation arises when a particular product is protected by a number of equivalent national patents, and imitation products are distributed in multiple countries. Here too, a bundle of different national laws will be applicable. In addition, applying the *lex loci protectionis* to space activities may lead to the situation that no law is applicable, given the absence of a legal system in outer space. The issues which result will be explored via the hypothetical cases discussed previously.

2.4   Hypothetical Cases

2.4.1   Case 1 (work created in outer space but infringed on the earth)[789]

A, B and C, a team of scientists from the UK, US and Thailand, respectively, are on board the International Space Station. During their mission, B formulates a medicinal compound under zero gravity which is an effective cure for lung cancer. Upon their return to earth, A, B and C each files patent applications covering the compound at their home patent offices. X and Y, domiciled in Germany and Thailand, respectively, jointly manufacture the patented compound in a laboratory in Italy, and then export it to the United States, where the product is sold to end-users by a local subsidiary established in the United States by X and Y. On learning about these activities, A, B and C each claim sole patent rights in the invention and insist that X and Y's unauthorized actions amount to patent infringement. Manufacturers X and Y counterclaim that any patent rights are invalid.

This hypothetical case raises three points worth closer examination. Firstly, is the new drug formulation produced in outer space protectable?

---

[789]   This hypothetical case does not mention jurisdiction in part because it does not give rise to any specific problems in terms of jurisdiction.

It was devised in an extraterritorial area where no law is applicable. However, we have already determined that the location where an invention is made is irrelevant to the granting of patent protection.[790] No provision in either the Paris Convention or national legislation prevents an invention from being patented, merely because it is invented in an extraterritorial area.[791] The law of the protecting country will apply to any disputed issues relating to acquisition of patent rights. The basic requirements for obtaining a patent are universal (novelty, inventive step and industrial application). Thus, if the new formulation is different enough to pass all the requirements, it would certainly be patentable.

The second question relates to ownership of the national patents, since Scientist B was the inventor, and yet A, B and C all claim to be entitled to file a patent application in their own sole name. Who is entitled to the patent? This may lead to an invalidity or entitlement issue, if the patent has been granted to the wrong persons (A and C). In assessing entitlement, which law should be applicable? It is suggested the law of the protecting country should be applied, since such an issue is closely related to devising the invention and the processing of the application itself.[792] It is assumed that any court asserting jurisdiction would apply the law of the protecting country (in this example: the UK, the US or Thailand) to determine entitlement of the national patent rights. Hence, whether the UK or Thai patent was wrongly granted to A and C, and its fate, if so, would depend upon the national substantive law of the UK and Thailand, respectively. If A is found to lack entitlement to the UK patent according to UK patent law and/or if C is found to lack entitlement to the Thai patent according to Thai law, then the patents may be revoked, and B afforded the opportunity to re-file new applications in his own name, without loss of the original priority date.

Moreover, there might be some differences in substantive law from country to country, but within the provision in the Paris Convention which permits independence of the granting states.[793] For example, ownership is decided differently in the case of an employee invention. Suppose that B is a scientist employed by the US Government. Now, the question arises which law would determine whether B (the employee) or the US government (the employer) is entitled to the patent. There is no consensus about whether the law of the protecting country or the law of the place connected to the employment relationship should decide on the

---

[790] Chapter 2 Section 2.2. and Chapter 3 Section 1.
[791] Ibid.
[792] Fawcett and Torremans (n 696) 730.
[793] Ibid 730.

entitlement in the case of an employee invention. The general choice-of-law rule is the law of the protecting country,[794] but different views exist, and others propose that such determination should be based on the employment relationship and contract.[795] The specific choice-of-law rule contained in Article 60 of the European Patent Convention (EPC) points to the law of the state in which the employee is mainly employed.[796] The outcome of who owns the patent in our case might be different depending on the substantive law in question. For example, if B files a patent application in the US, applying US law as the protecting country will lead to a finding that B is the owner of the patent,[797] whereas both the Thai Patent Act and the UK Patent Act stipulate that any inventions arising from an employee's employment duties belong to the employer.[798]

There is no available precedent to be found, either in the legislation or in the case-law in the US, UK and Thailand regarding the choice-of-law on the issue of patent ownership. I would, however, assume that these competent authorities would follow the international practice by applying the law of the protecting country to such case, if it were to arise.

Now, suppose that B produced his new medicine while in the Japanese module of the ISS. The fact that the invention arose while B was in the Japanese module is irrelevant. While in the case of a copyright work which is protected automatically, in this case, the act of an invention does not make Japan the protecting country (based upon quasi-territoriality) because protection only arises by the act of filing a patent application. Japan would only be the protecting country were B also to file his patent application in Japan.

The last issue to consider is infringement. Owing to the strict territorial nature of patent rights, there is no infringement beyond the territory of the granting state.[799] There is no issue where an unauthorized act occurs within the boundaries of the granting state, and clearly, the law of that state will be applicable.[800] However, when a patented invention is subject to unauthorized exploitation in another state beyond the territory of granting state, the state where the infringing act occurs (*lex loci delicti*)

---

[794]   Ibid 731.
[795]   Ibid.
[796]   Article 60(1) of the EPC (n 777).
[797]   37 C.F.R. §3.73 (a) states, 'The inventor is presumed to be the owner of a patent application, and any patent that may issue therefrom, unless there is an assignment'.
[798]   Section 11 of the Thai Patent Act and Section 39(1) of the UK Patent Act.
[799]   Sender (n 357) 213.
[800]   Ibid 213.

may have interest in applying its national law to the dispute. Hence, the law of the place where the infringement occurs could be another alternative.[801] However, in case of intellectual property rights infringement, the application of the *lex loci delicti* to disputes is limited because of the territoriality of intellectual property.[802] No infringement of rights arises unless protection has been secured for the work in that country.

In our hypothetical case, unauthorized conduct take place in Italy (manufacturing the product) and in the US (selling unauthorized product), respectively. If we apply the law of the protecting country to the case, this would lead to the application of the US law only in the United States. This means that unauthorized exploitation of the patented product in Italy will not amount to infringement because the invention is unprotected, since no patent application was filed in Italy. Although the patent in dispute is also protected in the UK and Thailand, this does not give rise to the operation of UK and Thai laws in this case, since the unauthorized acts occur beyond their territories as well. Italian law is not applicable either, even though the unauthorized conduct takes place within its border. This is because such work in question does not gain any protection under Italian law as the result of not filing an application there. Accordingly, there is no infringing act in Italy. Thus, the only available law in this case is the US law, as the law of the protecting country on the territorial basis.

So, let us further suppose that B had also filed a European patent application at the European Patent Office which designates Italy. Assuming the application proceeds to grant, and any local formalities are complied with, B will obtain a bundle of national patents covering multiple EPC states, including Italy. Now, Italy will become the protecting country for the Italian patent, and Italian law will also be applicable in this case as well.

Thus, in case of multiple registration and infringement, the *lex loci protectionis* is the choice-of-law rule that may lead to more than one applicable law.[803]

---

[801] Ibid 213–214.
[802] Ibid 213–215.
[803] Ibid 219.

2.4.2   Case 2 (work created in outer space but infringed on the earth)[804]

A is a US astronaut. While on a Moon walk, A films what he can see as he explores the Moon and then broadcasts the resulting motion picture back to earth via a control station located in the United States. As the signal is being transmitted, it is illicitly intercepted and rebroadcast to recipients in the United Kingdom and other European countries by B, a Thai resident.

We shall assume that US, UK and Thai courts have jurisdiction to try this case. Were A to bring his case before these three courts, it is likely that each court would elect to apply different law to the case, based upon the choice-of-law favored in these countries.

Applying the *lex loci protectionis* rule results in the dispute being adjudicated under the law of the place of infringement. Since the unauthorized transmission was made to a number of states, this would lead to multiple applicable laws of each protecting country; there is nothing to prevent the court seized from applying multiple domestic laws in a single case.

The first step is to determine where the infringing conduct occurs in this case, so we may determine the applicable law. There are a number of options. The place of infringement could be the place at the location where the uplink signal is transmitted, or it could be the place where the signal is received. There are various theories to consider when determining the applicable law in a satellite broadcasting case,[805] including the 'emission', 'Bogsch', 'effect' and 'root-copy' theories.[806] The emission theory advocates the place of infringement as the place where the signals are transmitted, whereas the Bogsch theory considers that infringement occurs in both the emission and reception countries.[807] According to the effect doctrine, whether infringement occurs in a particular country or not is determined based upon whether sufficient effect occurs.[808] The root-copy theory, as the name suggests, tries to locate the 'root' of the infringement, by identifying the country where the initial conduct takes place which leads onto the damage abroad.[809]

---

[804]   The factual background of this case has been modified from the hypothetical case 2 in Chapter 4 for the purpose of examining choice-of-law rule.

[805]   Matulionyte (n 780) 62.

[806]   Ibid.

[807]   Ibid. The Bogsch theory later has been modified and known as the communication theory. See also Makeen Fouad Makeen (n 556) 194–196.

[808]   Matulionyte (n 780) 62.

[809]   Ibid.

Applying each of these different theories to the case study suggests a number of alternative applicable laws, and the applicable law which will actually be selected will depend on the approach taken by the court of the tribunal where the dispute is being heard.

In case of the United States, taking previous court practice into consideration,[810] it is likely that a US court would apply the Bogsch theory for satellite broadcasting cases. This approach leads to the law of the country under the footprint of the satellite. As a result, the US court will likely need to apply multiple national laws in any one case.

If our dispute is brought before a court in the UK, it seems likely that it would adopt the emission theory. As a member state of the EU, the court would be influenced by adoption of this theory when determining choice-of-law issues in the EU Satellite Directive. Hence, in our hypothetical case, an English court would apply US law, since the United States is the place where the broadcasts at issue were emitted. However, now suppose that A's broadcast was transmitted directly from the Moon, without first sending signals back to a ground station. Applying the emission theory as the determining rule for the choice-of-law issue in these circumstances would be problematic, since it would point to no applicable law in this case. Here, the emission location is the Moon and, as we have already concluded, no IP law covering this 'territory' exists.

Pursuant to the Thai Conflict of Laws Act,[811] a Thai Court is likely to apply the law of the protecting country to this case. But the term of the protecting country has to be decided first. There is currently no precedent or guidance to indicate how a Thai court would define 'the place of infringement' for a satellite broadcast. In its decision no. 6359/2551 (2008), the Thai Supreme Court did, however, consider a claim for copyright infringement based upon an unauthorized re-broadcasting of protected television programs and found infringement in this case. The defendant, a hotel owner based in Thailand, intercepted the satellite signals and transmitted programs onto televisions in the guest rooms, thereby avoiding the subscription charges. Applying the reasoning in this decision, by analogy, Thai courts may deem the reception country to be the place of infringement. Hence, if presented with a conflict of laws issue arising from satellite broadcasting, it seems most likely that a Thai

---

[810] *National Football League* (n 623); *Los Angeles News Service v. Conus Communications Co.*, 969 F.Supp. 579 (USCD Cal., 1997); *Allarcom Pay TV* (n 623).

[811] Section 15, paragraph 1 of the Thai Conflict of Law Act states 'An obligation arising out of a wrongful act is governed by the law of the place where the facts constituting such wrongful act have been taken place'.

court would refer to the law of each country covered by satellite's footprint as being the law of the protecting country.

This example, combined with our earlier analysis, demonstrates that applying different national substantive law to the infringement scenario will likely lead to different outcomes. For example, application of US copyright law might result in a decision that there is no infringement because a broadcast is only protected under US law if it is simultaneously fixed during its transmission.[812]

The application of the law of each country covered by a satellite's footprint in satellite-broadcast cases tends to result in a need to consider numerous national laws because of a spillover effect. It is not practically possible to confine a satellite broadcast within territorial boundaries; rather, it is necessary for the broadcast signal to cover a wider area than is actually required, to ensure uniform coverage of the particular country or countries which are actually intended to be targeted. Owing to the practical difficulties which may result, the CLIP group has proposed a *de minimis* rule which limits consideration of national law to only those countries where there is either a substantial conduct or substantial effects.[813] Adopting this proposal would limit the scope of application to the law of the protecting country in which the broadcast is directed or targeted. This would eliminate application of additional states' law, resulting from unintended spillover, where the effects are insubstantial. The ALI group has also recognized this issue and has proposed a similar 'market effect' rule. In this proposal, the deciding court's focus is not on where the infringing conduct occurred, but where market effects were felt.[814]

Nevertheless, applying a *de minimis* rule as proposed, infringement could still be established in multiple locations: either those where substantial effects or where substantial conduct takes place. In such a situation, issues of conflicting and overlapping remedies arise.[815] In the case of *National Football League*,[816] for example, US law was applied (as the law of the country of emission), and as a result, reception of a broadcast was precluded in Canada, even though reception was legal under the Canadian law. This case identifies an issue with conflicting remedies which adopting the *de minimis* rule would not solve. In this

---

[812]   See the hypothetical case 2 in Chapter 4.
[813]   Article 3:602 of the CLIP group. See more in Fawcett and Torremans (n 696) 917–918; Matulionyte (n 780) 146–157.
[814]   Section 301(2) ALI principles, Preliminary Draft of 2005.
[815]   Matulionyte (n 780) 160–161.
[816]   *National Football League* (n 623).

example, US law could still be applicable, since it represents the place where a substantial conduct occurred.[817] In the German case, *Sender Felsberg*,[818] collecting societies demanded damages under both German law (as the law of the country of emission) and French law (as the law of the country of reception) for the same radio transmission. This illustrates the potential for unfair cumulative remedies. According to the *de minimis* rule, infringement could be established both in Germany (substantial conduct) and France (substantial effect). If full compensation were awarded under each law, this would lead to a double payment for the same infringing act.[819] In *Lagardere*, the CJEU held that although both German and French laws could be applied to determine issues concerning remedies in this case, any damages awarded should be proportional to the 'actual value of use' in each country.[820]

In conclusion, adopting a choice-of-law rule in satellite broadcast infringement cases based on the law of the protecting country approach would be well-supported. However, there is no consensus yet as to how the 'protecting country' would be defined, and proposed solutions to resolve inconsistencies between various competing theories do not yet exist.

2.4.3 Case 3 (works created on the earth and infringed in outer space)[821]

A team of astronauts lands on Mars. During the stay, one of the team members, B, uploads a selection of newly released (and copyright protected) songs from an unauthorized file-sharing website and then distributes copies to the rest of the team, to provide everyone with entertainment during their mission. The electronic copies are deleted on Mars, before the team returns to the earth. In this situation, do the copyright owners, acting through a rights management company, C, have

---

[817] Matulionyte (n 780) 160–161.

[818] German Supreme Court decision of 7 November 2002 – I ZR 175/00 Sender Felsberg, GRUR Int. 470 (2003) in Matulionyte, ibid 93–94 and 161.

[819] Ibid 161.

[820] CJEU case C–192/04 *Lagardere Active Broadcast v. SPRE and GVL* [2005] ECR I-07199 (14 July 2005).

[821] The factual background of this hypothetical case has been changed from the factual background in the hypothetical case 2 in the jurisdiction part. In addition, its factual background has also been modified from the hypothetical case 3 in Chapter 4. Such changing and modification are for the purpose of examining the choice-of-law rule.

any means for legal redress? The songs are protected by copyright in a number of countries, including Thailand, the UK and the US.

Let us consider the outcome if Company C initiates infringement proceedings before a Thai court. Pursuant to the Thai Conflict of Laws Act, determining whether Astronaut B's action constitutes an infringement will be decided by applying the law of the place where the wrongful act occurs (*lex loci*).[822] Similar approaches would be taken were the same case to be brought before courts in the UK or the USA. This is because the choice-of-law rule adopted in the United Kingdom and the United States also point to the law of the protecting country.[823]

However, whether B's unauthorized copying and distribution amounts to infringing use is questionable, since the use occurs on Mars, an extraterritorial area where there is no copyright law. Applying the law of protecting country (*lex loci protectionis*) leads to the same situation: that no law is applicable to the case. The absence of an adequate choice-of-law rule prevents this case for being heard on its merits. But is it fair that the copyright owner has no legal redress? One might argue that the rights holder has suffered no harm, since the unauthorized use occurred in outer space, and no unauthorized copies were brought back to earth. However, while this may be the situation where instances of use are few and limited, having regard to the likely development of the space industry, especially the anticipated growth of space tourism, it cannot be ruled out that in the future, unauthorized use of IP-protected products in extraterritorial areas of outer space might well affect the right holders' business. Although it is impossible to predict the likely scale of any impact at this point in time, now that we have become aware of the possible outcome of the strict territoriality rule in IP, it would seem prudent to give the matter some thought now.

But, if there *should* be a governing law in outer space, which law would be the most appropriate? Let us consider the alternative choice-of-law rules. Might the *lex originis* rule be adopted to determine the applicable law to this case? There is no reason, based upon international law, which prevents a court from applying the *lex originis* to an action for intellectual property infringement. Furthermore, applying the law of the place where the work was first created generally[824] points to a single locality which, in turn, leads to a single law to apply.[825] Additionally, this

---

[822]   Article 15 of the Thai Conflict of Laws Act.
[823]   See Article 8 of the Rome II Regulation and *Itar-Tass Russian News Agency* (n 688).
[824]   A collaborative work created online might still be problematic.
[825]   Matulionyte (n 780) 81.

would resolve the issue identified in our hypothetical case of finding no applicable law in outer space. However, as we have identified, operation of the *lex originis* appears to be contrary to the strict territorial nature of intellectual property rights, and at present only a minority of countries apply the *lex originis* rule to infringement cases.[826] However, it can be questioned whether applying the *lex originis* rule, or any other choice-of-law rules, to a situation which occurs in outer space is really contrary to the territoriality principle. While this may be the case on earth where territoriality is a fact, since there is currently no IP law, no IP protection and no territory in outer space, how can applying a choice-of-laws rule conflict with this territoriality rule?

Leaving this unresolved issue to one side, we shall attempt to find a better alternative governing law for our hypothetical case. To analyze a possible choice-of-law rule in outer space, we can look to Antarctica, as an analogous extraterritorial area. It seems a reasonable starting assumption, that any precedent set in Antarctica would be a good path for outer space to follow.

Beattie v. United States[827] is a case concerning an alleged wrongful death when an Air New Zealand plane crashed in Antarctica. The family of one of the victims brought wrongful death proceedings against the United States under the Federal Tort Claims Act (FTCA) in the United States. The US District Court for the District of Columbia considered that since there was no law in Antarctica, there was no conflict of laws at issue. Referring to Section 6 of the Second Restatement,[828] since it was not possible to select 'Antarctica' law as an alternative system of law, the case should be determined according to the law of the forum (*lex fori*); however, the case did not include detailed reasons for this decision.[829] While two further US cases have been identified relating to torts arising

---

[826]   Ibid 80.

[827]   *Beattie v. United States*, 756 F.2d 91, (1984).

[828]   Section 6 of the Second Restatement sets forth the following factors to be taken into account in determining the applicable law: (a) the needs of the interstate and international system; (b) the relevant policies of the forum; (c) the relevant policies of other interested states and the relative interests of those states in the determination of the particular issue; (d) the protection of justified expectations; (e) the basic policies underlying the particular field of law; (f) certainty, predictability and uniformity of result; and (g) ease in determination and application of the law to be applied.

[829]   Carl (n 766) 84; Jonathan Blum, 'The Deep Freeze: Torts, Choice of Law, and the Antarctic Treaty Regime' (1994) 8 *Emory International Law Review* 667, 682.

in Antarctica, *Smith v. United States*[830] and *EDF v. Massey*,[831] neither case explicitly addressed the choice-of-law issue, but rather the matter was dealt with indirectly, in the sense that the US courts decided upon the territorial scope of law.

The Antarctic Treaty of 1959 itself does not include a special choice-of-law rule. The main provisions of the treaty aim to regulate a peaceful use and exploitation of Antarctica's resources. Article VIII (1) of the Treaty indicates that proper jurisdiction over observers, scientific personnel and staff during their stay in Antarctica should be based upon their nationality,[832] but it makes no reference to applicable law. If the US court decision in *Beattie* represents an accurate reflection, then we might assume that US courts would adopt the law of the forum approach if faced with a case of relating to allegations of IP infringement in outer space.

It is the lack of IP law in outer space which prevents the use of the law of the protecting country (*lex loci protectionis*), the most widely accepted choice-of-law rule in IP infringement cases. In cases of infringement, the *lex loci contractus* is irrelevant, since by its very nature, there is no contract at issue. This leaves the two possible alternatives as the *lex originis* and *lex fori*. Each option has its own disadvantage. The merit of

---

[830]   *Smith v. United States*, 113 S.Ct. 1178 (1993). In this case, Mr. Smith, an employee of the contractor to the US government agency, worked in Antarctica at McMurdo Station, the US base in Antarctic, accidently died from hiking when he was in Antarctica, his widow sued the US government basing her claims on the FTCA. The US Supreme Court refused to grant any remedy, holding that the FTCA did not apply to event occurring in Antarctic since Antarctica is a 'foreign country' for the purpose of FTCA.

[831]   *Environmental Defense Fund v. Massey*, 986 F.2d 528, 529 (1993). In this case, EDF, a private environmental group sought declaratory and injunctive relief against the National Science Foundation (NSF) under the National Environmental Policy Act (NEPA) for failure to follow waste disposal procedures in Antarctica as required by law. The Court of Appeals for the District of Columbia held that since there was no law in Antarctica, there was no foreign law in conflict with NEPA. Therefore, the court applied NEPA to the case.

[832]   Article VIII (1) of the Antarctica Treaty states, 'In order to facilitate the exercise of their functions under the present Treaty, and without prejudice to the respective positions of the Contracting Parties relating to jurisdiction over all other persons in Antarctica observers designated under paragraph 1 of Article VII and scientific personnel exchanged under subparagraph 1(b) of Article III of the Treaty, and member of the staffs accompanying any such persons, shall be subject only to the jurisdiction of the Contracting Party of which they are nationals in respect to all acts or omissions occurring while they are in Antarctica for the purpose of exercising their functions'.

the *lex originis* approach is that it leads to application of a single law, but it has the disadvantage that the right holder might ensure any work is always first published in the country which has the most right holder-friendly IP protection. This might create an additional burden in terms of remedies for any defendant. It may not always be easy for a user of a protected work to determine where a work originated, and so determine whether a particular use of a work required authorization or not, since terms for permitted use varies greatly from country to country. Application of the *lex fori* rule would inevitably lead to forum shopping. This again would increase uncertainty for any would-be defendant, in terms of which applicable law[833] would govern their activity. In this regard, both these choice-of-law rules seem to benefit the right holder, rather than furthering fairness over all.

It is also possible that any trial court might hold that, given the absence of law in outer space, it is not possible for any unauthorized acts to constitute an infringement. In which case, no remedy is available. While our hypothetical case may seem to be far-fetched, let us instead consider the likely outcome in a scenario which is easier to imagine. Now, the unauthorized use of copyright material occurs not on Mars, but in modules forming the US element of the International Space Station instead. Can the law of the protecting country be applied in this case?

Recalling that the ISS is a quasi-territorial territory, the unauthorized use in this case could be deemed to have occurred in the territory of the United States.[834] Therefore, it is likely that an adjudicating court hearing C's case would apply US law, as the law of the protecting country, to the question of infringement. However, although ISS has its own governing agreement, as has been noted above, the position is not clear-cut in relation to other space objects, since (unlike ships and aircraft) a space object does not automatically become part of the territory of the state in which it is registered.[835] In addition, any jurisdiction which the state of registration has in the case of space objects does not cover third parties.[836] One might equally argue that the quasi-territory rule does not apply by analogy to a US-registered module in the ISS. In which case,

---

[833] For example, suppose that the work is already in the public domain in Thailand, but it is still protected in the US owing to the longer duration of protection under the US Copyright law. Different outcomes result from different terms of protection and will arise in this case depending on which law is applicable. See Chapter 4 under the duration section.

[834] Article 21(2) of the IGA.

[835] Ibid.

[836] Article VIII of the Outer Space Treaty.

unauthorized use of any protected work within the module would not take place within US boundaries, and US law would not be applicable by reference as the law of the protecting country.

While the choice-of-law issue in outer space is currently far from reaching a conclusion, allowing intellectual products protected by IP rights on earth to go unprotected in outer space would, to me, appear an undesirable result. It would discourage innovative activity in that extra-territorial area, as well leading to potential unfairness if innovations created on earth are freely exploited in outer space.

Given our awareness of the problems, solutions should be in place to ease them. Having explored the difficulties encountered when trying to apply national IP laws to outer space activities, a dedicated IP law to regulate outer space is an obvious alternative which should be considered. We shall examine possible solutions following examination of the next hypothetical case.

2.4.4   Case 4 (work created in outer space and infringed in outer space and on the earth)[837]

Astronaut A is on a Moon walk. As he explores the Moon's surface, he composes a long description of the landscape and features he encounters, and he stores it in his smartphone. Once completed, he sends it by text to all the other members of the team for their personal use, since they are also exploring the Moon surface at the same time as A. There are 50 astronauts and scientists in the group. Unbeknownst to A, Astronaut C sends this file of A's work to D. Despite knowing the origins of the work, D publishes the text in a magazine published on earth, claiming it as his own work of fiction. D is a national of country E, which is a Berne member country, while A is a national of country B, which is neither a signatory to the Berne Convention nor any other international copyright treaty or bilateral agreement.

This example raises questions whether A's work is protected by copyright – a question of initial ownership. There are two possible applicable laws: the law of the country of origin and the law of the protecting country. Applying the country of origin rule would point to no applicable law, since this work is created on the Moon. As to the law of the protecting country, we need to establish where copyright protection arises. Is A's work protected via the unauthorized actions of D? Can A be

---

[837]   The factual background of this case is similar to that of the hypothetical case 3 in the jurisdiction part and the hypothetical case 4 in Chapter 4. However, additional factual background has been added for the purpose of examining the choice-of-law rule.

protected under the law of country E; given that A is a national of a country which does not grant reciprocal copyright protection to nationals of other countries? Can A's distribution of his work to other team members on the Moon be considered as 'publication'? If A's work is protected, is C liable for infringement based upon his unauthorized act took place in outer space?

The first question to be addressed is the initial ownership of the work in dispute. If a court elects to determine ownership of the work based upon the law of the country of origin, which law will be applicable in this case? Considering the fact that work was created and first published in a location where no copyright law exists, would this lead to the answer that this work is unprotected, and C will thus be exonerated from any liability arising from his unauthorized act?

Although the location of creation is not relevant to the subsistence of copyright (we have already concluded that a work created in outer space is eligible for copyright, provided it passes all the requirements for subsistence), it is unlikely that an unpublished work of a non-member of the Berne Convention will gain any copyright protection since Article 3(1) (b) of the Berne Convention bases authorship on the nationality of the author and place of first, or simultaneous, publication. The fact that A's work has been distributed cannot satisfy the requirements for publication pursuant to the Berne Convention, since the treaty defines 'publication' in terms of publication in a Berne country. Thus, A's text is an 'unpublished work' within the meaning of the Berne Convention. The country of origin would then be determined by reference to his nationality, i.e., the law of country B. Thus, if the adjudicating court applies the law of the country of origin to the issue of initial ownership, it is the law of country B.

Alternatively, if the adjudicating court chooses to apply the law of the protecting country to this same issue, we have to determine which country is considered to be the protecting country. In this case unauthorized use occurs both on the Moon and in country E. In the case of the Moon, this would lead to no applicable law, so the only alternative is to adopt the law of country E. However, A's work is unpublished, and A is not a national of a Berne country. Thus, A's work is not qualified for protection under the Berne Convention. Accordingly, E is not a protecting country. In this situation, the only plausible answer is to fall back to the nationality of the author. Our hypothetical case has identified a scenario in which there is no applicable law if the law of the protecting country is adopted.

Considering the infringement issue in the case of C. C makes an unauthorized copy of A's work on the Moon. It is likely that applying the law of the protecting country would lead to the application of no law, since this would refer to copyright law in outer space. Assuming that a court in country B accepts that it has jurisdiction to hear this case, how might such a court proceed? Although A's work is protected by copyright in country B, operation of national copyright law in country B cannot go beyond its border, in light of the territoriality rule. Does this mean that C's act does not constitute an infringement? If the court in country B concludes that there is no copyright law on the Moon, then it follows that although C's act was unauthorized, C is not liable for infringement, since infringement can only arise when there is a right to be infringed. Alternatively, the court in country B might proceed by adjudicating based upon its own law (the law of the forum), as did the US court in the *Beattie* case, or adopt the law of the country of origin, which in this case also falls back to the law of country B.

Let us further suppose that C's unauthorized use takes place in the ISS in the ESA module, and not on the Moon. In this case, C's act might be deemed to occur in the territory of each ESA member state.[838] Thus, the copyright law of each ESA member state will be applicable as the law of the protecting country. But the question still remains whether such national law can give rise to extraterritorial infringement without an explicit provision, as is provided in the case of US patent law.[839]

Turning now to the actions of D; if proceedings were initiated against D for his unauthorized actions before the court in country E, what law should be applicable in this case? Let us assume first that the court decides to adopt the law of the protecting country, the most widely advocated choice-of-law rule in an infringement case. The copyright law of country E cannot be considered here as the law of the protecting country, since A's work is not protected in country E, because it is an unpublished work of a non-Berne country. So, in this case, can the court proceed by just applying its own law to the case? While adjudicating this case by the law of the forum might provide an alternative, in this case the work is unprotected in country E. Thus, D would not be liable, since he has copied an unprotected work. Hence, it is likely that the court would have to rule in favor of the defendant and dismiss the case.

As discussed above, it seems that the law of the protecting country would not be a good option for the choice-of-law rule in outer space, even though it is the most accepted choice-of-law rule in case of IP infringement. This is because the absence of IP law in outer space

---

[838]   Article 21(2) of the IGA.
[839]   See Chapter 3 under the infringement section.

prevents this choice-of-law rule from being operative. Since there is no authoritative guidance for the selection of the applicable law, it is possible that the Court would be unable to hear the case on its merits. Although other choice-of-law rules remain (either the law of the country of origin or the law of the forum) which a court can elect to determine the applicable law for the case, neither of these options finds wide support. Taking the rapid pace of development of space activities into consideration, it is time to think about the problems highlighted in our hypothetical cases above. Suggestions have been made to resolve similar choice-of-law issues in Antarctica which we could adopt for use in outer space.[840]

Creating a special IP law for outer space or establishing specific choice-of-law rules[841] are the best prospects for solutions. However, while theoretically the ideal solution, the first option seems unlikely to offer a short-term solution. Establishing an entirely new IP regime for outer space would involve establishing a new body which has the necessary legislative, executive and judicial powers to set up and operate a legal regime for IP rights in outer space.[842] Reaching international consensus on either practical or substantive issues, even if possible, would take many years to negotiate. Indeed, many states would be reluctant to derogate their sovereignty and jurisdiction to another organ.[843]

The latter option is likely to be more promising, since it could be promulgated in the form of a Protocol to the existing Outer Space Treaty. Such a Protocol could set forth a choice-of-law rule for national courts to determine the applicable law when adjudicating on IP cases involving outer space. The choice-of-law code could be accompanied with guidance, distinguishing between proprietary and infringement matters. In terms of proprietary matters, for works originating in outer space, it would not be practical to select either the law of the protecting country or the law of the country of origin as an applicable law to the case, given the lack of law in outer space. However, the law of the protecting country might have a role for patent cases (and indeed other registered rights, such as trademarks and designs) where recognition of protection requires the filing of an application in a patent office based on earth. Therefore, the law of registration or the law of the protecting country could be

---

[840] It was suggested that the choice-of-law issue in Antarctica could be solved by creating tort law for the Antarctic or having a unified choice-of-law code. See more in Blum (n 829) 696–698.

[841] Ibid 696–698, see also Sterling (n 483) 32.

[842] Blum (n 829) 692.

[843] Ibid.

applicable. (While these two rules will normally coincide, there might be circumstances when they do not.) Another possible connection would be that of the nationality of the creator. This would be particularly relevant in respect of copyright and other forms of unregistered rights. While the law of the forum provides a further alternative, this has the disadvantage that where the forum has no point of attachment to the case, it would seem ill-founded to apply that law, and indeed, the forum might be rightly reluctant to hear the case, given the lack of 'local' interest involved.

For the reasons outlined already, the law of the protecting country would not be appropriate as a method to decide the applicable law when determining infringement. The most probable option would be to adopt the law of the forum. However, this rule is also controversial, both because of likely forum shopping and possibility that the forum might have only a weak interest in adjudicating the case. The law of the country of origin also seems inappropriate, since sometimes it may not have a close connection to either of the parties involved, and the exact location where a work is created may be difficult to determine, in any event. This leaves us with the option of linking applicable law to the nationality of the parties, whether the plaintiff or the defendant. This option is worth due consideration, since it does have a connection to the case.[844] This approach would certainly eliminate issues with forum shopping, and a court might be more amenable to hear a case which involves a dispute which concerns an interest connected to its own nation.

3. RECOGNITION AND ENFORCEMENT OF FOREIGN JUDGMENTS

Once a judgment has been given, the next step for the successful party is to see that decision is enforced. Given the international nature of intellectual property rights, disputes sometimes involve a foreign element. As such, there is a real possibility that a decision issued by a court in one country will need to be enforced in another. Alternatively, if litigation has been pursued in one jurisdiction, it is expedient to have the outcome recognized in other jurisdictions where the same issues arise, to avoid the parties having to re-litigate the same case again.

In order to have a foreign judgment enforced, it is necessary for it to be recognized as binding in the state where the enforcement is sought. In

---

[844]   Jonathan Blum proposed this choice-of-law module in his article as another option. (n 829) 698.

this section, we shall examine recognition and enforcement of judgment arising from disputes regarding intellectual property rights in outer space activities. Since any such judgment will be granted by a court based on earth (currently, there is no special judicial body established in outer space), relevant rules of the recognizing court will be applied. Since neither the nature of outer space activities, nor the nature of intellectual property law, gives rise to any specific problems in terms of recognition and enforcement of an earlier judgment, the examination of this area will be brief.

Generally, the recognition and enforcement of foreign judgments are treated on the basis of international comity.[845] The recognition and enforcement of foreign judgments are subject to national legislation which shares similar requirements and exceptions. The private international rules which are applicable in our two jurisdictions: the United States, and the United Kingdom, will be examined below.[846, 847]

3.1 Requirement

There are two common requirements for the recognition and enforcement of foreign judgment. These are the jurisdiction of the rendering court and the finality of the foreign judgment. Let us look at each in turn.

---

[845]   The US Supreme Court in *Hilton v. Guyot* 159 US 113 (1895) held that foreign judgments were recognized on the basis of comity. However, the Court in this case refused to recognize the foreign judgment (in this case was French judgment) on the ground of lack of reciprocity. A literature review on the recognition and enforcement of foreign judgment in the US can be found in Symeon C. Symeonides, *American Private International Law* (Kluwer Law International 2008), Yoav Oestreicher, 'Recognition and Enforcement of Foreign Intellectual Property Judgments: Analysis and Guidelines for A New International Convention' (S.J.D. thesis, Duke University School of Law 2004); and Fritz Blumer, 'Jurisdiction and Recognition in Transatlantic Patent Litigation' (2001) 9 *Texas Intellectual Property Law Journal* 329; Thai Supreme Court decision no. 585/2461 (1918). There is no report that the international comity is taken into account for recognition and enforcement of foreign judgment in the UK.

[846]   US practice on the recognition of foreign judgments is presently guided by three documents which are the Uniform Foreign Money-Judgments Recognition Act of 1962; the Restatement (Third) of Foreign Relations; and the draft statute titled 'Foreign Judgments Recognition and Enforcement Act'. Symeonides (n 845) 334–335.

[847]   There are two different legal rules for recognition and enforcement of foreign judgments in the UK. These are the Brussels I Regulation (recast) and the traditional English rule. Fawcett and Torremans (n 696) 945.

3.1.1   Jurisdiction of the rendering court

There is general worldwide consensus that as a prerequisite for its judgment to be recognized in other jurisdictions, the rendering court must have properly established jurisdiction over the case.[848] This condition is required in the United States and the United Kingdom. As with matters of jurisdiction and choice of law, in the United Kingdom, there are two different sets of legal rules for recognition and enforcement of foreign judgments: the EU/EFTA rules and the traditional English rules.[849] The former are applicable to the case of recognition and enforcement of judgments originating from courts of other EU member states, whereas the latter apply to foreign judgment of non-members.[850]

3.1.2   Finality of the foreign judgment

In order to be recognizable and enforceable in other countries, a foreign judgment must be final according to the law of the country in which it was given.[851] However, there is no requirement that the judgment given by an EU member country has to be final where the recognition and enforcement are sought in another EU member country.[852] Usually, there is no judicial review on the merits of that foreign judgment.[853]

3.2   Exceptions

There are several exceptions applied to non-recognition and non-enforcement of foreign judgments. However, the two common exceptions are default judgments and matters which give rise to public policy concerns.

---

[848]   *Hilton* (n 845) 166–167; Article 35 of the Brussels I Regulation (recast); *Pemberton v Hughes* (1899) 1 Ch 781, 790 *et seq;* and *Salvesen v Administrator of Austrian Property* [1927] AC 641,659; Thai Supreme Court decision no. 585/2461 (1918).

[849]   Fawcett and Torremans (n 696) 945.

[850]   Articles 36 and 39 of the Brussels I Regulation (recast) and Fawcett and Torremans (696) 955.

[851]   *Kington Bros. v AFG Indus. Inc.*, 581 F. Supp. 1039, 1045 (D. Del 1984), reported in Ronald A. Brand, 'Recognition and Enforcement of Foreign Judgments' in Federal Judicial Center International Litigation Guide, (April 2012) 9, <http://www.fjc.gov/public/pdf.nsf/lookup/brandenforce.pdf/$file/brandenforce.pdf> (accessed 12 March 2016), *Nouvion v Freeman* (1889) 15 App Cas 1 and *Blohn v Desser* [1962] 2 QB 116, [1961] 3 All ER 1.

[852]   Case C–143/78 *De Cavel v De Cavel* [1979] ECR 1055.

[853]   Symeonides (n 845) 334; *Henderson v Henderson* (1844) 6 QB 288; and Thai Supreme Court decision no. 585/2461 (1918).

3.2.1 Default judgments

A judgment in a rendering court which has been issued in default of an appearance, and without allowing the defendant sufficient opportunity to present his case, will not be recognized and enforced in most countries, including the United States and the United Kingdom.[854]

3.2.2 Public policy

Another common exception for non-recognition of a foreign judgment is public policy.[855] Recognizing courts can refuse to recognize and enforce of a foreign judgment if to do so would be contrary to its public policy. What constitutes valid public policy concerns differ from country to country. For example, while US courts are permitted to award punitive damages in cases of willful intellectual property infringement, recognizing and enforcing such punitive awards against their own citizens might be seen as contrary to public policy in other countries, particularly in most civil law countries, where no punitive damages are available.[856,857]

---

[854]   In the case of the United States, see Symeonides (n 845) 338–339. In case of the UK, see Article 45(1)(b) of the Brussels I Regulation (recast). This requirement does not exist under the English Traditional Rules.

[855]   For the US, see Section 4(b)(3) of the Uniform Foreign Money Judgments Recognition Act (UFMJRA) and Section 482(2)(d) of the Restatement (Third) of Foreign Relations Law; see also Symeonides (n 845) 346; for the UK, see Article 45(1)(a) of the recast, *Israel Discount Bank of New York v Hadjipateras* [1984] 1 WLR 137 and *Vervaeke v Smith* [1983] 1 AC 145.

[856]   This was the position adopted by a German court, which ruled in 1992 that a US court decision was unenforceable to the extent that is the punitive damages awarded exceeded compensation for actual damage suffered. See Blumer (n 845) 385; Csongor Istvan Nagy, 'Recognition and Enforcement of US Judgment involving Punitive Damages in Continental Europe', (2012) Afl.1, 7–8 <http://www.nipr-online.eu/pdf/2012–149.pdf> (accessed 12 March 2016), citing *BGH* decision of 4 June 1992 Case IX ZR 149/91, ZIP 1992, 1256, 1261–62. The Japanese Supreme Court in *Mansei Kogyo* case recognized only compensatory damages, while punitive damages were refused as they violated Japanese public policy; N.T. Braslow, 'The Recognition and Enforcement of Common Law Punitive Damages in a Civil Law System: Some Reflections on the Japanese Experience' (1999) 16 *Arizona Journal of International and Comparative Law* 285, 288–294.

[857]   In Thailand, for example, there is uncertainty whether the Thai court would recognize and enforce the foreign judgment to the extent that it covered punitive damages. Punitive damages are rarely awarded under Thai law, and Section 438 of the Thai Civil and Commercial Code, dealing with the liability in tort, does not empower the Thai court to award punitive damages to the injured parties. Also, there is no mention of punitive damages in Thai patent and

3.3 Recognition and Enforcement of Foreign Judgment on Intellectual Property Rights in Space-related Activities

As there is neither law nor tribunal in outer space, the disputes relating to intellectual property rights in space-related activities would be brought before any competent courts on the earth. Hence, the recognition and enforcement of a foreign judgment on this matter are subject to the general principles under national law of respective countries.

The usual practice in the two jurisdictions under consideration is to recognize and enforce foreign judgments, although there are a few exceptions which lead to denial of recognition and enforcement. We shall examine some instances where refusal may arise, based upon the hypothetical cases introduced previously.

3.3.1 Different choice of law

The choice-of-law rule adopted by the rendering court may be one reason why another court may refuse to recognize and enforce a foreign judgment on an IP dispute related to outer space activities. As previously mentioned, due to the territorial scope of the intellectual property rights, unauthorized exploitation of IP right in outer space will generally not amount to an infringement, since no IP law applies in outer space. However, if the rendering court elects to apply the law of the forum, they may reach the opposite conclusion.[858]

Let us refer back to our case no. 3 in the choice-of-law section as a point of discussion. Suppose that C brings a case before a US court, claiming that B, by copying songs on Mars which are protected by copyright in the United States has infringed his copyright. The court, treating *Beattie v. United States* as a suitable precedent, may apply the law of the forum (US law). Considering C's acts as equivalent to unauthorized copying in the United States, they rule in favor of C, and order B to pay C compensatory damages totaling US$50,000. However,

---

copyright legislation. However, the possibility of a punitive damages award has been incorporated into some recent Thai legislation including in Section 13 of the Thai Trade Secret Act B.E. 2545 (A.D. 2002), an area of law which is closely associated with intellectual property law. Although there is no precedent, since it appears that punitive damages have become more widely accepted in Thai legal practice, I am of the view that any foreign punitive damages judgment might well be recognized by a Thai court, but based upon the provision in the Trade Secret Act, the level of award may be capped to a proportionate and reasonable amount, to avoid unjust enrichment of the claimant (e.g., not exceeding double amount of the actual damage).

[858]   *Beattie* (n 827).

B has no assets in the United States, but does have assets in Thailand. C applies to the Thai court and requests that the US court's decision is recognized and enforced. Assuming that the US court decisions satisfies all other requirements for recognition, would the Thai court recognize and enforce the judgment in favor of C?

Here, it seems doubtful that a Thai court would recognize the US judgment. This is because Section 15(1) of the Thai Conflict of Laws Act B.E. 2481 directs the Thai courts to apply the law of the protecting country to the case of IP infringement involving foreign element.[859] Since adopting this approach would lead to a finding of non-infringement, a position irreconcilable with the US ruling the Thai court is being requested to endorse, they may decline to recognize the US decision as contrary to public policy.

3.3.2 Jurisdiction

Although at this point in time, establishment of a space tribunal seems very far-fetched, for the purpose of this study let us mention briefly issues which might arise in the event that such a space tribunal did exist and renders a judgment.[860] Could such a judgment be considered as a foreign judgment and be recognized in a court on the earth?

The first question to be addressed is that whether a space tribunal decision is a 'foreign' judgment. It would be arguable that such a judgment is not a foreign judgment, since it is not a judgment of a sovereign entity – outer space belongs to no man. Alternatively, such a judgment could be analogous to a foreign judgment, based on the ground that it is not a judgment rendered within the territory of a recognizing state.

Even if a space tribunal judgment is considered as a foreign judgment, judgments might not be recognized and enforced in all states. Certain courts may consider that the tribunal lacked proper jurisdiction. This is possible, for example, if a recognizing state is not a party to the international treaty which has established the space tribunal. Such state might challenge the jurisdiction of that space tribunal and so decline to recognize any of its judgment if sought in that state.

---

[859] (n 811).

[860] A space tribunal does not need to be located in outer space. It could be located on earth but adjudicate on 'outer space IP law'.

However, a perceived lack of jurisdiction cannot give rise to non-recognition and non-enforcement of the foreign judgment under the Brussels I Regulation (recast),[861] whereas it can in the United States.[862]

To recap this section, recognition and enforcement of foreign judgments appear to be least problematic in the private international law sphere, in relation to the topic under consideration. Since rulings in relation to intellectual property rights in space-related matters are, and will be for the foreseeable future, issued by competent courts on the earth, there appears to be no need to have a specific 'space' regime in this regard. Thus, once a foreign judgment concerning an intellectual property rights dispute in space-related matter is issued, the judgment is entitled to be recognized and enforced in accordance with the rules of the respective recognizing states. The criteria used to deny recognition and enforcement of foreign judgments relating to space-related activities is similar to those applied when considering foreign judgments in other types of cases. Also, resolution of issues identified in other areas of public international law, such as more widespread agreement and consistent adoption of particular choice-of-law rules in intellectual property cases, would go some way to address some of the issues which then arise when parties seek to have one court's judgment recognized and enforced in other jurisdictions.

4. CONCLUSION

Private international law cannot sufficiently fill in all gaps for disputes arising from space activities.

In terms of jurisdiction, courts can normally find grounds to establish their adjudicative authority either based upon the domicile of the defendant or on the subject matter of the case. Additionally, exclusive jurisdiction can be established in certain circumstances, as in the case of registered IP rights under Article 24(4), independent of a defendant's domicile. Moreover, both quasi-territorial jurisdiction and nationality may provide alternative grounds for jurisdiction in some countries. The issue of jurisdiction seems to be resolved adequately through private international law, except in some rare situations where there is no connecting factor between the facts of the case and the forum. Similarly, although rare, issues relating to recognition and enforcement of an earlier

---

[861] This is relevant only if other EU courts recognize an EU court decision.
[862] Article 45(3) of the Brussels I Regulation (recast).

foreign court judgment might occur in disputes relating to IP rights in space activities.

The greatest point of concern in this area relates to applicable law. Because outer space belongs to no state, there is no governing law. Since the law of the protecting country applies to an IP infringement claim, any unauthorized use which occurs in outer space cannot constitute a tortious act, because the work is not protected. Although the law of the forum might be an alternative to bridge this gap, it is still uncertain whether national courts would be willing to adopt this practice. Thus, establishing a bespoke regime to govern the IP rights in space activities would be the most promising way to solve these problems efficiently.

6. Conclusion

In today's global world, boundary limitations seem meaningless. With the support of sophisticated technology, it is now straightforward for people to communicate simultaneously, not only around the globe, but also in outer space. Some of that technology used directly illustrates the role which space potentially plays in our daily lives, including telecommunication systems dependent upon telecommunication satellites and transportation devices, which rely upon remote sensing data. Clearly, outer space activities are the fruit of human intellectual creation, but further development of space technology is contingent upon those engaging in space activities receiving a reasonable return on their investment. Awareness of the protection of intellectual property rights in outer space activities has been raised as the direct result of the increasing involvement of private entities in the space sector. This is because the protection of intellectual property rights is recognized as an efficient legal mechanism which can ensure and secure the interest of the private enterprises engaging in space activities, as well as creating a fair and competitive environment in this field.[863]

However, space law and intellectual property law are founded upon different principles. The former focuses on the interest of the public, whereas the latter protects the private right holder. Moreover, the applicability of intellectual property law is limited to within the boundaries of the granting state. As described in the Introduction, the key question of this research is to examine the applicability of intellectual property law to space activities. This leads to four sub-questions; investigated in the earlier chapters:

(1) Do the fundamental principles in space law, namely the non-appropriation and the common heritage of mankind principles,[864]

---

[863] WIPO Doc. (n 118) 5.

[864] The province of all mankind principle is another fundamental principle in space law which also has been discussed in Chapter 1. However, since the said rule shares the common characteristics with the common heritage of mankind principle (only the latter requires an additional equitable sharing benefit), the

preclude protection of any intellectual fruits arising from outer space activities?

(2)   Can the key principles of existing international intellectual property treaties apply properly to outer space activities?

(3)   How and to what extent does national intellectual property law, using the exemplars of patent and copyright law, apply to outer space activities?

(4)   Are there any barriers for the applicability of national intellectual property law in outer space in term of jurisdiction, choice of law and enforcement?

This chapter will draw together the results of the discussions of the previous chapters to reach final conclusions, and respond to those questions.

QUESTION 1

Do the fundamental principles in space law, namely the non-appropriation and the common heritage of mankind principles, preclude the protection of intellectual fruits arising from outer space activities?

This first question was answered in Chapter 1. The study in Chapter 1 demonstrated that none of the space treaties contains explicit provisions relating to the protection of intellectual rights in outer space activities. In contrast, space law focuses upon protecting the utilization of outer space and its resources for the public interest. However, neither the non-appropriation nor the common heritage of mankind principles explicitly requires relinquishment of intellectual property rights in outer space, although undertaking certain space activities (which may give rise to intellectual property rights) may be interpreted as violating these two principles.

Regarding the non-appropriation principle, this rule prevents acquisition of outer space and its resources. Therefore, any work or invention created in outer space which does not physically appropriate any part of outer space, or any space resources, falls beyond the scope of this principle. However, some space activities might violate this principle as the result of their utilization of outer space resources. The examples discussed were a method of producing nuclear power in outer space

---

conclusion remark of these two principles in this chapter will refer only to the common heritage of mankind principle in order to avoid confusion and repetition.

using Helium-3, available on the Moon, as its input; and the use of geostationary orbits when placing satellites in outer space.[865] Both these scenarios could be interpreted as an appropriation of outer space, since both rely on outer space resources. Hence, if strictly interpreted, such activities are likely to contravene international space law, arising from a breach of the non-appropriation obligation.

Similar issues arise when applying the common heritage of mankind principle to the same space activities. This principle declares outer space and its resources are the common heritage of mankind, meaning that any country has the right to access, explore and use this spatial area and its resources freely, irrespective of its own contribution and investment. Also, any benefit arising from such activities must be equally shared. While the exact scope of this principle remains unclear, an interpretation which obligates all intellectual products (both space-related work and general work) created in outer space to be freely accessible to all would seem overly broad and unjustifiable. Otherwise, any invention or work would be unprotected merely because it is created in outer space. In contrast, some space activities would appear rightly to be subject to this principle, because they use outer space resources as part of their production. Examples of such activities are nuclear power generation using the Moon's supply of Helium-3 and methods for producing goods under zero gravity. Hence, in these cases, third parties may claim free access and use of the products, and a share of benefits arising therefrom, by availing themselves of the common heritage of mankind principle. In this way, the principle has the ability to impact the right holder's ability to enjoy exclusive rights in own inventions.

The obligations set forth in these two principles of space law certainly have the potential to jeopardize the development of space technology. Taking into account the potential advantages of space activities to humankind, some scholars have argued that the obligations imposed by these rules should not be interpreted so strictly as to bar the protection of IP rights. Instead, a compromise licensing scheme has been put forward which allows rights holders of relevant space technologies a reasonable reward, in exchange for a share in the benefits in their activities which exploit outer space. Not only is this proposal compliant with the obligations under the space law principles, but such a scheme would also encourage private entities to participate in space investment and thereby support the development of space technology.

---

[865]   See section 4.2 in Chapter 1.

This research has also identified that lack of a clear definition and delimitation of outer space is another problem which needs resolution, to eliminate legal uncertainty as to the applicable law. Presently, exactly where 'outer space' commences is ambiguous, and the status of a region located between 80 km to 120 km above sea level is uncertain, since it is considered to be air space in some situations and outer space in others.

The findings of Chapter 1 show that while none of the space treaty deals with the protection of intellectual property rights in outer space activities (presumably because no one foresaw the relevance of IP matters to space activities at the time these treaties were drafted), fundamental principles contained within those treaties seem to bar protection of certain space activities by intellectual property rights. Private ownership of products derived from space resources would appear to cut across the non-appropriation and common heritage of mankind principles. Therefore, it is necessary to investigate whether intellectual property law conventions deal adequately with this apparent conflict.

QUESTION 2

Can the key principles in the international intellectual property treaties be properly applied to outer space activities?

Chapter 2 answers this question. This chapter examined the implication to space activities of three fundamental principles (territoriality, national treatment and the most-favored nation principles) contained within international intellectual property law instruments. The research demonstrated that the territoriality principle sets limits to the application of intellectual property law in outer space. Even though some states have extended national law in this field extraterritorially,[866] the chapter explained why it is not clear whether such practice would be widely accepted. The principle of quasi-territorial jurisdiction was investigated as one solution. This principle of international law grants jurisdiction and control to a flag state over any space object which it registers. However, while it is advocated that this provides a sensible way forward, its scope is limited to only those activities which occur within a registered spacecraft. Beyond that, it has no effect in the pure extraterritorial area of outer space.

The national treatment and the most-favored nation principles share a common problem: neither is applicable in the case a copyright work

---

[866] The US Patent in Space Act and the IGA Agreement, see Section 4 in Chapter 3.

which is created in outer space by a non-member state national. Since outer space is not within the territorial reach of any state, both principles would be technically inoperative whenever the first fixation of a work, the habitual residence of the author and the work's first publication all take place in outer space. This is because in such case there is no point of attachment to render protection to a work created by a non-member state national.[867]

Chapter 2 reveals that there are still some difficulties when applying intellectual property treaties to space activities. Normally, qualifying conditions do not matter in term of location of creation, although problems still arise in the case of an author from a non-member country. Both the national treatment and the most-favored nation rules would be inoperative if the qualifying conditions in such a case are attached to the location in outer space. But this scenario occurs rarely. The key problem is the territoriality principle. This rule, which limits its application only in the granting state, bars application extraterritorially. This means there is no intellectual property protection in outer space. Chapters 3 and 4 illustrated how such rules may impact in the application of patent and copyright law.

QUESTION 3

How and to what extent do national patent and copyright laws apply to outer space activities?

As explained in the Introduction, while outer space activities may be protected by one or more forms of intellectual property rights, this research elected to focus on patents and copyright, since these rights are likely to be most pertinent for current outer space activities.[868] The study of the application of these two intellectual property rights to outer space activities was undertaken in Chapters 3 and 4, using a comparative analysis of the national patent and copyright laws in the United States and the United Kingdom, covering both the acquisition and enforcement of rights.

In terms of patent rights, the study illustrates that national patent law can apply appropriately to certain outer space activities. Chapter 3 commenced by identifying examples of particular space inventions which raised questions as to the patentability of their subject matter: namely a method of operating a telecommunication satellite by occupation of a

---

867   See Section 3.2 in Chapter 2.
868   WIPO (n 118) 13.

particular orbit; nuclear power generation using Helium-3 from the Moon; satellite navigation signals; and finally products, such as pharmaceuticals and electronics, manufactured under zero-gravity conditions. The analysis concludes that for the first three types of technology, the method of production is the potentially patentable subject matter, whereas both the end product and the manufacturing process represent patentable subject matters in the case of pharmaceutical and electronic products.

There is at least a theoretical risk that any invention devised within the ISS might face issues regarding novelty. Space law provides that third parties must be permitted access to the ISS,[869] and any invention which is disclosed 'in public' before a patent application is filed lacks novelty. However, it would appear that this problem would be resolved by use of a suitable confidentiality agreement, as is typically signed already by astronauts on board the ISS. With regard to products manufactured in space in a zero-gravity environment, it is currently unclear whether merely manufacturing known products using a known process, but under zero-gravity conditions would satisfy the novelty requirement. In my view, use of particular environmental conditions is one step in the process, and providing that this step is new, its adoption should be sufficient to render the process novel, (although the process may well lack inventive step). The assessment of the non-obviousness requirement does not raise any specific difficulties when applied to space inventions.

When assessing whether a space invention meets the requirement for industrial application, while utility does not generally need to be actually demonstrated, issues may be resolved by re-creating a weightless environment in an earth-based laboratory.

Therefore, it is the territorial characteristic of a patent which is the key issue to resolve when considering the nexus between space law and patent law. The territoriality of IP protection limits the scope of its protection within the boundary of the protecting country. This leads to uncertainty in enforcement issues and determining infringement when any unauthorized use takes place beyond national boundaries, especially in the extraterritorial area of outer space, where no national law is applicable. At present, the United States is the only country which has enacted patent law to give extraterritorial effect in outer space. In the absence of explicit statutory basis, as provided in US law, it is still uncertain whether other national patent laws would be applicable to their

---

[869] See Section 1.2.1 in Chapter 3.

nationally registered space objects, adopting by analogy, the quasi-territorial principle of the flag states used for shipping and aircraft. In addition, although in some jurisdictions, the doctrine relating to 'temporary presence' of vessels within a territory has been construed to include spacecraft, such an interpretation is questionable and does not appear to have gained wide support from the world community.

To sum up, even though territoriality appears more problematic than issues of patentability, there is still scope for further discussion with regard to the latter. In addition, extending domestic law to give extra-territorial effect may solve the issue of territoriality, but only to a degree, since use in outer space, other than in spacecraft, would still fall beyond the scope of any national law.

The relevance of copyright law to outer space activities was investigated in Chapter 4, by reference to two important space activities, namely: remote sensing data and satellite broadcasting. In each case, the activities were assessed to determine the eligibility as subject-matter for copyright protection in the two jurisdictions of interest. It was concluded that remote sensing data (which consists of three different types of data – raw data, processed data and analyzed information), may all be categorized as 'photographs', whereas satellite transmissions fall within the broadcast category. However, while potentially eligible for copyright protection, issues arise regarding satisfaction of the requirements of originality and authorship. With respect to remote sensing data, scholars have different opinions as to whether raw data can be original: it may simply not include sufficient creative human input in its creation.[870] Thus, whether copyright does subsist in raw data is arguable and still open for further discussion. For similar reasons, it is arguable whether remote sensing data is a work of authorship i.e., a work of human intellect, or whether it is a computer-generated work. In contrast, satellite broadcasting has no difficulty in satisfying either originality or authorship requirements.[871] It is clear that the process of its creation explicitly involves human intervention. Therefore, as with the conclusions of

---

[870]   It is still arguable that the process of obtaining raw data does not sufficiently involve human intellectual creation and thus does not merit for copyright. However, in my view, even though the raw data is automatically acquired through satellite's programming, such process involves human intervention in term of selecting location, time and angle for shooting. It is therefore justifiable for copyright protection. The discussion of this issue can be found in Chapter 4 under section 2.1.1.

[871]   Indeed, in some jurisdictions including the UK, a broadcast is not required to be original to gain copyright protection.

Chapter 4, the key problem in applying intellectual property law regimes to space activities is also the territorial scope of copyright law.

The investigations of Chapters 3 and 4 show that, despite certain complications applying patent and copyright law's requirements to outer space activities, it is the enforcement of such rights which presents the greatest problem owing to limitations arising from the territoriality principle. At present, private international law offers the only possible solution to these difficulties. Whether, and to what extent, private international law's rules can properly and sufficiently apply was reviewed specifically in Chapter 5.

QUESTION 4

Are there any barriers for the applicability of national intellectual property law in outer space in term of jurisdiction, choice of law and enforcement?

Chapter 5 examined likely difficulties when applying rules of private international law to space activities. The research identified that there is no specific problem in the context of recognition and enforcement of foreign judgment regarding IP rights in space activities. Here, the general rules are applicable. It was also established that in terms of jurisdiction, there is some scope for national courts to establish jurisdiction for disputes arising from outer space activities. Since jurisdiction is normally determined according to the domicile of the defendant or geographical factors related to the subject-matter of the case, the fact that an activity takes place in outer space is largely irrelevant when establishing jurisdiction, except in some rare instances where the defendant is not domiciled in any country on earth, or where the relevant 'harmful event' occurs in outer space. Another alternative is to establish exclusive jurisdiction based upon the country of registration of the IP rights at issue, irrespective of the defendant's domicile. In addition, in some countries the courts have jurisdiction based upon the plaintiff's domicile. The quasi-territorial jurisdictional principle, which also grants adjudicative authority to the court where the spacecraft is registered, provides another option.

The analysis of Chapter 5 also revealed the potential for issues in case of the applicable law. The analysis in this part was divided into two aspects: questions of proprietary issues and matters regarding infringement. In the context of IP rights, the law of the protecting country is widely accepted as the choice-of-law rule, both in case of propriety and infringement matters, except in case of initial ownership. Here two different approaches have been adopted: the law of the protecting country (*lex protectionis*) and the law of the country of origin (*lex originis*). But both *lex protectionis* and *lex originis* are technically inoperative when the place of creation (in case of copyright) and infringement are in outer space, since in outer space, no national law is applicable.[872] The law of the forum, as adopted by the US courts in the *Beattie* case[873] could be an option in the absence of governing law in outer space, but there is no widespread agreement on this matter. In the meantime, while the application of this choice-of-law rule is still uncertain, forum shopping may result. It has also been suggested that the law of the national country of the plaintiff or the defendant could be considered as possible alternatives. However, the application of these three choice-of-law rules will finally lead to an undesirable situation in which no infringement is found owing to the territoriality rules of IP rights.

To sum up, there are still live and unresolved issues when intellectual property rights are set in an outer space context. As has been highlighted, certain principles contained in both the international space law and intellectual property law treaties do not translate across satisfactorily to space activities, as has been illustrated with examples from national patent and copyright laws. Private international law was also found to be insufficient to fill certain gaps identified, especially in case of the applicable law. Therefore, taking into account the unique characteristic of space activities and its extraterritorial nature, this book proposes that the best solution would be a creation of a specially tailored regime for the protection of IP rights in outer space activities. In this regard, the proposal that any such international treaty agreement should establish a Space Tribunal and Space Bureau, tasked to adjudicate and administer any actions and issues relating to space activities, is endorsed.[874]

With respect to the issues as to applicable law, it is proposed that a new substantive IP law should be created to specifically apply in the

---

[872] See the hypothetical case no. 3 under the choice of law section in Chapter 5.

[873] See section 2.4.3, case 3 in chapter 5 and (n 827).

[874] This proposal is suggested in Sterling (n 483) 33. Professor Sterling proposed in his article that the Space Copyright Tribunal and Space Copyright Bureau should be established for the efficiency and clarity of exercising extraterritorial rights in relation to space activities. A similar proposal can be found at Hanneke van Traa-Engelman, 'The Need for a Uniform Law System Protecting Rights in Outer Space' (Proceedings of the International Institute of Space Law, 2008) and Bradford Lee Smith, 'Recent Development in Patents for Outer Space' (42nd Proceedings of Outer Space Amsterdam, 1999).

extraterritorial area of space, leaving the strict territoriality rule of national IP laws intact. In addition, the conflict when attempting to reconcile space law principles (non-appropriation and the common heritage of mankind principles) with IP protection in the case of certain space activities can be solved with a compulsory licensing scheme. This proposal both recognizes ownership of IP rights, while at the same time permitting others to share in the benefits. The failings regarding application of national treatment and most-favored nation principles can be replaced justifiably with a rule of non-discrimination.[875] Such a rule would guarantee that acquisition and enforcement of IP rights in relation to space activities is equitably accorded to any rights holder, irrespective of their nationality. Nonetheless, it is recognized that such a proposal may be difficult to achieve in practice, since states would be reluctant or unwilling to transfer their adjudicative and administrative power to a specific authority in which they may not be able to actively participate.

In this regard, a possible alternative would be the implementation of separate uniform substantive copyright and patent laws for space activities. States might find this solution more palatable, such that it would be easier for an agreement to be reached. It would even represent progress were states able to reach consensus in respect of particular space-related issues, such as whether raw data is an original work for the purposes of copyright protection.

Development of the space industry will definitely be hampered by the lack of legal certainty as to whether intellectual property rights can be acquired and then successfully enforced. This is not only detrimental to commercial entities interested in space activities, but also to the public as a whole. The position can only be clarified by a dedicated international treaty, or by separate agreements which address specific issues.

The closing remarks are directed to some recommendations for further research in this area. At present, the vast majority of scholarly discussion of intellectual property rights in the context of space activities relates to patent and copyright protection. But a whole new space tourism industry is close to becoming a reality,[876] and with it will follow trademark issues relating to souvenirs and advertising in space, which scholars will be required to address.[877] Similarly, with further growth in the commercialization of space activities, other forms of intellectual property rights protection will come to the foreground and be taken into account. In this

---

[875] This principle is also suggested in Sterling (n 483) 34.
[876] See the Introduction 1–2.
[877] WIPO (n 118) 5 and 13.

regard, the analysis provided in Chapters 3 (patentability) and 4 (copy-rightability) may provide a useful starting point for an examination of other forms of intellectual protection. It is also evident that the proposal for a specific legal regime for the protection of IP rights in outer space would require further and extensive research in respect of matters of detail; including aspects such as the structures, functions and powers of the Space Tribunal and Space Bureau, as well as the applicable law. The findings in this book are therefore only the starting point, which is intended to offer a useful contribution to future research in this area.

Bibliography

ARTICLES

Abeyrantne R., 'The Application of Intellectual Property Rights to Outer Space Activities' (2003) 29 *Journal of Space Law* 1.

Adolph J., 'The Recent Boom in Private Space Development and the Necessity of an International Framework Embracing Private Property Rights to Encourage Investment' (2006) 40 *International Lawyer* 961.

Arnold R., 'Content Copyrights and Signal Copyrights: the Case for a Rational Scheme of Protection' (2011) 1 *Queen Mary Journal of Intellectual Property* 272.

Asbell M.D., 'Progress on the WIPO Broadcasting and Webcasting Treaty' (2006) 24 *Cardozo Arts & Entertainment* 349.

Balsano A.M. and A.D. Clercq, 'The Community Patent and Space-Related Inventions' (2004) 30 *Journal of Space Law* 1.

Barbosa R.G., 'International Copyright Law and Litigation: A Mechanism for Improvement' (2007) 11 *Marquette Intellectual Property Law Review,* 78.

Black V., 'Canadian and the US Contemplate Changes to Foreign-Judgment Enforcement' (2007) 3 *Journal of Private International Law* 1.

Blount P.J., 'Jurisdiction in Outer Space: Challenges of Private Individuals in Space' (2007) 33 *Journal of Space Law* 299.

Blum J., 'The Deep Freeze: Torts, Choice of Law and the Antarctic Treaty Regime' (1994) 8 *Emory International Law Review* 667.

Blumer F., 'Jurisdiction and Recognition in Transatlantic Patent Litigation' (2001) 9 *Texas Intellectual Property Law Journal* 329.

Bockstiegel Karl-Heinz, Paul Michael Kramer and Isabel Polley, 'Patent Protection for the Operation of Telecommunication Satellite Systems in Outer Space? Part I' (1998) 47 *ZLW* 3.

Bockstiegel Karl-Heinz, Paul Michael Kramer and Isabel Polley, 'Patent Protection for the Operation of Telecommunication Satellite Systems in Outer Space? Part II' (1998) 47 *ZLW* 166.

Braslow N.T., 'The Recognition and Enforcement of Common Law Punitive Damages in a Civil Law System: Some Reflections on the

Japanese Experience' (1999) 16 *Arizona Journal of International and Comparative Law* 285.

Burk D.L., 'Application of United States Patent Law to Commercial Activity in Outer Space' (1990–1991) 6 *Santa Clara Computer & High Technology Law Journal* 295.

Burk D.L., 'Protection of Trade Secrets In Outer Space Activity: A Study in Federal Preemption' (1992–1993) 23 *Seton Hall Law Review* 560.

Buxton C.R., 'Property in Outer Space: The Common Heritage of Mankind Principles vs. The "First in Time, First in Right, Rule of Property Law"' (2004) 69 *Journal of Air Law and Commerce* 689.

'Chinese Space Station to Benefit World', Xinhua News Agency (16 June 2012) <http://news.xinhuanet.com/english/china/2012-06/16/c_12329 3484.htm> (accessed 12 March 2016).

Christol C.Q., 'The Common Heritage of Mankind Provision in the 1979 Agreement Governing the Activities of States on the Moon and Outer Celestial Bodies' (1980) 14 *International Lawyer* 429.

Cooper D.N., 'Circumventing Non-Appropriation: Law and Development of United States Space Commerce' (2009) 36 *Hastings Constitutional Law Quarterly* 457.

Cromer J.D., 'How on Earth Terrestrial Laws Can Protect Geospatial Data' (2006) 32 *Journal of Space Law* 253.

Dembert H., 'Securing Authors' Rights in Satellite Transmissions: US Efforts to Extend Copyright Protection Abroad' (1985–1986) 24 *Columbia Journal of Transnational Law* 73.

Derclaye E., 'Infopaq International A/S Danske Dagblades Forening (C–5/08): Wonderful or Worrisome? The Impact of the ECJ Ruling in Infopaq on UK Copyright Law' (2010) *European Intellectual Property Review* 247.

Desaussure H., 'Remote Sensing Satellite Regulation by National and International Law' (1989) 15 *Rutgers Computer & Technology Law Journal* 351.

Dickerson T.B., 'Patent Rights under Space Act Agreement and Procurement Contracts: A Comparison by the Examination of NASA's Commercial Orbital Transportation Services (COTS)' (2007) 33 *Journal of Space Law* 341.

Dinwoodie G.B., 'Developing a Private International Intellectual Property Law: The Demise of Territoriality?' (2009) 51 *William and Mary Law Review* 711.

Dinwoodie G.B., 'International Intellectual Property Litigation: A Vehicle for Resurgent Comparative Thought?' (2001) 49 *American Journal of Comparative Law* 429.

Durantaye K., S.J. Golla and L. Kuschel, 'Space Oddities: Copyright Law and Conflict of Laws in Outer Space' (2014) 9 *Journal of Intellectual Property Law and Practice* 521.

Engel J.A. and J.E. Fajkowski, 'Major Patent Law Changes: First-To-File Provisions' <http://www.klgates.com/major-patent-law-changes-first-to-file-provisions—effective-march-16–2013–12–18–2012/> (accessed 31 January 2016).

Ervin S., 'Law in a Vacuum: The Common Heritage Doctrine in Outer Space Law' (1984) 7 *Boston College International and Comparative Law Review* 403.

Ficsor M., 'Direct Broadcasting by Satellite and the Bogsch Theory' (1990) 18 *International Business Law* 258.

Field T.L., 'The Planes, Trains, and Automobiles Defense to Patent Infringement for Today's Global Economy: Section 272 of the Patent Act' (2006) 12 *Boston University Journal of Science & Technology Law* 26.

Freeland S., 'Up, Up ... Back: The Emergence of Space Tourism and Its Impact on the International Law of Outer Space' (2005–2006) 6 *Chicago Journal of International Law* 1.

Gabrynowicz J.I., 'The Perils of Landsat from Grassroots to Globalization: A Comprehensive Review of US Remote Sensing Law with a Few Thoughts for the Future' (2005–2006) 6 *Chicago Journal of International Law* 44.

Gallia C.R., 'To Fix or Not to Fix: Copyright's Fixation Requirement and the Rights of Theatrical Collaborations' (2007–2008) 92 *Minnesota Law Review* 231.

Gaudrat Ph., 'La terre vue en haut sur le puzzle des Amateurs d'en Bas: Brève Observations à propos Riom' (Com. 14 mai 2003), 2 RTD.com, 309 (2004).

Gillis J., 'Privacy Rights and Satellite Broadcasts' (1993) 27 *Israel Law Review* 384.

Ginsburg J.C., 'The Concept of Authorship in Comparative Copyright Law' (2002–2003) 52 *DePaul Law Review* 1063.

Guntrip E., 'The Common Heritage of Mankind: An Adequate Regime for Managing the Deep Seabed?' (2003) 4 *Melbourne Journal of International Law* 376.

Hammerle K.G. and T.U. Ro, 'The Extra-Territorial Reach of US Patent Law on Space-Related Activities: Does The "International Shoe" Fit As We Reach For The Stars?' (2008) 34 *Journal of Space Law* 241.

Handler M., 'The Panel Case and Television Broadcast Copyright' (2003) 25 *Sydney Law Review* 391.

Hayward C.M., 'Remote Sensing: Terrestrial Laws for Celestial Activities' (1990) 8 *Boston University International Law Journal* 157.

Henry N.L., 'The Convention Relating to the Distribution of Programme-Carrying Signals Transmitted by Satellite: A Potshot at Poaching' (1974) 7 *NYU Journal of International Law and Politics* 575.

Hertzfeld H.R. and F.G. Von der Dunk, 'Bringing Space Law into the Commercial World: Property Rights without Sovereignty' (2005–2006) 6 *Chicago Journal of International Law* 81.

Holbrook T.R., 'Extraterritoriality in US Patent Law' (2008) 49 *William and Mary Law Review* 2119.

Homiller D.P., 'From Deepsouth to the Great White North: The Extra-territorial Reach of United States Patent Law After Research in Motion' (2005) 17 *Duke Law and Technology Review* 1.

Hoover R.K., 'Law and Security in Outer Space from the Viewpoint of Private Industry' (1983) 11 *Journal of Space Law* 115.

Hopper T., 'Reproduction in Part of Online Articles in the Aftermath of Infopaq (C–5/08): *Newspaper Licensing Agency Ltd. v. Meltwater Holding BV*' (2011) *European Intellectual Property Review* 331.

Howell E., 'Virgin Galactic: Richard Branson's Space Tourism Company', Space.com (17 February 2016) <http://www.space.com/18993-virgin-galactic.html> (accessed 31 January 2016).

Howell R.G., 'Intellectual Property, Private International Law, and Issues of Territoriality' (1996) 13 *Canadian Intellectual Property Review* 209.

Irimis D., 'Promoting Space Ventures by Creating An International Space IPR Framework' (2011) 33 *European Intellectual Property Review* 35.

Kaplan L.G.C. and J.R. Bankoff, 'Of Satellites and Copyrights: Problems of Overspill and Choice of Law' (1993) 7 *Emory International Law Review* 727.

Karjala D.S., 'Copyright in Electronic Maps' (1994–1995) 35 *Jurimetrics Journal* 395.

Kesan J., 'Personal Jurisdiction in Cyberspace: Brief Summary of Personal Jurisdiction Law' <http://www.cyberspacelaw.org/kesan/keasan1.html> and <http://mycivpro.pbworks.com/w/page/21954161/cyberspace-jurisdiction> (accessed 3 February 2014 and 12 March 2016, respectively).

Kono T., 'Intellectual Property and Private International Law' General Report (Abbreviated version), International Academy of Comparative Law Washington Congress (1 December 2010) 1 <http://ssrn.com/abstract=1974124> (accessed 12 March 2016).

Kono T., 'Intellectual Property Rights, Conflict of Laws and International Jurisdiction: Applicability of ALI Principles in Japan?' (2005) 30 *Brooklyn Journal of International Law* 865.

Kravets L., 'First-To-File Patent Law Is Imminent, But What Will It Mean?' <http://techcrunch.com/2013/02/16/first-to-file-a-primer/> (accessed 31 January 2016).

Lafferranderie G., 'The United States Proposed Patent in Outer Space Legislation: An International Perspective' (1990) 18 *Journal of Space Law* 1.

Lee Y.H., 'Case Comment: Photograph and the Standard of Originality in Europe: *Eva-Maria Painer v. Standard Verlgas GmbH, Axel Springer AG, suddeutsche Zeitunung GmbH, Spiegel-Verlag Rudolf Augstein GmbH & Co KG, Verlag M. DuMont Schauberg Expedition der Kolnischen Zeitung GmbH & Co KG* (C–145/10)' (2012) *European Intellectual Property Review* 1.

Lockridge L.A.W., 'Comment: Intellectual Property in Outer Space: International Law, National Jurisdiction, and Exclusive Rights in Geospatial Data and Databases' (2006) 32 *Journal of Space Law* 319.

Lucanik J., 'Direct Broadcasting Satellites: Protecting Rights of Contributing Artists and Broadcasting Organizations' (1982) 12 *California Western International Law Journal* 204.

Manzione L.L., 'Multinational Investment in the Space Station: An Outer Space Model for International Cooperation?' (2002) 18 *American University International Law Review* 507.

Matulionyte R., 'IP and Applicable Law in Recent International Proposals' (2012) 3 *Journal of Intellectual Property, Information Technology and Electronic Commerce Law* 263.

Mauny C., 'High Court Applies "Emission Theory" to Database Infringement' (2011) 6 *Journal of Intellectual Property Law and Practice* 296.

McManis C.R., 'Satellite Dish Antenna Reception: Copyright Protection of Live Broadcasts and the Doctrine of Anticipatory Infringement' (1986–1987) 11 *Columbia-VLA Journal of Law & the Arts* 387.

Mejia-Kaiser M., 'Copyright Claims for METEOSAT and LANDSAT Images under Court Challenge' (2006) 32 *Journal of Space Law* 293.

Meredith P., 'Status of the "Patent in Space" Legislation in Congress-October 1989' (1989) 17 *Journal of Space Law* 163.

Michel S.T., 'The Experimental Use Exception to Infringement Applied to Federal Funded Inventions' available online at <file:///F:/juf/doc%20for%20thesis/articles/Patent%20exception%20in%20US%20law.pdf> (accessed 31 January 2016).

Miles C., 'Assessing the Need for an International Patent Regime for Inventions in Outer Space' (2008) 11 *Tulane Journal of Technology and Intellectual Property* 59.

Moenter Rochus, 'The International Space Station: Legal Framework and Current Status' (1998–1999) 64 *Journal of Air Law and Commerce* 1033.

Nagy C.I., 'Recognition and Enforcement of US Judgment Involving Punitive Damages in Continental Europe', (2012) Afl.1, 4 <http://www.nipr-online.eu/pdf/2012–149.pdf> (accessed 12 March 2016).

Neumann S., 'Intellectual Property Rights Infringements in European Private International Law: Meeting the Requirements of Territoriality and Private International Law' (2011) 7 *Journal of Private International Law* 583.

Oosterlinck R., 'The Intergovernmental Space Station Agreement and Intellectual Property Rights' (1989) 17 *Journal of Space Law* 23.

Piera A., 'Intellectual Property in Space Activities: An Analysis of the United States Patent Regime' (2004) 29 *Annals of Air and Space Law* 42.

Porras D.A., 'Comment the "Common Heritage" of Outer Space: Equal Benefits for Most of Mankind' (2006) 37 *California Western International Law Journal* 143.

Rahmatian A., 'Originality in UK Copyright Law: The Old "Skill and Labour" Doctrine under Pressure' (2013) *International Review of Intellectual Property and Competition Law* 4.

Rees R.D., 'Plaintiff Due Process Rights in Assertions of Personal Jurisdiction' (2003) 78 *NYU Law Review* 405.

Ro. T.U., M.J. Kleiman and K.G. Hammerle, 'Patent Infringement in Outer Space in Light of 35 U.S.C. section 105: Following the White Rabbit Down the Rabbit Loophole' <http://128.197.26.36/law/central/jd/organizations/journals/scitech/volume172/documents/Kleiman_Web.pdf>, at page 4 (accessed 31 January 2016).

Ruth S., 'The Regulation of Spillover Transmissions from Direct Broadcast Satellites in Europe' (1989–1990) 42 *Federal Communications Law Journal* 107.

Salin P.A., 'Proprietary Aspects of Commercial Remote-Sensing Imagery' (1992–1993) 13 *Northwestern Journal of International Law and Business* 349.

Samuelson P., 'Allocating Ownership Rights in Computer-Generated Works' (1985) 47 *University of Pittsburgh Law Review* 1185.

Schauwecker M., 'Extraterritorial Patent Jurisdiction: Can One Sue in Europe for Infringement of a U.S. Patent?' (TTLF Working Paper No. 10, 2011) <https://www.law.stanford.edu/sites/default/files/publication/205085/doc/slspublic/schauwecker_wp10.pdf> (accessed 12 March 2016).

Shackelford S.J., 'The Tragedy of the Common Heritage of Mankind' (2008) 27 *Stanford Environmental Law Journal* 101.

Sirinelli P., 'Originalité d'images satellites ou comment distinguer la carte du territoire' 40 *Recueil Dalloz* (13 November 2003) 2454.

Smith L.J. and C. Doldirina, 'Remote Sensing: A Case for Moving Space Data towards the Public Good' (2008) 24 *Space Policy* 24.

Smith T., 'A Phantom Menace? Patents and the Commercial Status of Space' (2003) 34 *Victoria University Wellington Law Review* 545.

'Space Foundation's 2013 Report Reveals 6.7 Percent Growth in the Global Space Economy in 2012', Space Foundation Press Release (2 April 2013) <http://www.spacefoundation.org/media/press-releases/space-foundations-2013-report-reveals-67-percent-growth-global-space -economy> (accessed 16 June 2013).

Sreejith S.G., 'The Pertinent Law for Outer Space Related Intellectual Property Issues: An Odyssey into TRIPs' (2005) 45 *Indian Journal of International Law* 180.

Sterling J.A.L., 'Space Copyright Law: the New Dimension, A Preliminary Survey and Proposals' <www.qmipri.org/research.html> (accessed 22 February 2016).

Struyen O., 'Exorbitant Jurisdiction in the Brussels Convention' <http://www.law.kuleuven.be/jura/art/35n4/struyven.htm> (accessed 12 March 2016).

Tan D., 'Towards a New Regime for the Protection of Outer Space as the "Province of All Mankind"' (2000) 25 *Yale Journal of International Law* 145.

Tennen L.I., 'Towards a New Regime for Exploration of Outer Space Mineral Resources' (2010) 88 *Nebraska Law Review* 794.

Torremans P.L.C., 'The Sense or Nonsense of Subject-matter Jurisdiction over Foreign Copyright' (2011) *European Intellectual Property Review* 1.

Traa-Engelman, H. von, 'The Commercial Exploitation of Outer Space: Issues of Intellectual Property Rights and Liability' (1991) 4 *Leiden Journal of International Law* 293.

Trimble J.J., 'International Law of Outer Space and Its Effect on Commercial Space Activity' (1984) 11 *Pepperdine Law Review* 521.

Tronchetti F., 'The Non-Appropriation Principles as a Structural Norm of International Law: A New Way of Interpreting Article II of the Outer Space Treaty' (2008) 33 *Air and Space Law* 277.

Ubertazzi B., 'Intellectual Property Rights and Exclusive (Subject Matter) Jurisdiction: Between Private and Public International Law' (2011) 15 *Marquette Intellectual Property Law Review* 357.

Uhram M.L., 'Microgravity-Related Patent History' <http://www.iss-casis.org/portals/0/docs/2012%20patent%20history.pdf> (accessed 31 January 2016).

Ullrich H., 'TRIPS: Adequate Protection, Inadequate Trade, Adequate Competition Policy' (1995) 4 *Pacific Rim Law & Policy Association* 153.

Vahrenwald A., 'Intellectual Property on the Space Station Freedom' (1993) 15 *European Intellectual Property Review* 318.

West J.R., 'Copyright Protection for Data Obtained By Remote Sensing: How the Data Enhancement Industry Will Ensure Access for Developing Countries' (1990–1991) 11 *Northwestern Journal of International Law and Business* 403.

Wolfrum R., 'The Principle of Common Heritage of Mankind' (1983) Max-Planck-Institut für ausländisches öffentliches Recht und Völkerrecht 312, <http://www.zaoerv.de> (accessed 31 January 2016).

Zhao Y., 'Patent Protection in Outer Space, with Particular Reference to the Patent Regime in Hong Kong' (2006) 14 *Asia Pacific Law Reviews* 161.

Zhao Y., 'Regulation of Remote Sensing Activities in Hong Kong: Privacy, Access, Security, Copyright and the Case of Google' (2010) 36 *Journal of Space Law* 547.

BOOKS

Aplin T., 'United Kingdom' in Linder B. and T. Shapiro (eds), in *Copyright in the Information Society: A Guide to National Implementation of the European Directive* (Edward Elgar 2011) 558.

Balsano A.M. and J. Wheeler, 'The IGA and ESA: Protecting Intellectual Property Rights in the Context of ISS Activities' in Von der Dunk F.G. and M. Brus (eds), in *The International Space Station* (Martinus Nijhoff 2006).

Baslar K., *The Concept of the Common Heritage of Mankind in International Law* (Martinus Nijhoff 1998).

Benkö M., W. De Graaff and G.C.M. Reijnen, *Space Law in the United Nations* (Martinus Nijhoff 1985).

Bently L. and B. Sherman, *Intellectual Property Law* (4th ed., OUP 2014).

Bhatt S., *Legal Controls of Outer Space* (S. Chand & Co. 1973).

Cane P. and M. Tushnet (ed.), *The Oxford Handbook of Legal Studies* (OUP 2003).

Carl B.M., 'The Need for a Private International Law Regime in Antarctica' in C.C. Joyner and S.K. Chopra (eds), *The Antarctic Legal Regime* (Martinus Nijhoff 1988).

Cheng B., *Studies in International Space Law* (Clarendon Press 1997).

Christol C.Q., *The Modern International Law of Outer Space* (2nd ed., Pergamon Press 1984).

Christol C.Q., *Space Law Past, Present and Future* (Kluwer 1991).

Chuvieco E. and A. Huete, *Fundamentals of Satellite Remote Sensing* (CRC Press/Taylor & Francis Group 2010).

Clarkson C.M.V. and J. Hill, *The Conflict of Laws* (4th ed., OUP 2011).

Diederiks-Verschoor I.H.Ph. and V. Kopal, *An Introduction to Space Law* (3rd ed., Wolters Kluwer Law & Business 2008).

Doldirina C., 'A Rightly Balanced Intellectual Property Rights Regime as a Mechanism to Enhance Commercial Earth Observation Activities' in C.M. Jorgenson, *Proceedings of the International Institute of Space Law: 52nd Colloquium on the Law of Outer Space* (American Institute of Aeronautics and Astronautics 2009).

Doldirina C., 'The Impact of Copyright Protection and Public Sector' in R. Purdy and D. Leung (eds), *Evidence from Earth Observation Satellites* (Martinus Nijhoff 2013).

Eechoud Mireille van, *Choice of Law in Copyright and Related Rights Alternative to the Lex Protectionis* (Kluwer Law International 2003).

Fawcett, J. and J.M. Carruthers, *Cheshire, North and Fawcett: Private International Law* (14th ed., OUP 2008).

Fawcett J.J. and P. Torremans, *Intellectual Property and Private International Law* (2nd ed., OUP 2011).

Fentiman R., 'Choice of Law and Intellectual Property' in J. Drexl and A. Kur (eds), *Intellectual Property and Private International Law* (Hart Publishing 2005).

Fumagalli L., 'Litigating Intellectual Property Rights Disputes Cross-Border: Jurisdiction and Recognition of Judgments under the Brussels I Regulation' in S. Bariatti (ed.), *Litigating Intellectual Property Rights Disputes Cross-Border: EU Regulations, ALI Principles, CLIP Project* (Wolters Kluwer Italia Srl 2010).

Garnett K., G.D.L. Davies and G. Harbottle, *Copinger and Skone James on Copyright* (16th ed., Thomson Reuters Limited 2011).

Gendreau Y., A. Nordeman and R. Oesch (eds), *Copyright and Photographs: An International Survey* (Kluwer Law International 1999).

Goldstein P. and P. Hugenholtz, *International Copyright: Principles, Law and Practice* (3rd ed., OUP 2013).

Halpern S.W., S.B. Seymore and K.L. Port, *Fundamentals of United States Intellectual Property Law: Copyright, Patent, Trademark* (4th ed., Wolters Kluwer Law International 2012).

Hartley T.C., *International Commercial Litigation* (Cambridge University Press 2009).

Heath C. and S. Kamperman, (eds), *Spares, Repairs and Intellectual Property Rights* (Wolters Kluwer Law and Business 2009).

Jasentuliyana N., (ed.), *Space Law Development and Scope* (Praeger Publishers 1992).

Jasentuliyana N., *International Space Law and the United Nations* (Kluwer Law International 1999).

Joyner C.C. and S.K. Chopra (eds), *The Antarctic Legal Regime* (Martinus Nijhoff 1988).

Kessler E.A., *Picturing the Cosmos: Hubble Telescope Images and the Astronomical Subline* (University of Minnesota Press 2012).

Kono T. (ed.), *Intellectual Property and Private International Law: Comparative Perspectives* (Hart Publishing 2012).

Kur A. and T. Dreier, *European Intellectual Property Law: Text, Cases & Materials* (Edward Elgar 2013).

Lamb D., *The Search for Extraterritorial Intelligence: A Philosophical Inquiry* (Routledge 2001).

Loewenheim U., 'The Principle of National Treatment in the International Conventions Protecting Intellectual Property' in M.J. Adelmann, R. Brauneis, J. Drexl and R. Nack (eds), *Patents and Technological Progress in a Globalized World* (Springer 2009).

Lyall F. and P.B. Larsen, *Space Law A Treaties* (Ashgate 2009).

Makeen F.M., *Copyright in a Global Information Society: The Scope of Copyright Protection under International, US, UK and French Law* (Kluwer Law International 2000).

Matos Gomez J., *Satellite Broadcast Systems Engineering* (Artech House 2002).

Matulionyte R., *Law Applicable to Copyright: A Comparison of the ALI and CLIP Proposals* (Edward Elgar, 2011).

Mayss A., *Principles of Conflict of Laws* (3rd ed., Cavendish Publishing, 1999).

Metzger A., 'Applicable Law under the CLIP Principles: A Pragmatic Revaluation of Territoriality' in J. Basedow, T. Kono and A. Metzger (eds.), *Intellectual Property in the Global Arena* (Mohr Siebeck GmbH KG 2010).

Michalos C., *The Law of Photography and Digital Images* (Sweet & Maxwell 2004).

Miller R., G. Burkill, C. Birss and D. Campbell, *Terrell on the Law of Patents* (17th ed. Sweet and Maxwell, 2011).

Mohri M., 'Repair and Recycle as Direct Patent Infringement?' in C. Heath and A.K. Sanders (eds), *Spares, Repairs and Intellectual Property Rights* (Wolters Kluwer 2009).

Mosteshar S., 'Intellectual Property Issues in Space Activities' in S. Mosteshar (ed.), *Research and Invention in Outer Space Liability and Intellectual Property Rights* (Martinus Nijhoff 1995).

Moufang F., 'The Extraterritorial Reach of Patent Law' in Martin J. Adelmann, Robert Brauneis and Josef Drexl (eds), *Patents and Technological Progress in a Globalized World* (Springer 2009).

Muller J.M., *Patent Law* (3rd ed., Aspen Publishers 2009).

Nard C., D. Barnes and M. Madison, *The Law of Intellectual Property* (2nd ed., Wolters Kluwer 2008).

Oduntan G., *Sovereignty and Jurisdiction in the Airspace and Outer Space* (Routledge 2012).

Prescott L. and M. Vitoria, *The Modern Law of Copyright and Designs* (4th ed., LexisNexis 2011).

Purdy R. and D. Leung (eds), *Evidence From Earth Observation Satellites* (Martinus Nijhoff 2013).

Reijnen B.C.M., *The United Nations Space Treaties Analysed* (Editions Frontieres 1992).

Reynolds G.H. and R.P. Merges, *Outer Space Problems of Law and Policy* (Westview 1997).

Rosati E., *Originality in EU Copyright: Full Harmonisation Through Case Law* (Edward Elgar 2013).

Salt D.J., 'Space Operations for a New Space Era' in C.A. Cruzen, J.M. Gunn and P.J. Amadiel (eds), *Progress in Astronautics and Aeronautics*, vol. 236: Exploration, Scientific Utilization and Technology Development (American Institute of Aeronautics and Astronautics, Inc. 2011).

Sender M.P., *Cross-Border Enforcement of Patent Rights* (OUP 2002).

Seville C., *EU Intellectual Property Law and Policy* (Edward Elgar Publishing Limited 2009).

Smith B.L., 'Problems and Realities in Applying the Provisions of the Outer Space Treaty to Intellectual Property Issues' in *Proceedings of the 40th Colloquium on the Law of Outer Space* (the International Institute of Space Law of the International Astronautical Federation 1997).

Space Foundation, *The Space Report, 2014*, <http://www.space foundation.org/sites/default/files/downloads/The_Space_Report_2014_ Overview_TOC_Exhibits.pdf> (accessed 5 July 2015).

Space Foundation, *The Space Report, 2015*, https://www.space foundation.org/sites/default/files/downloads/The_Space_Report_2015_ Overview_TOC_Exhibits.pdf (accessed 29 December 2015).

Sterling J.A.L., *World Copyright Law* (3rd edn, Sweet & Maxwell 2008)

Symeonides S.C., *American Private International Law* (Kluwer Law International 2008).

Tatley L., *Intellectual Property Law in Hungary* (Kluwer Law International 2010).

Torremans P., *Intellectual Property Law* (6th ed., OUP 2010).

Trimble M., *Global Patents* (OUP 2012).

Tronchetti F., *The Exploitation of Natural Resources of the Moon and Other Celestial Bodies* (Martinus Nijhoff 2009).

Ulmer E., 'Territorial Limitation of Intellectual Property Rights', *International Encyclopedia of Comparative Law: Copyright* vol. 14 (2007).

Van De Wouwer J.L. and F. Lambert, *European Trajectories in Space Law* (European Commission 2008).
Wadegaonkar D., *The Orbit of Space Law* (Stevens & Sons 1984).
WIPO, *WIPO Intellectual Property Handbook* (2nd ed., WIPO 2008).
Zhao Y., *Space Commercialization and the Development of Space Law from a Chinese Legal Perspective* (Nova Science 2009).
Zweigert K. and H. Kotz, *An Introduction to Comparative Law* (Oxford: Clarendon Press 1998).

CASES

United Kingdom

Actavis Group HF and Eli Lilly and Company [2013] EWCA Civ 517 (21 May 2013). *See also* the High Court (Patent Court) decision in this case at [2012] EWHC 3316 (Pat) (High Court 2012).
Bauman v. Fussell and others (1978) R.P.C.
Blohn v. Desser [1962] 2 QB 116 [1961] 3 All ER 1.
Def Lepp Music v. Stuart-Brown [1986] R.R.C. 273.
Eli Lilly v. Human Genome Sciences [2008] RPC 29 confirmed on appeal [2010] EWCA CSU 33.
Genentech's Patent [1989] RPC 147 (C.A.).
Henderson v. Henderson (1844) 6 QB 288
Hubbard v. Vosper [1972] 2 QB 84.
Israel Discount Bank of New York v. Hadjipateras [1984] 1 WLR 137.
John Walker & Sons Ltd v. Ost [1970] 2 All ER 106.
Kirin-Amgen Inc. v. Hoechst Marion Roussel [2003] RPC 31.
Kirin-Amgen Inc. v. Hoechst Marion Roussel [2005] RPC 9.
Knorr-Bremse Systems for Commercial Vehicles Ltd v. Haldex Brake Products GmbH [2008] EWHC 156 (Pat).
Ladbroke v. William Hill [1964] 1 W.L.R. 273, 278, [1964] 1 All ER 465, 469.
Lucasfilm Ltd. v. Andrew Ainsworth, [2011] UK SC 39. See the Court of Appeal decision of this case in [2008] EWHC 1878, [2009] FSR 2, Ch; [2009] EWCA Civ 1328, [2010] FSR 10, CA.
Maharanee of Baroda v. Wildenstein [1972] 2QB 283.
Missing Link Software v. Magee [1989] FSR 361.
Newspaper Licensing Agency v. Marks & Spencer plc [1999] EMLR 369.
Newspaper Licensing Agency Ltd and Others v. Meltwater Holding BV and Others [2010] EWHC 3099 (Ch).
Nouvion v. Freeman (1889) 15 App Cas 1.
Pemberton v. Hughes (1899) 1 Ch. 781.

Pozzoli v. BDMD SA & Anor [2007] FSR 37 (CA), [2007] EWCA Civ 588 (22 June 2007).

Salvesen v. Administrator of Austrian Property [1927] AC 641.

Spiliada Maritime Corp. v. Cansulex Ltd [1987] AC 460.

Synthon BV v. SmithKline Beecham [2006] RPC 10.

Temple Island Collections Limited v. New English Teas Limited and Nicholas John Hougton [2012] EWPCC 1.

United Wire Limited v. Screen Repair Service Ltd [2001] RPC 439, [2001] FSR 24.

University of London Press, Limited v. University Tutorial Press [1916] 2 Ch. 601.

Vervaeke v. Smith [1983] 1 AC 145.

Walter v. Lane [1900] A.C. 539.

Windsurfing International Inc. v. Tabur Marine (Great Britain) Ltd. [1985] RPC 59(CA).

United States

Aalumhammed v. Lee 202 F.3d 1227 (9th Cir. 2000).

Akro Corp. v. Luker, 45 F. 3d 1541 (Fed. Cir. 1995).

Allarcom Pay TV Ltd. v. Gen Instrument Corp., 69 F.3d 381,387 (9th Cir. 1995).

American Cotton-Tie Co. v. Simmons, 106 U.S. (16 Otto.) 89 (1882).

Andrien v. Southern Ocean County Chamber of Commerce, 927 F.2d. 132 (3d Cir. 1991).

Aro Mfg. Co. v. Convertible Top Replacement Co., 365 U.S. 338 (1961).

Asahi Metal Industry Co. v. Superior Court, 480 U.S. 102 (1987).

Baltimore Orioles v. Major League Baseball Players, 805 F.2d. 663 (7th Cir. 1986).

Beattie v. United States, 756 F.2d 91, (1984).

Blue Ribbon Pet Prods. v. Hagen Corp., 66 F.Supp.2d. 454 (E.D.N.Y. 1999).

Brenner v. Manson, 388 U.S. 519 (1966).

Bridgeman Art, Inc. v. Corel, Inc., 25 F.Supp. 2d 191 (S.D.N.Y. 1999), aff'd on reconsideration, 36 F.Supp. 2d 191 (S.D.N.Y. 1999).

Brown v. Duchesne 60 U.S. 183 (1856).

Burger King Corp v. Rudzewicz 471 US 462 (1985).

Burnham v. Superior Court, 495 U.S. 604.

Burrow-Giles Lithographing Co. v. Sarony, 111 U.S. 53, 4 S.Ct. 279 (1884).

Coin Controls v. Suzo International et al. [1999] Ch 33.

Cordon Holding B.V. v. Northwest Publishing Corp., 49 U.S.P.Q. 2d 1697 (S.D.N.Y. 1998).

Creative Technology Ltd v. Aztech Sys PTE 61 F 3d 696 (9th Cir. 1995).

Deepsouth Packing Co. v. Laitram Corp., 406 U.S. 518 (1972).

Diamond v. Chakrabarty 447 U.S. 303 (1980).

Dow Chemical Co., 837 F.2d 469, 473 (Fed. Cir. 1988).

Eli Lilly v. Generic Drug Sales, 460 F2d 1096, 174 USPQ 65 (5th Cir 1972).

Environmental Defense Fund v. Massey, 986 F.2d 528, 529 (1993).

Ex Parte McKay (1975) 200 USPQ (BNA) 324 (PTO BA).

Feist Publications, Inc. v. Rural Telephone Service Co. 499 U.S. 340, 348, 111 S.Ct. 1282,1289 (1991).

Gardner v. Howe (1865), 9 Feb Cases 1157 (Federal Case no. 5,219).

Gayler v. Wilder, 51 U.S. (10 How.) 477 (1980).

Geo. M. Martin Co. v. Alliance Machine Systems International LLC., 618 F.3d 1294 (Fed. Cir. 2010).

Gulf Oil Corp. v. Gilber, 330 U.S. 501 (1947).

Harper & Row Publishers, Inc. v. Nation Enterprises 471 U.S. 539, 105 S.Ct. 2218 (1985).

Helicopteros Nacionales de Colombia v. Hall, 466 US 408 (1984).

Hilton v. Guyot 159 US 113 (1895).

Hughes Aircraft Co. v. United States, 29 Fed Cl. 197 (1993).

ICOS Corporation/Seven Transmembrane Receptor, [2002] 6 OJPEO 293.

International Shoe Co. v. Washington 326 U.S. 310 (1945).

Itar-Tass Russian News Agency v. Russian Kurier Inc., 153 F 3d 82, 47 USPQ 2D 1810 (2d Cir 1998).

Kington Bros. v. AFG Indus. Inc., 581 F. Supp. 1039.

Los Angeles News Service v. Conus Communications Co., 969 F.Supp. 579 (USCD Cal., 1997).

MAI System Corp. v. Peak Computer, Inc. 991 F.2d 511 (9th Cir 1993).

Marconi Wireless Telco v. USA (1942), 53 USPQ 246, 81 CCI 671.

Mars Inc. v. Kabushiki-Kaisha Nippon Conlux, 24 F.3d 1368, 62 USLW 2720, 30 U.S.P.Q. 2d 1621.

Meshwerk, Inc. v. Toyota Motor Sales U.S.A., Inc., 528F.3d 1258 (2008).

National Football League v. McBee & Bruno's Inc. 792 F.2d 726 (8th Cir., 1986).

National Football League v. Primetime 24 Joint Venture 211 F.3d 10 (2nd Cir. 2000).

NTP v. RIM 418 F.3d 1282 (2005).

Pennoyer v. Neff, 95 U.S. 714, 729 (1877).

Rite-Hite Corp v. Kelly Co., 56 F.3d 1538, (Fed. Cir 1995).

Rosen v. NASA, 152 USPQ 757 (1966).

Sawin v. Guild, 21 F Cas 554, 555 (C.C.D. Mass 1813) (No. 12,391).

Sewall v. Walters, 21 F.3d 411, (Fed. Cir. 1994).

Smith v. United States, 113 S.Ct. 1178 (1993).

Sony Corp. of America v. Universal City Studios, Inc. 464 U.S. 417, 104 S.Ct. 774 (1984).

Steele v. Bulova Watch Co. 344 U.S. 280 (1952).

SubaFilms, Ltd. v. MGM-Pathe Communications Co. 24 F.3d. 1008 (9th Cir. 1994).

Therasense v. Becton Dickinson & Co., 593 F.3d 1289 (Fed. Cir 2010).

Tyburn v. Conan Doyle [1991] Ch. 5 (Ch D).

Voda M.D. v. Cordis Corp. 476 F.3d 887 (Fed. Cir 2007).

Westcode v. RBE Electronics, 2000 U.S. Dist. LEXIS 815 (E.D. Pa. Feb. 1, 2000).

Wilbur-Ellis Co., v. Kuther, 377 U.S. 422 (1964).

Williams Electronics, Inc. v. Artic International, Inc. 685 F.2d 870 (3d Cir. 1982).

Wilson v. Simpson, 50 U.S. 109 (1850).

World Film Services v. RAI Radiotelevisione Italiano, 50 U.S.Q. 2D. 1187 (S.D.N.Y. 1999).

Worldwide Volkswagen Corp. v. Woodson, 444 U.S. 286 (1980).

ICJ

Ethiopia v. S. Africa; Liberia v. S. Africa (Second Phase) [1966] ICJ Rep 6.

CJEU

Case C–364/93 *Antonio Marinari v. Lloyds Bank plc and Zubaidi Trading Company* [1995] ECR I–2709.

Case C–143/78 *De Cavel v. De Cavel* [1979] ECR 1055.

Case C–509/09 *eDate Advertising v. X* [2012] QB 654.

Case C–145/10 *Eva-Maria Painer v. Standard VerlagsGmbH and others* (CJEU 7 March 2013).

Case C–288/32 *Duijnstee v. Goderbauer* [1983] ECR 3663.

Case C–4/03 *GAT v. LuK* [2006] ECR I-6509.

Case C–21/76 *Handelskwekerij Bier Bv v. Mines de Potasse d'Alsace* [1978] QB 708, [1976] ECR 1735.

Case C–5/08 *Infopaq International A/S v. Danske Dagblades Forening* [2012] Bus. L.R. 102; [2009] E.C.R. I-6569; [2009] E.C.D.R. 16; [2010] F.S.R. 20.

Case C–192/04 *Lagardere Active Broadcast v. SPRE and GVL* [2005] ECR I-07199.

Case C–189/87 *Kalfelis v. Bankhaus Schoder,* [1988] ECR 5565.

Case C–161/10 *Martinez v. MGN Ltd* [2011] WLR (D) 330.

Case C–228/11 *Melzer v. MF Global UK Ltd*, [2013] EUECJ C–228/11, ECLT:EU:C2013:305, [2013] WLR (D) 196, EU:C:2013:305, [2013] CEC 1023, [2013] 3 WLR 883, [2013] ILPr 30, [2013] 1 QB 1112.
Case C–281/02 *Andrew Owusu v. N.B. Jackson* OC 2005, I–1383.
Case C–170/12 *Pinckey v. KDG Mediatech AG*, [2013] EUECJ, [2013] WLR (D) 367, [2013] Bus LP 1313.
Case C–539/03, *Roche Nederland v. Frederick Primus and Milton Goldenberg*, [2006] ECR I–6535.
Case C–68/93 *Shevill and Others v. Press Alliance SA* [1995] 2 WLR 499.
Case C–616/10 *Solvay v. Honeywell* (CJEU 12 July 2012).
Case C–523/10 *Wintersteiger AG v. Products 4U Sondermaschinenbau GmbH*. [2012] WLR (D) 117.

CONFERENCE PAPERS AND DOCUMENTS

Austin G., 'Private International Law and Intellectual Property Rights A Common Law Overview' (WIPO Forum on Private International Law and Intellectual Property, Geneva, January 2001) (WIPO/PIL/01/5).
Blumer F., 'Patent Law and International Private Law on Both Sides of the Atlantic' (WIPO Forum on Private International Law and Intellectual Property, Geneva, January, 2001) (WIPO/PIL/01/3).
Christol, C., 'Judicial Protection of Intellectual Property: Hughes Aircraft vs. US' (Proceedings of 37th Colloquium on the Law of Outer Space, Jerusalem, October 1994).
Christol, C., 'Persistence Pays Off: The Case of Hughes Aircraft Company v. USA (Proceedings of 42nd Colloquium on the Law of Outer Space, Amsterdam, October 1999).
Derby B., 'Industrial Property Rights and Space Activity: An EPO Perspective' (Proceedings of an ESA Workshop on Intellectual Property Rights and Space Activities, Paris, December 1994).
Doldirina C., 'A Rightly Balanced Intellectual Property Rights Regime as a Mechanism to Enhance Commercial Earth Observation Activities' (Proceedings of the International Institute of Space Law, 52nd Colloquium on the Law of Outer Space, Daejeon, October 2009).
Gantt J.B., 'Space Station Intellectual Property Rights and U.S. Patent Law' (Proceedings of an International Colloquium on the Manned Space Stations – Legal Issues, Paris, November 1989) 109.
Gervais D. (Proceedings of an ESA Workshop on Intellectual Property Rights and Space Activities, Paris, December 1994).
Ginsburg J.C., 'Private International Law Aspects of the Protection of Works and Objects of Related Rights Transmitted Through Digital

Network (2000 Update)' (WIPO Forum on Private International Law and Intellectual Property, Geneva, January 2001) (WIPO/PIL/01/2) 1.

Hearsey C.M., 'A Review of Challenge to Corporate Expansion into Outer Space' (AIAA Space 2008 Conference & Exposition, San Diego, September 2008) available online at <http://www.astrosociology.org/Library/PDF/Hearsey_CorporateExpansion.pdf> (accessed 12 March 2016).

Jurcys P., 'The Role of the Territoriality Principle in Modern Intellectual Property Regimes: Institutional Lessons from Japan' (New Spaces, New Actors and the Institutional Turn in Contemporary Intellectual Property Law conference, Kyushu, February 2010).

Kopal V., 'The Geostationary Orbit: A Limited Natural Resource or A Precious Part of Outer Space' (Proceedings of 26th Colloquium On The Law Of Outer Space, Budapest, October 1983).

Max-Planck-Gesellschaft, 'Exclusive Jurisdiction and Cross Border IP (Patent) Infringement Suggestions for Amendment of The Brussels I Regulations' available online at <http://www.ip.mpg.de/files/pdf1/Comments-JurisdictionCrossBorderIPInfringement2.pdf> (accessed 1 August 2013).

Okolie C.C., 'Applicability of International Law to Telecommunication Satellites in Geostationary Orbit and the Interest of the Developing Countries' (Proceedings of the 26th Colloquium on the Law of Outer Space, Budapest, October 1983).

Osterlinck R., 'Intellectual Property and Space Activities' (Proceedings of 26th Colloquium on the Law of Outer Space, Budapest, October 1983).

Oosterlinck R., 'Tangible and Intangible Property in Outer Space' (Proceedings of 39th Colloquium on the Law of Outer Space, Beijing, October 1996).

Sgrosso G.C., 'Applicable Jurisdiction Conflicts in the International Space Station' (Proceedings of 43rd Colloquium on the Law of Outer Space. Rio de Janeiro, October 2000).

Smith B.L., 'Recent Developments in Patents for Outer Space' (Proceedings of the 42nd Colloquium on the Law of Outer Space Amsterdam, October 1999).

Traa-Engelman, von H., 'The Need for a Uniform Law System Protecting Rights in Outer Space' (Proceedings of the International Institute of Space Law, 2008).

Tramposch A., 'International Aspects of Protection for Inventions Made or Used in Outer Space' (Proceedings of an ESA Workshop on Intellectual Property Rights and Space Activities, Paris, December 1994).

U.S. Congress, Office of Technology Assessment, 'Space Station and the Law: Selected Legal Issues-Background Paper', OTA-BP-ISC–41 (Washington, DC: US Government Printing Office, August 1986).

Walker C.H., 'Potential Patent Problem on the ISS' (Proceedings of the 42nd Colloquium on the Law of Outer Space Amsterdam, October 1999).

WIPO, 'Intellectual Property and Space Activities' (April 2004) <http:// www.wipo.int/export/sites/www/patent-law/en/developments/pdf/ip_space. pdf> (accessed 31 January 2016).

WIPO, 'Meeting of Consultants on Inventions Made or Used in Outer Space' <http://www.wipo.int/export/sites/www/patent-law/en/ developments/pdf/inventions_space.pdf> (accessed 31 January 2016).

INTERVIEWS

Interview with Dr. Sompong Liangrocapart, Lecturer, Department of Physics, Mahanakorn University of Technology (Bangkok, Thailand, 3 January 2012).

Interview with Professor Christopher Conselice, Professor of Astrophysics, School of Physics and Astronomy, the University of Nottingham (Nottingham, 29 March 2012).

LEGISLATION

United Kingdom

Copyright Designs and Patents Act 1988.
Patent Act 1977.
Private International Law (Miscellaneous Provisions) Act 1995.

United States

Copyright Act 1976.
Patent Act 1977.

Treaties, Conventions and Other Instruments

Agreement Governing the Activities of States on the Moon and Other Celestial Bodies 1979.

Berne Convention for the Protection of Literary and Artistic Works 1886.
Brussels Convention on Jurisdiction and Enforcement of Judgments in Civil and Commercial Matters 1968.
Convention on Registration of Objects Launched into Outer Space 1975.
Convention relating to the Distribution of Programme-Carrying Signals Transmitted by Satellite 1974.
European Patent Convention (EPC) 1973 (2000).
Paris Convention for the Protection of Industrial Property 1883.
Rome Convention on the Law Applicable to Contractual Obligations (EEC) 1980.
Rome Convention for the Protection of Performers, Producers of Phonograms and Broadcasting Organizations 1961.
Treaty on Principles Governing the Activities of States in the Exploration and Use of Outer Space including the Moon and Other Celestial Bodies 1967.
TRIPs Agreement on Trade-related Aspects of Intellectual Property Rights, WTO, 1994.

Theses

Doldirina C., 'The Common Good and Access to Remote Sensing Data' (D.C.L. thesis, McGill University 2010).
Monahan R., 'The Sky's the Limit? Establishing a Legal Delimitation of Airspace and Outer Space' (D.Phil thesis, Durham University 2008).
Oestreicher Y., 'Recognition and Enforcement of Foreign Intellectual Property Judgments: Analysis and Guidelines for A New International Convention' (S.J.D. thesis, Duke University 2004).
Yang F., 'Infringement of Intellectual Property Rights over the Internet and Private International Law', (M.Phil thesis, University of Nottingham, 2010).

Index